Basic Matrix Theory

PRENTICE-HALL MATHEMATICS SERIES

Albert A. Bennett, EDITOR

Basic Matrix Theory

LEONARD E. FULLER

Professor of Mathematics
Kansas State University

PRENTICE-HALL, INC.

Englewood Cliffs, N. J., 1962

Library of Congress Catalog No. 62-12104

Printed in the United States of America

06518—C

Preface

This book has been written for the person who needs to use matrices as a tool; therefore, the mathematics involved has been kept at as simple a level as possible. Any person who has had elementary algebra and has a desire to learn something about matrices can understand the contents. To help the reader, many numerical examples are included to illustrate principles and techniques. Since matrices are viewed as a mathematical tool, throughout the book the emphasis is placed on developing skill in their use. No attempt has been made to give specific applications of the theory discussed because these are so varied that one cannot economically do justice to all of them for a given technique. The reader is urged to refer to the literature in his special area of interest for applications of the topics discussed.

The audience for which this text is intended is quite heterogeneous as can be seen by noting the backgrounds of the students in classes using the notes for this book. There were both undergraduate and graduate students enrolled for credit. The undergraduates were chiefly majors in mathematics, some of whom were planning to be high school teachers. The graduate students were in the various fields of engineering, the physical sciences, the social sciences, statistics, and plant and animal genetics, but no graduate students in mathematics were permitted to take the course. In addition to this group, there were several students and faculty members who audited the course. The faculty members were in the fields of engineering, statistics, mathematics, and genetics.

The material covered falls into two categories. The first four chapters contain the basic concepts of matrix theory, whereas the next three chapters are concerned with numerical computation techniques. The first chapters include topics that form the foundation for the remainder of the book. One of the most important of these topics is the concept of elementary operations. For each type, an easy to remember standard notation is given that also facilitates checking for errors in the reduction of matrices. A systematic procedure is outlined for simplifying matrices using elementary row or elementary column operations, or both. This basic procedure is then modified to give a method for evaluating the determinant of a given square matrix. Some of the numerical computation techniques that are considered also utilize the basic elementary operation process.

Chapters 5 through 7 contain a few of the many standard numerical techniques with no pretense at completeness. Again a standard notation is developed and used throughout to make it easier to apply the processes. Both direct and iterative techniques for inverting matrices and solving systems of linear equations are considered. Detailed numerical examples are worked out to show how to apply each of these methods. The emphasis in these chapters is on understanding not only how to use the procedures but also why they are valid.

The author wishes to express his thanks to his wife Frances for her valuable assistance and her patience during the preparation of this book. He is also deeply indebted to Dr. R. G. Sanger for his careful reading of the manuscript and his many valuable suggestions and comments.

L.E.F.

Contents

1

Basic Properties
of Matrices

1.1 Introduction

One of the most widely used mathematical concepts is that of a system of linear equations in certain unknowns. Such a system arises in many diverse situations and in a variety of subjects. For such a system, a set of values for the unknowns that will "satisfy" all the equations is desired. In the language of matrices, a system of linear equations can be written in a very simple form. The use of properties of matrices then makes the solution of the system easier to find.

However, this is not the only reason for studying matrix algebra. The sociologist uses matrices whose elements are zeros or ones in talking about dominance within a group. Closely allied to this application are the matrices arising in the study of communication links between pairs of people. In genetics, the relationship between frequencies of mating types in one generation and those in another can be expressed using matrices. In electrical engineering, network analysis is greatly aided by the use of matrix representations.

Today the language of matrices is spreading to more and more fields as its usefulness is becoming recognized. The reader can probably already call to mind instances in his own field where matrices are used. It is hoped that many more applications will occur to him after this study of matrix algebra is completed.

1.2 The Form of a Matrix

A proper way to being a discussion of matrices would be to give a definition. However, before doing this, it should be noted that a simple definition cannot begin to convey the concept that is involved. For this reason, a two part discussion will follow the definition. The first part will be concerned with trying to convey the nature of the form of a matrix. The second part of the discussion will be concerned with the properties of what are called matrix addition, matrix multiplication, and scalar multiplication. This will establish the basic algebra of matrices. Consider the following definition.

Definition 1.1. A matrix is a rectangular array of numbers of some algebraic system.

What does this mean? It simply means that a matrix is first of all a set of numbers arranged in a pattern that suggests the geometric form of a rectangle. Most of the time this will actually be a square. The algebraic system from which the numbers are chosen will be discussed in more detail later. Some simple examples of matrices are as follows:

$$C = \begin{bmatrix} 1 & 3 & 4 \\ 2 & 1 & 3 \end{bmatrix} \qquad D = \begin{bmatrix} 4 \\ 1 \\ 3 \end{bmatrix} \qquad E = \begin{bmatrix} 3 & 2 \\ 1 & 4 \\ 5 & 2 \end{bmatrix} \qquad F = \begin{bmatrix} 2 & -1 & 3 \\ 5 & 7 & 9 \\ 4 & 13 & 16 \end{bmatrix}$$

The [] that are used to enclose the array bring out the rectangular form. Sometimes large () are used, whereas other authors prefer double vertical lines instead of the []. Regardless of the notation, the numbers of the array are set apart as an entity by the symbolism. These numbers are often referred to as the *elements* of the matrix. The numbers in a horizontal line constitute a *row* of the matrix, those in a vertical line a *column*. The rows are numbered from the top to the bottom, while the columns are numbered from left to right.

It is sometimes necessary in a discussion to refer to a matrix that has been given. To avoid having to write it out completely every time, it is customary to label matrices with capital letters A, B, C, etc. as was done in the example above. In case the matrix being referred to is a general one, then its elements are often denoted with the corresponding small letters with numerical subscripts. The next example will illustrate this symbolism. With this notation one knows at once that capital letters refer to matrices and small letters to the elements.

When it is necessary in a discussion to talk about a general matrix A, it will be assumed that A consists of a set of mn numbers arranged in n rows with m numbers in each row. The individual elements will be denoted as a_{rs} where the r denotes the row in which the element belongs, and the s denotes the column. In other words, a_{23} will be the element in the second row and third column. The double subscript is the *address* of the element; it tells in which row and in which column the element may be found. This is definite since there can be, in each row, only one element that is also in a given column. Consider then the following examples.

$$A = \begin{bmatrix} a_{11} & a_{12} & a_{13} \\ a_{21} & a_{22} & a_{23} \\ a_{31} & a_{32} & a_{33} \\ a_{41} & a_{42} & a_{43} \end{bmatrix} \qquad B = \begin{bmatrix} b_{11} & b_{12} & b_{13} & b_{14} \\ b_{21} & b_{22} & b_{23} & b_{24} \\ b_{31} & b_{32} & b_{33} & b_{34} \end{bmatrix}$$

In these general matrices, notice that the first subscript does denote the row in which the element occurs, whereas the second indicates the column of the entry. When the number of rows and the number of columns are known, the shorter notation $A = (a_{rs})$ is often used. The real significance of this idea will appear several times in this chapter.

Another quite useful concept connected with the form of matrices is given by the following definition.

Definition 1.2. The dimension of a matrix A with n rows and m columns is $n \times m$.

In the numerical examples given before, the dimensions are 2×3, 3×1, 3×2, and 3×3, respectively. In the examples of the general matrices, A is of dimension 4×3 and B is of dimension 3×4. The dimension of a matrix is often referred to as the "size" of the matrix.

A special kind of a matrix is one that has only one row or only one column. These are useful enough to have a special name given to them. This designation is indicated in the next definition.

Definition 1.3. A row vector is a $1 \times m$ matrix. A column vector is an $n \times 1$ matrix.

Using these concepts, a matrix can be thought of as being composed of a set of row vectors placed one under the other. These can be numbered in order from top to bottom so that, in the double subscript notation, the first number refers to the row vector to which the element belongs. Similarly, a matrix can be considered as a set of column vectors placed side by side. If these are numbered from left to right, the second subscript of the address of each element would then refer to a column vector in this set.

There are occasions when reference will be made to the row vectors of a matrix or to the column vectors. In this case, the matrix is to be considered as indicated above. Sometimes the term "vectors" of a matrix will be used. In this case, the reference is to either row vectors or column vectors or both.

1.3 The Transpose of a Matrix

Associated with every $1 \times m$ row vector is an $m \times 1$ column vector. This column vector has the same numbers appearing in the same order as in the row vector. The only difference is that they are written vertically for the column vector and horizontally for the row vector. The column vector is referred to as the *transpose* of the row vector. Also, the row vector is called the transpose of the column vector.

This concept is readily extensible to matrices. With a given matrix A, one can associate a matrix A' known as the transpose of A. The column vectors of A' are the transposes of the corresponding row vectors of A; or, viewed another way, the row vectors of A' are the transposes of the corresponding column vectors of A. This concept is expressed in the next definition in terms of the addresses of the elements.

Definition 1.4. If $A = (a_{rs})$, then $A' = (a_{sr})$.

This definition says that the elements in A' are the same as those of A, with reversed interpretation of the subscripts. In other words, the element of A with the address (r, s) in A' has (s, r) as its address in A.

The concept of the transpose can be made clearer by referring to the previous examples. The matrix C is made up of two row vectors. The transposes of these two vectors are

$$\begin{bmatrix} 1 \\ 3 \\ 4 \end{bmatrix} \quad \text{and} \quad \begin{bmatrix} 2 \\ 1 \\ 3 \end{bmatrix}$$

respectively. This means that C' has these two vectors as its column vectors. In other words,

$$C' = \begin{bmatrix} 1 & 2 \\ 3 & 1 \\ 4 & 3 \end{bmatrix}$$

Similarly, the transposes of the other matrices are

$$D' = \begin{bmatrix} 4 & 1 & 3 \end{bmatrix} \qquad E' = \begin{bmatrix} 3 & 1 & 5 \\ 2 & 4 & 2 \end{bmatrix} \qquad F' = \begin{bmatrix} 2 & 5 & 4 \\ -1 & 7 & 13 \\ 3 & 9 & 16 \end{bmatrix}$$

For the two general matrices, the transposes are

$$A' = \begin{bmatrix} a_{11} & a_{21} & a_{31} & a_{41} \\ a_{12} & a_{22} & a_{32} & a_{42} \\ a_{13} & a_{23} & a_{33} & a_{43} \end{bmatrix} \qquad B' = \begin{bmatrix} b_{11} & b_{21} & b_{31} \\ b_{12} & b_{22} & b_{32} \\ b_{13} & b_{23} & b_{33} \\ b_{14} & b_{24} & b_{34} \end{bmatrix}$$

In all of these examples notice how the address of the elements of the original matrix are reversed. Of course, the elements whose row and column addresses are the same have their address unchanged in the transpose. Note too, how the column vectors of the transpose are the corresponding row vectors of the original matrix. This also applies to the row vectors of the transpose, for they are the same as the corresponding column vectors of the original matrix.

It is apparent that if the dimension of A is $n \times m$, then the dimension of A' is $m \times n$. This is a consequence of the definitions of transpose and dimension. For instance, the dimensions of the transposes of the numerical examples are 3×2, 1×3, 2×3, and 3×3, respectively. Similarly, the dimension of A' is 3×4, whereas that of B' is 4×3.

Another consequence of the definition of transpose is $(A')' = A$. In other words, the transpose of the transpose of A is A itself. This becomes apparent on considering the row vectors of A. They form the corresponding column vectors of A'. The column vectors of A' in turn determine the corresponding row vectors of its transpose $(A')'$. But this means that the row vectors of A and $(A')'$ are the same so they are the same matrix.

1.4 Submatrices

The last topic concerned with the form of a matrix to be considered is based on the next definition.

Definition 1.5. A submatrix of a matrix A is an array formed by deleting one or more vectors of A.

The definition does not specify whether the vectors deleted are row vectors or column vectors. It also allows the deletion of a combination of row vectors and column vectors. Some examples of what is meant will illustrate the concept.

The deletion of the second column vector of F gives the submatrix

$$\begin{bmatrix} 2 & 3 \\ 5 & 9 \\ 4 & 16 \end{bmatrix}$$

If the third row vector were also deleted, the resulting submatrix would be

$$\begin{bmatrix} 2 & 3 \\ 5 & 9 \end{bmatrix}$$

If the first and third row vectors and the first column vector of F were deleted, there would result the row vector $[7 \quad 9]$. It can be easily seen that there are a variety of submatrices that can be formed from a given matrix.

If the matrix is square, one can draw a diagonal from the upper left corner to the lower right corner. This line would pass through those elements whose row and column subscripts are the same. These elements are known as the *diagonal* elements. For the matrix F, 2, 7 and 16 are the diagonal elements. One can form submatrices by deleting corresponding row and column vectors. If the original matrix is square, the submatrices formed are also square. More important however, their diagonal elements are diagonal elements of the original matrix. These are called principal submatrices. For the matrix F, the principal submatrices are

$$\begin{bmatrix} 2 & -1 \\ 5 & 7 \end{bmatrix} \quad \begin{bmatrix} 2 & 3 \\ 4 & 16 \end{bmatrix} \quad \begin{bmatrix} 7 & 9 \\ 13 & 16 \end{bmatrix} \quad [2] \quad [7] \quad [16]$$

In the first three of these principal submatrices, a single row and column are deleted from the original matrix; in the last three, two rows and columns are deleted. In all six of these matrices, the diagonal elements are diagonal elements of F.

1.5 The Elements of a Matrix

In the definition of a matrix it was stated that the elements belong to an algebraic system. In nearly all of the work that follows, the elements will be real numbers; however, on occasion, they may be complex numbers. In either of these cases, the elements will belong to an algebraic system known as a *field*. These numbers of the algebraic system are often referred to as *scalars*. In the section of this chapter on partitioning, the elements will be matrices of smaller size. This way of considering a matrix can be very useful. Later chapters will have sections depending upon partitioning of matrices.

For matrices whose elements belong to the same algebraic system it is possible to define equality of matrices. Notice that the following definition gives this in terms of equality among the elements.

Definition 1.6. If A and B are both of dimension $n \times m$, and $a_{rs} = b_{rs}$ for all r and s then $A = B$.

This definition says that the matrices must be of the same size and equal element by element. The first requirement is actually implied by the second and is included only for clarity. It should be noted how the definition is made to depend upon the corresponding property of the elements. This will be characteristic of nearly all of the properties of matrices that will be discussed.

1.6 The Algebra of Real Numbers

The arrays of numbers that form a matrix are of little use by themselves. One has to be able to manipulate them according to a set of rules. The set of rules in this case consists of the definitions of three operations. As a consequence of these definitions each of the operations has some important properties. These operations will be known as *addition of matrices, multiplication of matrices*, and *scalar multiplication of matrices*. It should be obvious that the first two cannot be the familiar operations upon real numbers that bear these names. However, these new operations will be

defined in terms of multiplications and additions of the real number elements of the matrices. This is the justification for using the terminology
addition and multiplication.

Before going to these definitions, a review of some topics in the algebra
of real numbers will be made. The purpose will be twofold: first, the properties of the operations of addition and multiplication need to be written
down for reference; second, the same pattern of discussion will be used for
the operations with matrices. It will be found that not all of the properties
for real numbers will carry over to matrices because of the definitions of
the operations that are used. These points will be brought out later on as
they arise.

Assume, then, that the familiar operations of addition and multiplication of real numbers are known. These are called closed binary operations
or just binary operations because the result of operating with two real
numbers is a third real number. Addition and multiplication are actually
defined only for two real numbers, that is why they are called binary
operations. In order to add three numbers, one adds two of them, and then
to this sum one adds the third. In order to add four numbers, one adds to
the sum of two of them a third number. Then, to this sum the fourth number is added. The same is true for multiplication. If more than four numbers are added or multiplied, the above process is simply continued a step
at a time.

The operation of addition of real numbers has the following properties.

1. Addition is *commutative*, that is,

$$a + b = b + a.$$

We can add two real numbers in either order.

2. Addition is *associative*, that is,

$$(a + b) + c = a + (b + c).$$

If to the sum of two real numbers a third real number is added, then
the result is the same as if to the first number the sum of the last
two numbers is added.

3. For addition there is a unique *identity element* 0, that is,

$$a + 0 = 0 + a = a.$$

The number 0 added to any real number or any real number added
to 0 always gives the real number.

4. For every real number a there exists a unique real number denoted as $-a$, such that

$$a + (-a) = (-a) + a = 0.$$

This is known as the *additive inverse* of a. It is also called the negative of a.

Any system having a binary operation defined with the last three properties is called a *group*. In case the first property is also satisfied, it is called a *commutative group*. This means then that the real numbers form a commutative group under the binary operation of addition.

With respect to the operation of multiplication, the number 0 is usually omitted. It is then noted that multiplication by 0 gives 0, and if a product of two real numbers is 0, at least one of them is 0. The following properties are true for this operation.

1. Multiplication is *commutative*, that is,

$$a \cdot b = b \cdot a.$$

We can multiply two real numbers in either order.

2. Multiplication is *associative*, that is,

$$(a \cdot b) \cdot c = a \cdot (b \cdot c).$$

If the product of two real numbers is multiplied by a third real number then the result is the same as if the first number is multiplied by the product of the last two numbers.

3. For multiplication there is a unique *identity element* 1, that is,

$$a \cdot 1 = 1 \cdot a = a.$$

The number 1 multiplied by any real number gives that number.

4. For every nonzero real number a there exists a unique real number denoted as a^{-1} such that

$$a \cdot a^{-1} = a^{-1} \cdot a = 1.$$

This element is known as the *multiplicative inverse* of a. It is also called the reciprocal of a.

It follows that the real numbers without 0 also form a commutative group with respect to multiplication.

Finally, the two operations are related by the final property known as the distributive law.

D. Multiplication is distributive with respect to addition, that is,

$$(a + b) \cdot c = a \cdot c + b \cdot c \quad \text{or} \quad c \cdot (a + b) = c \cdot a + c \cdot b.$$

This latter property says that one can multiply the sum of two numbers by a third and get the same result as multiplying each of the two by the third and then adding the products.

Any system consisting of a set of elements and two closed binary operations on the set with all of the above properties is known as a field. This means that the system of real numbers forms a field. Other familiar examples of a field are the system of rational numbers and the system of complex numbers. These far from exhaust all the possible fields, but they are the best known.

1.7 Addition of Matrices

The following definition will bring out a difference between ordinary and matrix addition. In the real number system, any two numbers can be added but not in a matrix system. Addition of matrices as given here, will have meaning only when the matrices are of the same size and have elements from the same system.

Definition 1.7. If the matrices A and B are of the same dimension, then $A + B = (a_{rs} + b_{rs})$.

This type of matrix addition is known as "elementwise addition." It adds together elements in the same relative position in the two matrices. This makes addition a very simple operation. As an example of the operation if

$$A = \begin{bmatrix} 2 & 1 & 3 \\ 4 & -1 & 2 \end{bmatrix} \quad \text{and} \quad B = \begin{bmatrix} -3 & 2 & 0 \\ 1 & 5 & 2 \end{bmatrix}$$

then

$$A + B = \begin{bmatrix} 2 + (-3) & 1 + 2 & 3 + 0 \\ 4 + 1 & -1 + 5 & 2 + 2 \end{bmatrix} = \begin{bmatrix} -1 & 3 & 3 \\ 5 & 4 & 4 \end{bmatrix}$$

Also

$$B + A = \begin{bmatrix} -3 + 2 & 2 + 1 & 0 + 3 \\ 1 + 4 & 5 + (-1) & 2 + 2 \end{bmatrix} = \begin{bmatrix} -1 & 3 & 3 \\ 5 & 4 & 4 \end{bmatrix}$$

This illustrates the property that matrix addition is commutative. It can be easily seen from the definition that in general

$$A + B = (a_{rs} + b_{rs}) = (b_{rs} + a_{rs}) = B + A$$

This property holds for matrices with real numbers as elements because it holds for the real numbers.

If C is the matrix given by

$$C = \begin{bmatrix} -2 & 5 & -4 \\ 2 & 1 & -3 \end{bmatrix}$$

then it follows that

$$(A + B) + C = \begin{bmatrix} -3 & 8 & -1 \\ 7 & 5 & 1 \end{bmatrix}$$

It is also true that,

$$A + (B + C) = \begin{bmatrix} 2 & 1 & 3 \\ 4 & -1 & 2 \end{bmatrix} + \begin{bmatrix} -5 & 7 & -4 \\ 3 & 6 & -1 \end{bmatrix} = \begin{bmatrix} -3 & 8 & -1 \\ 7 & 5 & 1 \end{bmatrix}$$

This illustrates the fact that matrix addition is associative. It can be readily shown for the general case since

$$(A + B) + C = (a_{rs} + b_{rs}) + (c_{rs}) = ((a_{rs} + b_{rs}) + c_{rs})$$

$$= (a_{rs} + (b_{rs} + c_{rs})) = A + (B + C)$$

Again, since addition of real numbers is associative, addition of matrices with real numbers as elements is associative.

One important class of matrices consists of those whose elements are all zero. These are called zero matrices and are denoted with the symbol 0 if the dimension of the matrix is known. When this symbol is used, the context will show that it is a matrix rather than the symbol for the real number zero. For a given matrix A of dimension $n \times m$, there will be a zero matrix of the same size. For this zero matrix it will be true, that

$$A + 0 = 0 + A = A$$

This follows at once since all the elements of the zero matrix are zero, and when zero is added to any real number, that real number is obtained. Or, in other words, from the definition

$$A + 0 = (a_{rs}) + (0) = (a_{rs} + 0) = (a_{rs}) = A$$

Notice that again this property is a consequence of the corresponding property of real numbers.

Associated with any matrix A is a second matrix which can be denoted as $-A$ such that

$$A + (-A) = (-A) + A = 0$$

Define $-A = (-a_{rs})$. Then by the definition of addition

$$A + (-A) = (a_{rs} + (-a_{rs})) = (0) = 0$$

and

$$-A + A = ((-a_{rs}) + a_{rs}) = (0) = 0$$

Once again the property for matrices follows at once from the same property for the real numbers. That this should be true for all the properties of matrix addition is not surprising for it is a direct consequence of the definition of elementwise addition of matrices.

The above properties of matrix addition are those that are necessary for a set to form a commutative group. Therefore, the set of all matrices of the same dimension forms a commutative group under the given definition of addition. There will be more than one group of matrices under addition, because each set of matrices of the same size will be a group.

1.8 Multiplication of Matrices

The next operation to be considered is that of multiplication of matrices. How should it be defined? One way would be to define it as elementwise multiplication as was done for addition. However, if this were done, the dimension concept would lose significance and only the number of elements involved would be important. A justification for the definition that will be given will be brought up and discussed later. This is sometimes used to arrive at the definition.

Before proceeding to the general situation, a special type of matrix multiplication will be defined. This will then be used as the basis for the general definition. The special type of multiplication is that of a row vector by a column vector where each has the same number of elements.

Definition 1.8. The product of a $1 \times m$ row vector by an $m \times 1$ column vector is given by

$$[a_1 \quad a_2 \quad \cdots \quad a_m] \begin{bmatrix} b_1 \\ b_2 \\ \cdot \\ \cdot \\ \cdot \\ b_m \end{bmatrix} = a_1b_1 + a_2b_2 + \cdots + a_mb_m = \sum_{k=1}^{m} a_kb_k*$$

---

* See the appendix at the end of this chapter for a further discussion of this notation.

The following example will illustrate the general situation.

$$[2 \quad 1 \quad 3] \begin{bmatrix} -3 \\ 2 \\ 0 \end{bmatrix} = 2 \cdot -3 + 1 \cdot 2 + 3 \cdot 0 = -6 + 2 + 0 = -4$$

Some things should be noted about the definition. First of all, the two vectors must be *compatible*, that is, they must have the same number of elements. Secondly, the result of the multiplication is a single element. The importance of this fact will become apparent in the definition of matrix multiplication. In case either vector is a zero vector the result is the element zero.

Recall that in the discussion of the form of a general matrix a double subscript was used. The first subscript denoted the row vector to which the element belongs whereas the second indicated the column vector to which the element belongs. If the rth row vector of a matrix A is multiplied by the sth column vector of B, then by the Definition 1.8

$$[a_{r1} \quad a_{r2} \quad \cdots \quad a_{rm}] \begin{bmatrix} b_{1s} \\ b_{2s} \\ \cdot \\ \cdot \\ \cdot \\ b_{ms} \end{bmatrix} = \sum_{k=1}^{m} a_{rk} b_{ks}$$

With these preliminaries, the following definition of matrix multiplication can be made.

Definition 1.9. The product of two matrices A and B of dimension $n \times m$ and $m \times p$, respectively, is given by

$$AB = \left(\sum_{k=1}^{m} a_{rk} b_{ks} \right)$$

where AB is of dimension $n \times p$.

What does this say? It says the element in the rth row and sth column in the product matrix is the product of the rth row vector of A by the sth column vector of B. The address of a given element in the product matrix is thus given by the indices of the row vector of A and the column vector of B that are used to form the element. Since there are n row vectors in A

one can form n row vectors in the product. Similarly, with p column vectors in B, the product matrix can have p column vectors. The dimension of AB requires that one forms all possible products of the row vectors of A with the column vectors of B. The condition that the number of columns of A be the same as the number of rows of B insures that one can form these products of row vectors of A with column vectors of B.

It was noted above that if either the row vector or the column vector is zero, then their product is zero. This means that if a row vector of A should happen to be a zero vector, then the corresponding row vector of AB would also be a zero vector. Also if a column vector of B is a zero vector, the same column vector of AB would be a zero vector.

In the definition also notice that the column index of a_{rs} and the row index of b_{rs} are replaced by k, the *summation index*. This simple fact is useful in proving properties of matrix multiplication.

The following example will illustrate the concept of the product of two matrices.

$$\begin{bmatrix} 2 & 1 & 3 \\ 4 & -1 & 2 \end{bmatrix} \begin{bmatrix} -3 & 1 \\ 2 & 5 \\ 0 & 2 \end{bmatrix} = \begin{bmatrix} 2\cdot-3+ & 1\cdot2+3\cdot0 & 2\cdot1+ & 1\cdot5+3\cdot2 \\ 4\cdot-3+ & -1\cdot2+2\cdot0 & 4\cdot1+ & -1\cdot5+2\cdot2 \end{bmatrix}$$

$$= \begin{bmatrix} -4 & 13 \\ -14 & 3 \end{bmatrix}$$

On careful examination, note the -4 is the product of the first vectors; the 13 comes from the product of the first row vector of A by the second column vector of B. The other two can be easily checked. In this example, the number of column vectors of A is three, which is the number of row vectors of B so the vectors of these two matrices are compatible. Since A is of dimension 2×3 and B is of dimension 3×2, the dimension of the product AB is 2×2.

Consider the product of the two matrices above in the reverse order,

$$BA = \begin{bmatrix} -3\cdot2+1\cdot4 & -3\cdot1+1\cdot-1 & -3\cdot3+1\cdot2 \\ 2\cdot2+5\cdot4 & 2\cdot1+5\cdot-1 & 2\cdot3+5\cdot2 \\ 0\cdot2+2\cdot4 & 0\cdot1+2\cdot-1 & 0\cdot3+2\cdot2 \end{bmatrix}$$

$$= \begin{bmatrix} -2 & -4 & -7 \\ 24 & -3 & 16 \\ 8 & -2 & 4 \end{bmatrix}$$

The result here is a 3×3 matrix! Comparing this with the fact that AB is a 2×2 matrix points up the striking property of matrix multiplication that it is not always commutative. As a matter of fact, only matrices that are "doubly compatible" can be multiplied in either order, that is, only if the number of rows of either is the same as the number of columns of the other one as in the example above. In other words, if A is $n \times m$, then B must be $m \times n$ in order for them to be doubly compatible. In this case AB will be of dimension $n \times n$, whereas BA will be of dimension $m \times m$. Among the matrices that are doubly compatible are the square matrices.

The next property of matrix multiplication to be considered is that of "associativity." For matrices whose dimensions are properly related, multiplication is associative. This might best be illustrated starting with the A and B used above. Suppose that a third matrix is now defined as

$$C = \begin{bmatrix} -1 & 2 & 3 & 4 \\ 0 & -1 & 2 & 3 \end{bmatrix}$$

then

$$(AB)C = \begin{bmatrix} 4 & -21 & 14 & 23 \\ 14 & -31 & -36 & -47 \end{bmatrix}$$

This can be readily verified by performing the multiplication indicated. It is also true that,

$$A(BC) = \begin{bmatrix} 2 & 1 & 3 \\ 4 & -1 & 2 \end{bmatrix} \begin{bmatrix} 3 & -7 & -7 & -9 \\ -2 & -1 & 16 & 23 \\ 0 & -2 & 4 & 6 \end{bmatrix}$$

$$= \begin{bmatrix} 4 & -21 & 14 & 23 \\ 14 & -31 & -36 & -47 \end{bmatrix}$$

Since the final two results agree, this illustrates the property of associativity of matrix multiplication.

The general proof for this property of matrix multiplication is given in the appendix of this chapter. In the exercises, the reader is asked to show this for general matrices of small dimensions.

There is a special type of square matrix that has ones for the diagonal elements and zeros for all others. These are called *identity matrices* and are denoted as I_n where n indicates they are of dimension $n \times n$. The reason for the name will become apparent on considering the following example using the matrix A defined before,

$$\begin{bmatrix} 1 & 0 \\ 0 & 1 \end{bmatrix}\begin{bmatrix} 2 & 1 & 3 \\ 4 & -1 & 2 \end{bmatrix} = \begin{bmatrix} 2 & 1 & 3 \\ 4 & -1 & 2 \end{bmatrix}\begin{bmatrix} 1 & 0 & 0 \\ 0 & 1 & 0 \\ 0 & 0 & 1 \end{bmatrix} = \begin{bmatrix} 2 & 1 & 3 \\ 4 & -1 & 2 \end{bmatrix}$$

The I_2 used on the left is known as the *left identity*; the I_3 used on the right is called the *right identity* matrix. The adjective right or left indicates on which side the identity matrix is placed. These identity matrices can be written in the form

$$I_n = (\delta_{rs})$$

where

$$\delta_{rs} = 0 \quad \text{if} \quad r \neq s$$

and

$$\delta_{rs} = 1 \quad \text{if} \quad r = s$$

Of course, the dimension has to be known to use the second way of writing the identity matrices. Using this concept with the general matrix for the left identity,

$$I_n A = \left(\sum_{k=1}^{n} \delta_{rk} a_{ks} \right) = (a_{rs})$$

Since δ_{rk} is zero for all values of k except $k = r$, there will be just one term in the sum. This term will be $1 \cdot a_{rs}$ which is equal to a_{rs}. This means that the identity matrix depends upon the identity of multiplication of the real numbers. In a similar manner, it can be shown that $A I_m = A$. In case the matrix A is square, then the left and right identity matrices are the same.

The next concept to be considered is that of an inverse. The inverse of a matrix under addition was easy to define and compute. The situation for multiplication is quite different. From the discussion of the identity matrix above, it might be suspected that for a given matrix A, there could be left inverses and right inverses. It is shown in advanced textbooks on matrix theory that when a matrix is square and has a left inverse, it has a right inverse, and for such matrices, these are the same. This common matrix is called the *inverse* of the given matrix and is denoted as A^{-1}. Not all square matrices have inverses as the following example shows,

$$C = \begin{bmatrix} 1 & 0 & 0 \\ 0 & 1 & 0 \\ 0 & 0 & 0 \end{bmatrix}$$

has no inverse. The product of the third row vector of C with any column vector will always give zero so one can never obtain a 1 in the third row vector for the product. Hence, there can be no right inverse. A similar observation about the third column vector of C would show there could be no left inverse.

Even when a matrix does have an inverse, its computation is not always an easy task. Later chapters will be devoted to ways of finding the inverse for a square matrix when it exists. The problem for the nonsquare matrix will not be considered.

From the above results, it is now apparent that matrices do not form a group under multiplication. This is not a closed binary operation except for sets of square matrices of the same size. In such systems there are nonzero matrices that do not have inverses.

This leaves only a consideration of the distributive law. It is true for matrices of the proper dimensions, that $(A + C)B = AB + CB$. The matrices A and C have to be of the same dimension in order to be able to add them so let them be of dimension $n \times m$. Then the matrix B must have m rows so that the products AB and CB can be formed. Under these conditions it is true that

$$(A + C)B = (a_{rs} + c_{rs})(b_{rs}) = \left(\sum_{k=1}^{m} (a_{rk} + c_{rk})b_{ks} \right)$$

$$= \left(\sum_{k=1}^{m} a_{rk}b_{ks} + c_{rk}b_{ks} \right) = \left(\sum_{k=1}^{m} a_{rk}b_{ks} + \sum_{k=1}^{m} c_{rk}b_{ks} \right)$$

$$= \left(\sum_{k=1}^{m} a_{rk}b_{ks} \right) + \left(\sum_{k=1}^{m} c_{rk}b_{ks} \right) = AB + CB$$

This property again depends upon the corresponding property for real numbers.

It is apparent from the discussion above that matrices do not behave like the real numbers. The matrices must be both square and of the same size, in order to have addition and multiplication as closed binary operations. It was noted that multiplication is not always commutative even in this restricted set. Furthermore, there are some matrices without multiplicative inverses. Actually, it is possible for the product of two matrices to be the zero matrix when neither is a zero matrix. This is illustrated by the simple product

$$\begin{bmatrix} 1 & 0 \\ 5 & 0 \end{bmatrix} \begin{bmatrix} 0 & 0 \\ -1 & 2 \end{bmatrix} = \begin{bmatrix} 0 & 0 \\ 0 & 0 \end{bmatrix}$$

It is interesting to note that the product of these two matrices in the opposite order is no longer the zero matrix.

The discussion above shows that a set of all square matrices of the same size is an example of an algebraic system known as a *ring with unit element*. Any system that is a commutative group under addition, closed and associative under multiplication, and obeys the distributive law, is called a *ring*. If the identity of multiplication is also present, it is called a ring with unit element.

1.9 Scalar Multiplication

The third operation with matrices is known as scalar multiplication. It is of a different character for now the matrix is multiplied by a number from the same system as the elements of the matrix. The operation is characterized by the next definition.

Definition 1.10. The product of a scalar c and a matrix A is given by

$$cA = (ca_{rs})$$

That is, to multiply a matrix by a scalar, one multiplies each element of the matrix by the scalar. This can be done since c is in the same algebraic system as the elements of the matrix.

It is not difficult to prove that this operation has the properties:

1. $(c + d)A = cA + dA$

2. $c(A + B) = cA + cB$

3. $c(dA) = (cd)A$

4. $A(cB) = (cA)B = c(AB)$

The first two are referred to as the *distributive properties*, the third as the *associative property*, and the last as the *commutative property*.

In the definition, the scalar was always placed on the left of the matrix. Scalar multiplication may also be defined as

$$Ac = (a_{rs}c)$$

Since $a_{rs}c = ca_{rs}$ in the algebraic system of the elements, the results will be the same. This could be summed up in an additional property

5. $cA = Ac$

It is possible to define scalar multiplication as matrix multiplication. To see this, a special kind of matrix has to be defined.

Definition 1.11. A diagonal matrix is a square matrix that has all zeros for all elements not on the diagonal.

As an example, the matrix

$$A = \begin{bmatrix} 1 & 0 & 0 \\ 0 & 0 & 0 \\ 0 & 0 & 3 \end{bmatrix}$$

is diagonal. Notice that all the elements not on the diagonal are zero. The definition does not exclude zero elements on the diagonal as shown.

Multiplication on the left by this diagonal matrix is quite simple. Consider for example

$$\begin{bmatrix} 1 & 0 & 0 \\ 0 & 0 & 0 \\ 0 & 0 & 3 \end{bmatrix} \begin{bmatrix} 1 & -2 & 3 \\ 2 & -1 & 4 \\ 4 & 1 & -3 \end{bmatrix} = \begin{bmatrix} 1 & -2 & 3 \\ 0 & 0 & 0 \\ 12 & 3 & -9 \end{bmatrix}$$

The elements of the first row vector are multiplied by one, those of the second row vector by zero, and the third row vector by three. Multiplication on the right by this diagonal matrix gives

$$\begin{bmatrix} 1 & -2 & 3 \\ 2 & -1 & 4 \\ 4 & 1 & -3 \end{bmatrix} \begin{bmatrix} 1 & 0 & 0 \\ 0 & 0 & 0 \\ 0 & 0 & 3 \end{bmatrix} = \begin{bmatrix} 1 & 0 & 9 \\ 2 & 0 & 12 \\ 4 & 0 & -9 \end{bmatrix}$$

The corresponding column vectors of the matrix are multiplied in the same manner as row vectors were when the diagonal matrix was used as a multiplier on the left.

In case all the possible nonzero elements of a diagonal matrix are equal, the matrix is called a *scalar matrix*. The identity matrix previously considered is a scalar matrix whose nonzero elements are one. The zero matrix is also scalar since all of its diagonal elements are zero. As an example of a scalar matrix consider

$$S = \begin{bmatrix} 2 & 0 & 0 \\ 0 & 2 & 0 \\ 0 & 0 & 2 \end{bmatrix}$$

When S is used as a left multiplier, it will multiply all the components of the row vectors of a matrix by 2. If used on the right, it will do the same for all the column vectors. However, in either case, all elements of the matrix will be multiplied by 2. This is a reason for calling these scalar matrices; they accomplish scalar multiplication using ordinary matrix multiplication. In this example $AS = SA = 2A$.

1.10 Special Kinds of Matrices

There are some special types of square matrices that need to be defined and discussed. The most important kind are those that have multiplicative inverses. The next definition gives these a name.

Definition 1.12. A square matrix A is said to be nonsingular if there exists a matrix B such that $BA = AB = I$.

This definition says that a nonsingular matrix is one that has an inverse. In section 1.8, this inverse was denoted as A^{-1}. There will be many references to nonsingular matrices throughout the remainder of this book.

Another special type of a square matrix is the *triangular matrix*. These matrices have all zeros either above or below the diagonal elements. They are sometimes further classified as being *upper* or *lower triangular*. An example of an upper triangular matrix is

$$A = \begin{bmatrix} 1 & 0 & 0 \\ -1 & 3 & 0 \\ 2 & 0 & 4 \end{bmatrix}$$

Another type of square matrix that is very useful is the *symmetric* matrix. A matrix A is said to be symmetric if $A' = A$, that is, if the transpose of A is the same as A. This would mean that $a_{sr} = a_{rs}$ for all elements of A. Viewing the matrix as a square, this requirement says that elements that are symmetrically placed with respect to the diagonal are equal. This is the reason for the use of the adjective symmetric. All diagonal matrices satisfy this requirement for if $s \neq r$, the elements are zero and, hence, are equal. As an example of a more general symmetric matrix, consider

$$A = \begin{bmatrix} 1 & 1 & 2 \\ 1 & 3 & -1 \\ 2 & -1 & -2 \end{bmatrix}$$

Then

$$A' = \begin{bmatrix} 1 & 1 & 2 \\ 1 & 3 & -1 \\ 2 & -1 & -2 \end{bmatrix}$$

and so $A' = A$.

A symmetric matrix can be formed from any $n \times m$ matrix A by forming either the product AA' or $A'A$. These matrices are symmetric for

$$(AA')' = (A')'A' = AA'$$

and, similarly, $(A'A)' = A'A$. It is interesting to note what the elements of this matrix are. For example,

$$\begin{bmatrix} a_{11} & a_{12} & a_{13} \\ a_{21} & a_{22} & a_{23} \end{bmatrix} \begin{bmatrix} a_{11} & a_{21} \\ a_{12} & a_{22} \\ a_{13} & a_{23} \end{bmatrix} = \begin{bmatrix} \sum_{i=1}^{3} a_{1i}a_{1i} & \sum_{i=1}^{3} a_{1i}a_{2i} \\ \sum_{i=1}^{3} a_{2i}a_{1i} & \sum_{i=1}^{3} a_{2i}a_{2i} \end{bmatrix}$$

In statistics, the moment matrix of covariance can be expressed in this manner as the product of the deviation matrix and its transpose.

Closely related to the symmetric matrix is the *skew symmetric matrix*. A square matrix A is said to be skew symmetric if $A' = -A$. This requires that $a_{sr} = -a_{rs}$ for all elements of A. In particular, if

$$s = r, \quad a_{rr} = -a_{rr}$$

so $a_{rr} = 0$ for all r. This implies that all diagonal elements of a skew symmetric matrix are zero. As an example of this type of matrix, if

$$A = \begin{bmatrix} 0 & 1 & 2 \\ -1 & 0 & -1 \\ -2 & 1 & 0 \end{bmatrix}$$

then

$$A' = \begin{bmatrix} 0 & -1 & -2 \\ 1 & 0 & 1 \\ 2 & -1 & 0 \end{bmatrix} = -A$$

For the skew symmetric matrix, the elements that are symmetric with respect to the diagonal are the negatives of each other.

As a matter of interest, any matrix A can be expressed as the sum of a symmetric and a skew symmetric matrix. For the symmetric matrix, choose

$$S = \frac{A + A'}{2}$$

and for the skew symmetric, choose

$$T = \frac{A - A'}{2}$$

Then it is easy to see by addition that $S + T = A$. The matrix S is symmetric and T is skew symmetric since

$$S' = \frac{(a_{rs} + a_{sr})'}{2} = \frac{(a_{sr}) + (a_{rs})}{2} = \frac{A' + A}{2} = S$$

and

$$T' = \frac{(a_{rs} - a_{sr})'}{2} = \frac{(a_{sr}) - (a_{rs})}{2} = \frac{A' - A}{2} = -T$$

The concepts of symmetric and skew symmetric matrices have a simple generalization in case the elements are complex numbers. Involved in the extension is the idea of the *conjugate* of a complex number. Associated with every complex number $a = x + yi$, is another complex number $x - yi$. This second number is called the conjugate of the first one and is often denoted as $\bar{a}$. The first number can also be considered to be the conjugate of the second. A complex number and its conjugate differ only in that the coefficients of i are opposite in sign. It is easy to see that the sum of a complex number and its conjugate is just $2x$ and that their product is the non-negative real number $x^2 + y^2$. If a complex number and its conjugate are equal, then the coefficient of i must be zero. In other words, the complex number must be real.

The conjugate matrix $\bar{A}$ of A has as elements the complex conjugates of the corresponding elements of A. In symbols, this says that $\bar{A} = (\bar{a}_{rs})$. In case

$$\bar{A}' = A, \quad \text{that is,} \quad (\bar{a}_{sr}) = (a_{rs})$$

the matrix A is called *Hermitian*. Thus, if the symmetrically placed elements of A are complex conjugates, the matrix is Hermitian. The condition that $\bar{a}_{rr} = a_{rr}$ implies that in particular the diagonal elements must be real numbers. In case all the elements are real the matrix is symmetric, for if any element is real, its conjugate is equal to it. This is why the Hermitian matrix is said to be a generalization of the symmetric matrix.

As an example of a Hermitian matrix, if

$$A = \begin{bmatrix} 1 & 2+i & 3+2i \\ 2-i & 3 & -3i \\ 3-2i & 3i & -2 \end{bmatrix}$$

then

$$\bar{A}' = \begin{bmatrix} 1 & 2-i & 3-2i \\ 2+i & 3 & 3i \\ 3+2i & -3i & -2 \end{bmatrix}' = \begin{bmatrix} 1 & 2+i & 3+2i \\ 2-i & 3 & -3i \\ 3-2i & 3i & -2 \end{bmatrix}$$

and $\bar{A} = A$.

A matrix is said to be *skew Hermitian* if $\bar{A}' = -A$, that is, if $\bar{a}_{sr} = -a_{rs}$. For $r = s$, this gives $\bar{a}_{rr} = -a_{rr}$; this is possible only if a_{rr} is a pure imaginary number or zero. Consider for an example

$$A = \begin{bmatrix} i & 2+i & 3+2i \\ -2+i & 3i & -3i \\ -3+2i & -3i & 0 \end{bmatrix}$$

Then,

$$\bar{A}' = \begin{bmatrix} -i & 2-i & 3-2i \\ -2-i & -3i & 3i \\ -3-2i & 3i & 0 \end{bmatrix}'$$

$$= \begin{bmatrix} -i & -2-i & -3-2i \\ 2-i & -3i & 3i \\ 3-2i & 3i & 0 \end{bmatrix} = -A$$

For this type of matrix, the symmetrically placed elements are the negatives of the conjugates of each other. In case an element is a real number, it would be the negative of its symmetric element. If all the elements are real, the diagonal elements would be zero, and all symmetric pairs would be negatives of each other. In other words, the matrix would be skew symmetric.

As before, any matrix can be expressed as the sum of a Hermitian and a skew Hermitian matrix. Take for the Hermitian matrix, $S = \frac{1}{2}(A + \bar{A}')$ and for the skew Hermitian matrix, $T = \frac{1}{2}(A - \bar{A}')$. That this works can be readily verified as was done for the symmetric and skew symmetric cases.

The next special type of a matrix to be considered has real numbers as elements and is nonsingular. The matrix A is said to be *orthogonal* if $A'A = I = AA'$. Since A is nonsingular, there will exist a matrix A^{-1} such that $A^{-1}A = AA^{-1} = I$, so these conditions say that $A' = A^{-1}$. In other words the transpose of the orthogonal matrix is also its inverse. If A has complex numbers as elements, then A is orthogonal if $\bar{A}'A = I = A\bar{A}'$, that is, $\bar{A}' = A^{-1}$. Notice that this agrees with the first definition in case the elements of A are real, for then $\bar{A}' = A'$. As examples of this kind of matrix, note the following,

$$AA' = \begin{bmatrix} \cos\theta & \sin\theta \\ -\sin\theta & \cos\theta \end{bmatrix} \begin{bmatrix} \cos\theta & -\sin\theta \\ \sin\theta & \cos\theta \end{bmatrix} = \begin{bmatrix} 1 & 0 \\ 0 & 1 \end{bmatrix}$$

$$BB' = \begin{bmatrix} 1 & 0 & 0 \\ 0 & \dfrac{1}{2} & \dfrac{\sqrt{3}}{2} \\ 0 & -\dfrac{\sqrt{3}}{2} & \dfrac{1}{2} \end{bmatrix} \begin{bmatrix} 1 & 0 & 0 \\ 0 & \dfrac{1}{2} & -\dfrac{\sqrt{3}}{2} \\ 0 & \dfrac{\sqrt{3}}{2} & \dfrac{1}{2} \end{bmatrix} = \begin{bmatrix} 1 & 0 & 0 \\ 0 & 1 & 0 \\ 0 & 0 & 1 \end{bmatrix}$$

There are other special kinds of matrices, but the above listing covers the more important ones. Reference will be made to these in later chapters, especially to the nonsingular matrix.

1.11 Partitioning of Matrices

The column vectors of a matrix A can be divided into sets by lines drawn vertically between some of the columns. Similarly, the row vectors can be broken up into sets by horizontal lines. The matrix A is said to be *partitioned vertically* in the first case and *partitioned horizontally* in the second case. The partitioning lines in both cases define submatrices of A formed by deleting only column or only row vectors. If both horizontal and vertical lines are drawn, other submatrices are formed that can be obtained by deleting both row and column vectors. To illustrate this consider the general 4×5 matrix A. A vertical partitioning could be the following.

$$A = \begin{bmatrix} a_{11} & a_{12} & a_{13} & a_{14} & a_{15} \\ a_{21} & a_{22} & a_{23} & a_{24} & a_{25} \\ a_{31} & a_{32} & a_{33} & a_{34} & a_{35} \\ a_{41} & a_{42} & a_{43} & a_{44} & a_{45} \end{bmatrix}$$

Now the matrix A can be written as the row vector

$$[A_{11} \quad A_{12} \quad A_{13}]$$

where A_{11} is the first column vector of A, A_{12} is the matrix formed from the second and third column vectors of A, and A_{13} is the matrix formed by the last two column vectors of A. Here is an example of a matrix whose elements are matrices! Notice that the capital letter is used indicating that one is talking about matrices while the subscripts are used to give the address. These two then indicate that one is considering submatrices of A. It is necessary to know the partitioning in order to know exactly what the submatrices are.

The matrix A could be partitioned horizontally so that

$$A = \begin{bmatrix} a_{11} & a_{12} & a_{13} & a_{14} & a_{15} \\ a_{21} & a_{22} & a_{23} & a_{24} & a_{25} \\ a_{31} & a_{32} & a_{33} & a_{34} & a_{35} \\ a_{41} & a_{42} & a_{43} & a_{44} & a_{45} \end{bmatrix}$$

In this case, the matrix A can be written as the column vector

$$\begin{bmatrix} A_{11} \\ A_{21} \end{bmatrix}$$

where A_{11} is a matrix composed of the first row vector of A and A_{21} is composed of the last three row vectors of A. The A_{11} here is not the same as the A_{11} obtained by the vertical partitioning.

If both partitionings are made simultaneously on A, then

$$
A = \begin{bmatrix}
a_{11} & a_{12} & a_{13} & a_{14} & a_{15} \\
a_{21} & a_{22} & a_{23} & a_{24} & a_{25} \\
a_{31} & a_{32} & a_{33} & a_{34} & a_{35} \\
a_{41} & a_{42} & a_{43} & a_{44} & a_{45}
\end{bmatrix}
$$

Writing A as a matrix whose elements are the submatrices thus formed,

$$
A = \begin{bmatrix}
A_{11} & A_{12} & A_{13} \\
A_{21} & A_{22} & A_{23}
\end{bmatrix}
$$

It is easily verified that A_{21} is a column vector, A_{12} and A_{13} are row vectors, A_{22} and A_{23} are 3×2 matrices, and A_{11} is a 1×1 matrix.

Partitioning of matrices is sometimes used to lessen the work in matrix multiplication. If the matrices are large, partitioning gives smaller matrices that are easier to handle. Some of these may be zero matrices in which case any product involving them is a zero matrix. Partitioning is also used as a technique for finding the inverse of a matrix. This topic will be discussed in a later chapter.

The problem of partitioning, as related to products, is tied up with questions of compatability for multiplication of row vectors by column vectors. Suppose that a matrix A is partitioned vertically, how should a matrix B be partitioned in order to be able to form the product AB? In this case, A is written as a row vector whose elements are matrices. Then B is going to have to be written as a column vector with the same number of elements as A. In other words, the matrix B will have to be partitioned horizontally into the same number of submatrices as A. Perhaps an example will clarify this and also show another condition that must be imposed. Suppose A is partitioned as was done at the beginning of this section. Let B be the general 5×3 matrix, and let it be partitioned by two horizontal lines so that

$$
B = \begin{bmatrix}
B_{11} \\
B_{21} \\
B_{31}
\end{bmatrix}
$$

Then the formal product

$$AB = \begin{bmatrix} A_{11} & A_{12} & A_{13} \end{bmatrix} \begin{bmatrix} B_{11} \\ B_{21} \\ B_{31} \end{bmatrix} = A_{11}B_{11} + A_{12}B_{21} + A_{13}B_{31}$$

In order for $A_{11}B_{11}$ to be defined, B_{11} must contain one row vector since A_{11} by choice has only one column vector. Similarly, B_{21} and B_{31} must be made up of two row vectors because A_{12} and A_{13} have two column vectors. This implies that B must be partitioned as follows.

$$\begin{bmatrix} b_{11} & b_{12} & b_{13} \\ \hline b_{21} & b_{22} & b_{23} \\ b_{31} & b_{32} & b_{33} \\ \hline b_{41} & b_{42} & b_{43} \\ b_{51} & b_{52} & b_{53} \end{bmatrix}$$

Notice that the horizontal partitioning of B is the same as the vertical partitioning of A! This should not be too surprising because the number of column vectors of A must be the same as the number of row vectors of B.

This can be illustrated by considering the following numerical example. Let the matrices E and F be partitioned as indicated, then

$$EF = \begin{bmatrix} 2 & 1 & 3 \\ 0 & -1 & 2 \end{bmatrix} \begin{bmatrix} 3 & -7 & -7 & 2 \\ \hline -2 & 1 & 4 & 0 \\ 0 & 2 & 4 & 0 \end{bmatrix} = \begin{bmatrix} E_{11} & E_{12} \end{bmatrix} \begin{bmatrix} F_{11} \\ F_{21} \end{bmatrix}$$

$$= E_{11}F_{11} + E_{12}F_{21}$$

$$= \begin{bmatrix} 2 \\ 0 \end{bmatrix} \begin{bmatrix} 3 & -7 & -7 & 2 \end{bmatrix} + \begin{bmatrix} 1 & 3 \\ -1 & 2 \end{bmatrix} \begin{bmatrix} -2 & 1 & 4 & 0 \\ 0 & 2 & 4 & 0 \end{bmatrix}$$

$$= \begin{bmatrix} 6 & -14 & -14 & 4 \\ 0 & 0 & 0 & 0 \end{bmatrix} + \begin{bmatrix} -2 & 7 & 16 & 0 \\ 2 & 3 & 4 & 0 \end{bmatrix} = \begin{bmatrix} 4 & -7 & 2 & 4 \\ 2 & 3 & 4 & 0 \end{bmatrix}$$

The reader may want to verify that this is the product that would be obtained in the usual manner.

Now consider the horizontal partitioning of the general matrix A given before; does this place any requirements on how B is partitioned? The answer is no. Similarly, any vertical partitioning of B can be made without regard to A. This might be expected, since there is no necessary relation between the number of row vectors of A and the number of column vectors of B.

Suppose that A and B are partitioned both ways, A as illustrated above, and B as follows

$$
B = \begin{bmatrix}
b_{11} & b_{12} & b_{13} \\
b_{21} & b_{22} & b_{23} \\
b_{31} & b_{31} & b_{33} \\
b_{41} & b_{42} & b_{43} \\
b_{51} & b_{52} & b_{53}
\end{bmatrix}
=
\begin{bmatrix}
B_{11} & B_{12} \\
B_{21} & B_{22} \\
B_{31} & B_{32}
\end{bmatrix}
$$

The formal product is

$$
AB = \begin{bmatrix}
A_{11} & A_{12} & A_{13} \\
A_{21} & A_{22} & A_{23}
\end{bmatrix}
\begin{bmatrix}
B_{11} & B_{12} \\
B_{21} & B_{22} \\
B_{31} & B_{32}
\end{bmatrix}
$$

$$
= \begin{bmatrix}
A_{11}B_{11} + A_{12}B_{21} + A_{13}B_{31} & A_{11}B_{12} + A_{12}B_{22} + A_{13}B_{32} \\
A_{21}B_{11} + A_{22}B_{21} + A_{23}B_{31} & A_{21}B_{12} + A_{22}B_{22} + A_{23}B_{32}
\end{bmatrix}
$$

Suppose that the product AB is designated as C and, further, that C is partitioned into four submatrices

$$
C = \begin{bmatrix}
C_{11} & C_{12} \\
C_{21} & C_{22}
\end{bmatrix}
$$

If this is to be the product, then

$$
C_{11} = A_{11}B_{11} + A_{12}B_{21} + A_{13}B_{31}
$$

$$
C_{12} = A_{11}B_{12} + A_{12}B_{22} + A_{13}B_{32}
$$

$$
C_{21} = A_{21}B_{11} + A_{22}B_{21} + A_{23}B_{31}
$$

$$
C_{22} = A_{21}B_{12} + A_{22}B_{22} + A_{23}B_{32}
$$

A check of dimensions will show that C_{11} is 1×2, C_{12} is 1×1, C_{21} is 3×2, and C_{22} is 3×1. This indicates that the horizontal partitioning of C is the same as that of A while its vertical partitioning is the same as that for B. (The computation of each of the four submatrices of C is left as an exercise. From this it will follow that the matrix C is the same as the product matrix formed in the usual manner). It can be verified for this A and B that, as long as the vertical partitioning of A is the same as the horizontal partitioning of B, the product AB can be found using the submatrices of A and B.

Returning to the numerical example, suppose the matrices E and F are further partitioned as shown on page 30.

The product is again the same as computed before. If one noted that E_{21} and F_{23} are zero matrices then the product could be written simply as

$$\begin{bmatrix} E_{11}F_{11} + E_{12}F_{21} & E_{11}F_{12} + E_{12}F_{22} & E_{11}F_{13} \\ E_{22}F_{21} & E_{22}F_{22} & 0 \end{bmatrix}$$

This illustrates how partitioning can simplify forming a product of two matrices.

As a special case of partitioning, one could partition the matrix B between each of its rows. Then the submatrices of B are its row vectors. If the matrix A is also partitioned between each of its rows and columns, then the submatrices formed would be all 1×1. In other words, they could be thought of as being scalar matrices; thus, one can use the old designation for these submatrices. The product then becomes,

$$AB = \begin{bmatrix} a_{11} & a_{12} & a_{13} & a_{14} & a_{15} \\ a_{21} & a_{22} & a_{23} & a_{24} & a_{25} \\ a_{31} & a_{32} & a_{33} & a_{34} & a_{35} \\ a_{41} & a_{42} & a_{43} & a_{44} & a_{45} \end{bmatrix} \begin{bmatrix} B_{11} \\ B_{21} \\ B_{31} \\ B_{41} \\ B_{51} \end{bmatrix}$$

$$= \begin{bmatrix} a_{11}B_{11} + a_{12}B_{21} + a_{13}B_{31} + a_{14}B_{41} + a_{15}B_{51} \\ a_{21}B_{11} + a_{22}B_{21} + a_{23}B_{31} + a_{24}B_{41} + a_{25}B_{51} \\ a_{31}B_{11} + a_{32}B_{21} + a_{33}B_{31} + a_{34}B_{41} + a_{35}B_{51} \\ a_{41}B_{11} + a_{42}B_{21} + a_{43}B_{31} + a_{44}B_{41} + a_{45}B_{51} \end{bmatrix}$$

$$EF = \left[\begin{array}{c|cc} 2 & 1 & 3 \\ \hline 0 & -1 & 2 \end{array}\right] \left[\begin{array}{c|cc} 3 & -7 & -7 & 2 \\ \hline -2 & 1 & 4 & 0 \\ 0 & 2 & 4 & 0 \end{array}\right] = \left[\begin{array}{c|cc} E_{11} & E_{12} \\ \hline E_{21} & E_{22} \end{array}\right] \left[\begin{array}{ccc} F_{11} & F_{12} & F_{13} \\ F_{21} & F_{22} & F_{23} \end{array}\right]$$

$$= \left[\begin{array}{ccc} E_{11}F_{11} + E_{12}F_{21} & E_{11}F_{12} + E_{12}F_{22} & E_{11}F_{13} + E_{12}F_{23} \\ E_{21}F_{11} + E_{22}F_{21} & E_{21}F_{12} + E_{22}F_{22} & E_{21}F_{13} + E_{22}F_{23} \end{array}\right]$$

$$= \left[\begin{array}{c:cc} [2][3 \quad -7] + [1 \quad 3]\begin{bmatrix} -2 & 1 \\ 0 & 2 \end{bmatrix} & [2][-7] + [1 \quad 3]\begin{bmatrix} 4 \\ 4 \end{bmatrix} & [2][2] + [1 \quad 3]\begin{bmatrix} 0 \\ 0 \end{bmatrix} \\ \hdashline [0][3 \quad -7] + [-1 \quad 2]\begin{bmatrix} -2 & 1 \\ 0 & 2 \end{bmatrix} & [0][-7] + [-1 \quad 2]\begin{bmatrix} 4 \\ 4 \end{bmatrix} & [0][2] + [-1 \quad 2]\begin{bmatrix} 0 \\ 0 \end{bmatrix} \end{array}\right]$$

$$= \left[\begin{array}{c:cc} [6 \quad -14] + [-2 \quad 7] & [-14] + [16] & [4] + [0] \\ \hdashline [0 \quad 0] + [2 \quad 3] & [0] + [4] & [0] + [0] \end{array}\right] = \left[\begin{array}{c:cc} 4 & -7 & 2 & 4 \\ \hdashline 2 & 3 & 4 & 0 \end{array}\right]$$

Since the matrix B was partitioned between its row vectors, the matrix AB is partitioned the same way. The row vectors of the product AB are given in terms of the row vectors of B. These expressions are sums of scalar multiples of the row vectors of B. They are known as a linear combination of the vectors. It is sometimes helpful to think of the row vectors of a product as linear combinations of the row vectors of the second matrix. One can also partition A into its column vectors and B into its elements. Then the column vectors of the product AB are linear combinations of the column vectors of the matrix A.

PROBLEMS

1. Write out completely the following general matrices whose dimensions are given.

   (a) A which is 3×5 (b) B which is 3×3 (c) C which is 5×2

   (d) D which is 5×1 (e) E which is 1×5

   These five general matrices and the following five numerical matrices will be referred to by letter in the problems to follow.

$$F = \begin{bmatrix} 1 & -3 & 2 & 4 \end{bmatrix} \quad G = \begin{bmatrix} -3 \\ 2 \\ 0 \\ 1 \end{bmatrix} \quad H = \begin{bmatrix} 4 & -2 & 5 & 1 \\ 2 & -10 & 3 & 0 \\ -1 & 4 & 0 & 7 \end{bmatrix}$$

$$J = \begin{bmatrix} 2 & 1 & -4 \\ 2 & -1 & 3 \\ 4 & 4 & -1 \\ 1 & 0 & -1 \end{bmatrix} \quad K = \begin{bmatrix} 5 & -2 & -3 & 5 \\ 2 & 1 & 1 & 4 \\ 4 & -2 & 2 & 3 \\ 1 & -1 & 0 & 1 \end{bmatrix}$$

2. What are the dimensions of the matrices F through K?

3. What are the row vectors of the matrix A? of the matrix K? the column vectors of B? of H?

4. Find the transposes of the matrices A through K.

5. Find the transpose of the transpose of each of the matrices A, C, E, G, J.

6. Verify that:

(a) $(H + J')' = H' + J$ (b) $(F + G')' = F' + G$

(c) $(D + E')' = D' + E$

What property of the transpose does this illustrate?

7. Verify that:

(a) $H' + J = J + H'$ (b) $F' + G = G + F'$

(c) $D + E' = E' + D$

What property of addition does this illustrate?

8. What are the identity matrices of addition for A through K?

9. Find the additive inverses of the matrices F through K and verify that they are the inverses with respect to addition.

10. Form the following products: FG, ED, FJ, HG, KG, EC, AD, HJ, JH, HK, GF, DE, BA, AC.

11. What is the dimension of the product of an $n \times 1$ column vector by a $1 \times m$ row vector?

12. Verify that

(a) $(HJ)' = J'H'$ (b) $(KG)' = G'K'$ (c) $(BA)' = A'B'$

What property of the transpose does this illustrate?

13. Verify that

(a) $(JH)K = J(HK)$ (b) $(FK)G = F(KG)$

(c) $(BA)C = B(AC)$

14. What are the dimensions of the left and right identity matrices of multiplication for A through K?

15. Prove the four properties of scalar multiplication.

16. Express K as a sum of a symmetric and a skew symmetric matrix.

17. Let Q be the 3×3 diagonal matrix whose nonzero elements are 3, -1, and 2 respectively. Form the following products.

(a) QH (b) JQ (c) QB

18. Let R be the 4×4 scalar matrix whose nonzero elements are 3. Form the following products.

(a) RK (b)KR (c) RJ (d) HR

19. What is the inverse of each of the matrices Q and R used above?

20. Which of the following matrices are Hermitian? Skew Hermitian?

$$S = \begin{bmatrix} i & 2-i & 3-4i & 4 \\ -2-i & 3i & -5i & -3+2i \\ -3-4i & -5i & -2i & -2 \\ -4 & 3+2i & 2 & 0 \end{bmatrix}$$

$$T = \begin{bmatrix} 1 & 2-i & 3-4i & 4 \\ 2+i & 3 & -5i & -3+2i \\ 3+4i & 5i & -2 & 2 \\ 4 & -3-2i & 2 & 0 \end{bmatrix}$$

21. Verify that the following two matrices are orthogonal.

$$U = \begin{bmatrix} \dfrac{\sqrt{2}}{2} & \dfrac{\sqrt{2}}{2} & 0 \\ -\dfrac{\sqrt{2}}{2} & \dfrac{\sqrt{2}}{2} & 0 \\ 0 & 0 & 1 \end{bmatrix} \qquad V = \begin{bmatrix} \dfrac{\sqrt{14}}{14} & \dfrac{2\sqrt{14}}{14} & \dfrac{3\sqrt{14}}{14} \\ \dfrac{3\sqrt{10}}{10} & 0 & -\dfrac{\sqrt{10}}{10} \\ -\dfrac{\sqrt{35}}{35} & \dfrac{5\sqrt{35}}{35} & -\dfrac{3\sqrt{35}}{35} \end{bmatrix}$$

22. Partition the matrix H between the second and third columns. How must J be partitioned to be able to form the product HJ as a vector product? Find this product. Suppose H is also partitioned between the second and third rows and J between the first and second columns. Form the product of the H and J in terms of the submatrices formed. Verify that simplification of this will give the product HJ.

23. Compute the submatrices of C in Section 1.1. Show that the matrix C thus formed is the same as the product AB.

APPENDIX TO CHAPTER 1

A1.1 Finite Summation

One concept in mathematics that is quite useful is that of a sum of a set of elements of the form

$$a_1 + a_2 + a_3 + a_4 + a_5$$

It is convenient to indicate such a sum by the shorthand notation

$$\sum_{k=1}^{5} a_k.$$

The saving in space and writing may not be too great in this example but consider the following sum,

$$\sum_{k=3}^{100} b_k = b_3 + b_4 + b_5 + \cdots + b_{100}$$

where the "$\cdots$", called an ellipsis, stands for the terms that are left out. The ellipsis is a standard notation that is also quite necessary for something like

$$\sum_{k=10}^{n} a_k = a_{10} + a_{11} + \cdots + a_n$$

In this example the letter n is used to represent any general integer. The ellipsis indicates the terms that are left out for any particular value of n. If $n = 15$, there would be three terms left out, whereas if $n = 111$, there would be 99 omitted, but if $n = 12$, there would be no terms omitted.

In all of the examples above, the symbolism used has a definite purpose. The $\sum$ sign means that a sum is to be formed, whereas the a_k indicates the elements to be added together. These elements are numbered consecutively in some manner so that they can be referred to by an integer. The letter k beneath the summand and in the subscript is called the "index of summation." The index is not always written if it is clearly understood what it is. The number under the summation symbol gives the initial value for the index, and the one on top gives the final value. The symbol

$$\sum_{k=r}^{m} a_k$$

is then read as the summation of a_k from $k = r$ to $k = m$. The initial value can be any positive or negative integer or zero. The terminal value is then any larger integer.

A slightly more complicated example is given by the definition of multiplication of a row vector by a column vector. Here the 1×1 product is given by

$$\sum_{k=1}^{m} a_k b_k = a_1 b_1 + a_2 b_2 + \cdots + a_m b_m$$

In other words, the set to be summed is a special product of two sets of elements. When this definition was extended to a product of a row vector of a matrix with a column vector of a second matrix, the result was written as

$$\sum_{k=1}^{m} a_{rk} b_{ks}$$

This is an example of where the index of summation must be indicated because of the three letters involved in the subscripts. For this product if $m = 4$, then

$$\sum_{k=1}^{4} a_{rk} b_{ks} = a_{r1} b_{1s} + a_{r2} b_{2s} + a_{r3} b_{3s} + a_{r4} b_{4s}$$

Notice that the inner subscripts are the "running index," that is, in this sum they range from one to four. The outer subscripts are constant and are used to denote the row vector and the column vector used in this particular multiplication. In forming this product the column index of the element from the first matrix and the row index of the element of the second matrix are replaced by the index of summation.

A more complicated summation is the double finite sum. Consider

$$\sum_{t=1}^{3} \sum_{k=1}^{2} c_{tk} = \sum_{t=1}^{3} (c_{t1} + c_{t2}) = (c_{11} + c_{12}) + (c_{21} + c_{22}) + (c_{31} + c_{32})$$

By a simple rearrangement of terms, this sum could be expressed as

$$(c_{11} + c_{21} + c_{31}) + (c_{12} + c_{22} + c_{32})$$

However, this is the written out form of the sum

$$\sum_{k=1}^{2} (c_{1k} + c_{2k} + c_{3k}) = \sum_{k=1}^{2} \sum_{t=1}^{3} c_{tk}$$

This illustrates the important property of finite double sums: that the order of addition may be reversed. One way to see this is to write the elements for this example in the form

$$c_{11} \quad c_{12}$$
$$c_{21} \quad c_{22}$$
$$c_{31} \quad c_{32}$$

The first order of summation indicates the numbers in each row are to be added, that is, find $c_{t1} + c_{t2}$. Then these three sums are added together. The second order of summation indicates the two columns are to be added to obtain the $c_{1k} + c_{2k} + c_{3k}$. These two sums are then added to obtain the final sum. The same final result is obtained either way, since the same numbers are added but in a different order. This property of the finite double sum is needed in the proof of the associative law of matrix multiplication $(AB)C = A(BC)$.

A1.2 The Associative Law of Matrix Multiplication

The associative law of matrix multiplication is best illustrated by an example to show the general procedure for the proof. Suppose the three matrices A, B, and C are to be multiplied together in that order. Assume that A is 2×4, that B is 4×3, and that C is 3×2. The dimensions of the matrices involved might be checked to be sure that the products can be formed and to determine the size of the final product. The dimension of AB will be 2×3 so that the dimension of $(AB)C$ will be 2×2. In contrast, the dimension of BC will be 4×2, so the size of $A(BC)$ will be 2×2. Therefore, at least the dimensions of the final product in both cases will be the same.

Forming the product the first way

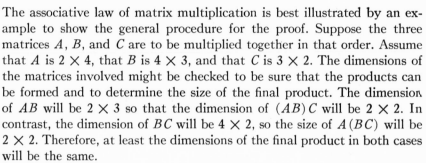

$$(AB)C = \begin{bmatrix} a_{11} & a_{12} & a_{13} & a_{14} \\ a_{21} & a_{22} & a_{23} & a_{24} \end{bmatrix} \begin{bmatrix} b_{11} & b_{12} & b_{13} \\ b_{21} & b_{22} & b_{23} \\ b_{31} & b_{32} & b_{33} \\ b_{41} & b_{42} & b_{43} \end{bmatrix} C$$

$$= \begin{bmatrix} \sum_{k=1}^{4} a_{1k}b_{k1} & \sum_{k=1}^{4} a_{1k}b_{k2} & \sum_{k=1}^{4} a_{1k}b_{k3} \\ \sum_{k=1}^{4} a_{2k}b_{k1} & \sum_{k=1}^{4} a_{2k}b_{k2} & \sum_{k=1}^{4} a_{2k}b_{k3} \end{bmatrix} \begin{bmatrix} c_{11} & c_{12} \\ c_{21} & c_{22} \\ c_{31} & c_{32} \end{bmatrix}$$

$$= \begin{bmatrix} \sum_{t=1}^{3}\sum_{k=1}^{4} (a_{1k}b_{kt})c_{t1} & \sum_{t=1}^{3}\sum_{k=1}^{4} (a_{1k}b_{kt})c_{t2} \\ \sum_{t=1}^{3}\sum_{k=1}^{4} (a_{2k}b_{kt})c_{t1} & \sum_{t=1}^{3}\sum_{k=1}^{4} (a_{2k}b_{kt})c_{t2} \end{bmatrix}$$

For the product

$$
A(BC) = A \begin{bmatrix} b_{11} & b_{12} & b_{13} \\ b_{21} & b_{22} & b_{23} \\ b_{31} & b_{32} & b_{33} \\ b_{41} & b_{42} & b_{43} \end{bmatrix} \begin{bmatrix} c_{11} & c_{12} \\ c_{21} & c_{22} \\ c_{31} & c_{32} \end{bmatrix}
$$

$$
= \begin{bmatrix} a_{11} & a_{12} & a_{13} & a_{14} \\ a_{21} & a_{22} & a_{23} & a_{24} \end{bmatrix} \begin{bmatrix} \sum_{t=1}^{3} b_{1t}c_{t1} & \sum_{t=1}^{3} b_{1t}c_{t2} \\ \sum_{t=1}^{3} b_{2t}c_{t1} & \sum_{t=1}^{3} b_{2t}c_{t2} \\ \sum_{t=1}^{3} b_{3t}c_{t1} & \sum_{t=1}^{3} b_{3t}c_{t2} \\ \sum_{t=1}^{3} b_{4t}c_{t1} & \sum_{t=1}^{3} b_{4t}c_{t2} \end{bmatrix}
$$

$$
= \begin{bmatrix} \sum_{k=1}^{4} a_{1k}\left(\sum_{t=1}^{3} b_{kt}c_{t1}\right) & \sum_{k=1}^{4} a_{1k}\left(\sum_{t=1}^{3} b_{kt}c_{t2}\right) \\ \sum_{k=1}^{4} a_{2k}\left(\sum_{t=1}^{3} b_{kt}c_{t1}\right) & \sum_{k=1}^{4} a_{2k}\left(\sum_{t=1}^{3} b_{kt}c_{t2}\right) \end{bmatrix}
$$

$$
= \begin{bmatrix} \sum_{k=1}^{4}\sum_{t=1}^{3} a_{1k}(b_{kt}c_{t1}) & \sum_{k=1}^{4}\sum_{t=1}^{3} a_{1k}(b_{kt}c_{t2}) \\ \sum_{k=1}^{4}\sum_{t=1}^{3} a_{2k}(b_{kt}c_{t1}) & \sum_{k=1}^{4}\sum_{t=1}^{3} a_{2k}(b_{kt}c_{t2}) \end{bmatrix}
$$

The quantities to be summed in these two results are the same because of the associativity of multiplication of real numbers. The sums involved are finite double sums in the two expressions and differ only in the order of summation. Hence, these two results are the same and the general elements in the two final product matrices are identical. Thus associativity of multiplication has been shown in this case.

For the general proof assume that the dimensions of A, B, and C are $n \times m$, $m \times p$, and $p \times q$ respectively. From the definition of the product of two matrices

$$AB = \left(\sum_{k=1}^{m} a_{rk}b_{ks} \right)$$

In this product the rth row vector has for its components the finite sums

$$\sum_{k=1}^{m} a_{rk}b_{k1}, \ \sum_{k=1}^{m} a_{rk}b_{k2}, \ \cdots, \ \sum_{k=1}^{m} a_{rk}b_{ks}, \ \cdots, \ \sum_{k=1}^{m} a_{rk}b_{kp}$$

Notice that the column index is given by the second subscript of the b. To form the product of this row vector with the sth column vector of C, the column index must be replaced by an index of summation, say t. Then, the row index of the column vector of C must also be replaced by t, the products formed and added to give the general element in the desired product $(AB)C$. This would yield

$$(AB)C = \left(\sum_{t=1}^{p} \sum_{k=1}^{m} (a_{rk}b_{kt})c_{ts} \right)$$

Working with the other side of the equation that is to be established and using t as the index of summation, the first product to be obtained is

$$BC = \left(\sum_{t=1}^{p} b_{rt}c_{ts} \right)$$

In this product the row index of the sth column vector is the first subscript of b. Replacing this and the column index of the rth row vector of A by the index k,

$$A(BC) = \left(\sum_{k=1}^{m} a_{rk} \sum_{t=1}^{p} b_{kt}c_{ts} \right) = \left(\sum_{k=1}^{m} \sum_{t=1}^{p} a_{rk}(b_{kt}c_{ts}) \right)$$

Because the multiplication of real numbers is associative, the quantities to be summed in both cases are the same. Since these are finite double sums, the same sum is obtained with either order of summation. Therefore, the general element of the triple product is the same in both cases and hence, the multiplication of matrices is associative.

2

Elementary   Matrix
Operations

2.1 Systems of Linear Equations

At the beginning of Chapter 1, reference was made to the widely used concept of a system of linear equations. It shall be the purpose of this chapter to consider the problem of how to find a solution for such a given system. First this will be done by an ordinary method, then the language of matrices will be used to simplify and organize the process of finding the solution. This approach will give a motivation for the important matrix theory that is developed. The entire discussion will be used in a later chapter to gain a better understanding of the numerical techniques for finding the solution of a system of linear equations and for finding the inverse of a matrix.

It will be necessary from time to time to refer to what will be called the *general system of linear equations*. This will be written in the following form:

$$a_{11}x_1 + a_{12}x_2 + \cdots + a_{1m}x_m = g_1$$

$$a_{21}x_1 + a_{22}x_2 + \cdots + a_{2m}x_m = g_2$$

$$\cdot \quad \cdot \quad \cdot \quad \cdot \quad \cdot \quad \cdot \quad \cdot \quad \cdot \quad \cdot \quad \cdot$$

$$a_{n1}x_1 + a_{n2}x_2 + \cdots + a_{nm}x_m = g_n$$

Notice that there are m unknowns indicated, written in the same order in each of the n equations. The coefficients will be assumed to be real numbers, positive, negative, or zero. In case an unknown is missing in an equation, it is written with a zero coefficient. Another important thing to observe is that only the multiples of the variables are shown on the left so that the constant term is always on the right.

Using concepts of the first chapter, these equations can be thought of as equality of components of two vectors. Thus, one can express the system in terms of equality of two vectors. If these are assumed to be column vectors, the system can be written in the form

$$
\begin{bmatrix}
a_{11}x_1 + a_{12}x_2 + \cdots + a_{1m}x_m \\
a_{21}x_1 + a_{22}x_2 + \cdots + a_{2m}x_m \\
\cdot \quad \cdot \quad \cdots \quad \cdot \\
\cdot \quad \cdot \quad \cdots \quad \cdot \\
\cdot \quad \cdot \quad \cdots \quad \cdot \\
a_{n1}x_1 + a_{n2}x_2 + \cdots + a_{nm}x_m
\end{bmatrix}
=
\begin{bmatrix}
g_1 \\
g_2 \\
\cdot \\
\cdot \\
\cdot \\
g_n
\end{bmatrix}
$$

A closer inspection of the vector on the left shows that each component is a product of a row vector of a matrix by the same column vector. In other words, the vector equation can be written as the matrix equation

$$
\begin{bmatrix}
a_{11} & a_{12} & \cdots & a_{1m} \\
a_{21} & a_{22} & \cdots & a_{2m} \\
\cdot & \cdot & \cdots & \cdot \\
\cdot & \cdot & \cdots & \cdot \\
\cdot & \cdot & \cdots & \cdot \\
a_{n1} & a_{n2} & \cdots & a_{nm}
\end{bmatrix}
\begin{bmatrix}
x_1 \\
x_2 \\
\cdot \\
\cdot \\
\cdot \\
x_m
\end{bmatrix}
=
\begin{bmatrix}
g_1 \\
g_2 \\
\cdot \\
\cdot \\
\cdot \\
g_n
\end{bmatrix}
$$

If the dimensions of the matrices involved are known, this could be simplified to the compact form

$$AX = G$$

where $A = (a_{rs})$ is an $n \times m$ matrix, X is an $m \times 1$ column matrix, and G is an $n \times 1$ column matrix. Furthermore, the components of the row vectors of A are the same as the coefficients of the unknowns in the system of equations. This of course can be done only if the unknowns are written in the same order in each equation with positive, negative, or zero coefficients. The matrix A is called the *coefficient matrix* of the system of equations. The vector G is known as the *constant vector* of the system.

In the simplest form, the solution for the system of equations can be expressed in the language of matrices. What is sought is a column vector

X which, when multiplied by the matrix A, gives the column vector G. In other words, the problem becomes one of solving a linear matrix equation!

To illustrate the general situation, consider the following system,

$$x_1 - x_2 + x_3 + 2 = 0$$
$$2x_1 + 3x_3 - 4x_2 + 3 = 0$$
$$3x_3 - 2x_2 = 7$$

First of all, this system needs to be put into standard form. For the first equation, 2 is subtracted from both sides to put the constant on the right. To express the left side as a sum of the unknowns, the coefficients must be 1, -1, and 1. Thus this equation written in standard form is

$$(1)x_1 + (-1)x_2 + (1)x_3 = -2$$

The second equation needs to be handled in much the same manner. The constant 3 is subtracted from both sides and the middle terms are interchanged. This would give the standard form of

$$(2)x_1 + (-4)x_2 + (3)x_3 = -3$$

For the third equation, the x_1 is added with a zero coefficient and the other two terms on the left are interchanged. This equation is then written as

$$(0)x_1 + (-2)x_2 + (3)x_3 = 7$$

Now that the equations are all in standard form, the system can be expressed as the matrix equation

$$\begin{bmatrix} 1 & -1 & 1 \\ 2 & -4 & 3 \\ 0 & -2 & 3 \end{bmatrix} \begin{bmatrix} x_1 \\ x_2 \\ x_3 \end{bmatrix} = \begin{bmatrix} -2 \\ -3 \\ 7 \end{bmatrix}$$

The reader may want to verify that the product on the left side gives a vector whose components are the left sides of the given equations.

2.2 Solution for the System of Linear Equations

The finding of a solution for a system of linear equations requires the determination of a set or sets of values for the unknowns which will reduce the left side of each equation to the constant value given on the right. Usually one replaces the given system by an equivalent one whose solution is readily found. This is accomplished in a series of steps so that each new system has exactly the same solutions as the original set of equations. In this chapter, instead of noting that one is finding a new set of equations each time, reference will be made only to equations that replace those of the previous set. Most of the changes will involve making coefficients of certain unknowns zero in some of the equations. The new equations are obtained by having this unknown "eliminated" from the original equations.

One method of finding a solution for a set of equations is known as the "triangular" method. In this procedure, one equation is used to eliminate one unknown from each of the other equations. The process is then repeated on the new set of equations without this first unknown to obtain equations without two unknowns. This technique is repeated over and over until one equation with only one unknown is obtained. At each step there is one equation that is used to simplify the others and then is never used again. The equations of this set have a decreasing number of unknowns starting with the first equation that was used. Since the last equation in the set involves only one unknown, its solution is readily found. When this value is substituted for this variable in the next to last equation it becomes an equation in one unknown that can be solved. The results from these two equations are then used in the next preceding equation in the set to reduce it to an equation in one unknown. This process is continued on up through the set, determining another unknown with each equation.

The technique described can best be shown by working out the solution for the system illustrated above. In this reduction, one might use the first equation to eliminate x_1 in the other equations. The reason for this choice is simply that there is no x_1 in the third equation and, secondly, the coefficient of x_1 is 1 in the first equation. This elimination is done by adding (-2) times the first equation to the second. The altered system then becomes

$$x_1 + (-1)x_2 + x_3 = -2$$
$$(-2)x_2 + x_3 = 1$$
$$(-2)x_2 + 3x_3 = 7$$

Note that the last two equations do not involve x_1. The x_2 can be eliminated from the third equation by adding -1 times the second equation to the third equation. If this is done, the system reduces to the form

$$x_1 + (-1)x_2 + x_3 = -2$$
$$(-2)x_2 + x_3 = 1$$
$$2x_3 = 6$$

Notice that the third equation involves only the unknown x_3. The other two equations were used in the two steps of the simplification. On solving the last equation for x_3 it is found that $x_3 = 3$. With this value used in the second equation, it is seen that $x_2 = 1$. Substitution of these two results into the first equation shows that $x_1 = -4$. One can easily verify that these values for the unknowns will satisfy all three original equations.

Assuming no errors are made, this process will yield a new system of equations with the same solution as the original system. This is easier to see if the operations that can be used are spelled out. These are:

1. Any two equations may be interchanged in the system.

2. Both sides of any equation may be multiplied by the same nonzero constant.

3. A multiple of any equation may be added to a second equation.

These are called the *elementary operations* on systems of linear equations. The most useful of the three is the last one, for this is the way unknowns are eliminated in the equations. The second one will simplify a coefficient of an unknown in an equation. This is often helpful when the equation is used to eliminate that unknown from the other equations in the set. The importance of the first operation will appear later.

These elementary operations are reversible. For the first operation, a repetition of it would give the original system, for a repeated interchange of two equations leaves the system in its original form. To restore an equation modified by an elementary operation of type two, a second elementary operation of the same type using the reciprocal of the constant will suffice when applied to the altered equation. For the last elementary operation, the negative of the multiple of the equation added to the second equation would reproduce its original form.

It is easy to see that the first elementary operation will not change the set of equations. Any solution of the resulting system is also a solution for the original system. For the second elementary operation, the new equation will still be satisfied by the solution of the original system since both sides of the equation are multiplied by the same constant. The solution to the original system will also be a solution for a new system obtained by a type three operation. Here the new equation can be thought of as consisting of two parts, the original equation and a multiple of another equation. A solution of the original system will satisfy each of these parts and hence their sum. Because the operations are reversible, the reasoning above can be applied starting with the altered system and using elementary operations to obtain the original system. In other words, the solutions for the system of equations are unchanged when the equations are altered by elementary operations.

2.3 *Finding the Solution Utilizing Matrices*

The technique above can be carried out more efficiently by utilizing the language of matrices. To see this, consider the following simplifications of the problem. First of all, if one is careful to have all the equations in the suggested standard form, there is no need to write the unknowns or the connective plus signs. Furthermore, with the constants always on the right, the equality sign is unnecessary. Then, in order to keep these coefficients and constants as a unit, brackets are placed around them. For the system illustrated in the last section, this would give

$$\begin{bmatrix} 1 & -1 & 1 & -2 \\ 2 & -4 & 3 & -3 \\ 0 & -2 & 3 & 7 \end{bmatrix}$$

A look at this result reveals that it is the coefficient matrix A of the system enlarged by adjoining the column vector of constants. The following definition describes this for the general case.

Definition 2.1. The augmented matrix for the system $AX = G$ is the matrix formed by placing the constant column vector G to the right of the column vectors of A.

The elementary operations are readily adaptable for use with the augmented matrix. Note that each row vector of this matrix contains all the coefficients and the constant of the given equations of the system. Thus, instead of referring to an equation, one can apply the elementary operations to the row vectors of the augmented matrix and accomplish the same result. Since these operations are to be used later without reference to a system of linear equations, they need to be repeated in an altered form. Also, a shorthand notation to describe each will be adopted. The following are called the "elementary row operations" for a matrix.

1. Interchange of the ith and jth row vectors denoted by $R(i, j)$.

2. Multiplication of the ith row vector by the nonzero constant c, denoted by cRi.

3. Adding to the ith row vector, k times the jth row vector, denoted by $Ri + kRj$.

Using this shorthand notation, the solution to the system of equations used above can now be written in the following form. The two-headed arrow is used to emphasize that the steps are reversible. Consider then

$$
\begin{bmatrix} 1 & -1 & 1 & -2 \\ 2 & -4 & 3 & -3 \\ 0 & -2 & 3 & 7 \end{bmatrix}
\underset{R2-2R1}{\longleftrightarrow}
\begin{bmatrix} 1 & -1 & 1 & -2 \\ 0 & -2 & 1 & 1 \\ 0 & -2 & 3 & 7 \end{bmatrix}
$$

$$
\underset{R3-1R2}{\longleftrightarrow}
\begin{bmatrix} 1 & -1 & 1 & -2 \\ 0 & -2 & 1 & 1 \\ 0 & 0 & 2 & 6 \end{bmatrix}
$$

A comparison of this result with the solution given in section 2.2, shows that the same system is represented here. In that section the last equation was multiplied by 0.5 to give the solution for x_3. The value obtained was substituted for this variable in the first two equations. The second equation then involved only x_2 so its solution could be found. When this result was substituted for x_2 in the first equation, it became an equation involving only x_1 so a solution for x_1 could be found. These changes are accomplished by using the elementary row operations as follows,

$$
\begin{bmatrix} 1 & -1 & 1 & -2 \\ 0 & -2 & 1 & 1 \\ 0 & 0 & 2 & 6 \end{bmatrix}
\underset{0.5R3}{\longleftrightarrow}
\begin{bmatrix} 1 & -1 & 1 & -2 \\ 0 & -2 & 1 & 1 \\ 0 & 0 & 1 & 3 \end{bmatrix}
$$

$$
\underset{\substack{R1-1R3 \\ R2-1R3}}{\longleftrightarrow}
\begin{bmatrix} 1 & -1 & 0 & -5 \\ 0 & -2 & 0 & -2 \\ 0 & 0 & 1 & 3 \end{bmatrix}
\underset{-0.5R2}{\longleftrightarrow}
\begin{bmatrix} 1 & -1 & 0 & -5 \\ 0 & 1 & 0 & 1 \\ 0 & 0 & 1 & 3 \end{bmatrix}
$$

$$
\underset{R1+1R2}{\longleftrightarrow}
\begin{bmatrix} 1 & 0 & 0 & -4 \\ 0 & 1 & 0 & 1 \\ 0 & 0 & 1 & 3 \end{bmatrix}
$$

Notice carefully the final form that is obtained. Each equation represented in this final form involves only one unknown with a coefficient 1 so the constant term is the solution for that unknown. Thus, in this process one strives to alter the coefficient matrix in order to obtain the identity matrix. The technique can be modified to decrease the number of steps required. Consider the following series of operations,

$$
\begin{bmatrix} 1 & -1 & 1 & -2 \\ 2 & -4 & 3 & -3 \\ 0 & -2 & 3 & 7 \end{bmatrix}
\underset{R2-2R1}{\longleftrightarrow}
\begin{bmatrix} 1 & -1 & 1 & -2 \\ 0 & -2 & 1 & 1 \\ 0 & -2 & 3 & 7 \end{bmatrix}
$$

$$
\underset{-0.5R2}{\longleftrightarrow}
\begin{bmatrix} 1 & -1 & 1 & -2 \\ 0 & 1 & -0.5 & -0.5 \\ 0 & -2 & 3 & 7 \end{bmatrix}
\underset{\substack{R1+1R2 \\ R3+2R2}}{\longleftrightarrow}
\begin{bmatrix} 1 & 0 & 0.5 & -2.5 \\ 0 & 1 & -0.5 & -0.5 \\ 0 & 0 & 2 & 6 \end{bmatrix}
$$

$$
\underset{0.5R3}{\longleftrightarrow}
\begin{bmatrix} 1 & 0 & 0.5 & -2.5 \\ 0 & 1 & -0.5 & -0.5 \\ 0 & 0 & 1 & 3 \end{bmatrix}
\underset{\substack{R1-0.5R3 \\ R2+0.5R3}}{\longleftrightarrow}
\begin{bmatrix} 1 & 0 & 0 & -4 \\ 0 & 1 & 0 & 1 \\ 0 & 0 & 1 & 3 \end{bmatrix}
$$

Notice that the essential difference between the two methods is the elimination of the coefficient of x_2 in the first equation at the same time it was eliminated in the third equation. Also, the coefficient of x_2 in the second equation was made 1 at an earlier step.

Before trying to state the procedure in words, another example of a larger system should be shown. For this consider the equations,

$$
\begin{aligned}
x_1 - x_2 - x_3 - x_4 &= 2 \\
4x_2 - 2x_1 + 3x_3 + 3 &= 0 \\
3x_4 - 4x_2 - 2x_3 + 1 &= 0 \\
2x_1 - 3x_2 + 4x_4 &= 6
\end{aligned}
$$

Putting this system into standard form gives

$$
\begin{aligned}
(1)x_1 + (-1)x_2 + (-1)x_3 + (-1)x_4 &= 2 \\
(-2)x_1 + (4)x_2 + (3)x_3 + (0)x_4 &= -3 \\
(0)x_1 + (-4)x_2 + (-2)x_3 + (3)x_4 &= -1 \\
(2)x_1 + (-3)x_2 + (0)x_3 + (4)x_4 &= 6
\end{aligned}
$$

This system will have an augmented matrix that can be simplified as follows,

$$
\begin{bmatrix}
1 & -1 & -1 & -1 & 2 \\
-2 & 4 & 3 & 0 & -3 \\
0 & -4 & -2 & 3 & -1 \\
2 & -3 & 0 & 4 & 6
\end{bmatrix}
\quad
\underset{\substack{R2 + 2R1 \\ R4 - 2R1}}{\longleftrightarrow}
\quad
\begin{bmatrix}
1 & -1 & -1 & -1 & 2 \\
0 & 2 & 1 & -2 & 1 \\
0 & -4 & -2 & 3 & -1 \\
0 & -1 & 2 & 6 & 2
\end{bmatrix}
$$

$$
\underset{R(2,4)}{\longleftrightarrow}
\quad
\begin{bmatrix}
1 & -1 & -1 & -1 & 2 \\
0 & -1 & 2 & 6 & 2 \\
0 & -4 & -2 & 3 & -1 \\
0 & 2 & 1 & -2 & 1
\end{bmatrix}
\quad
\underset{-1R2}{\longleftrightarrow}
\quad
\begin{bmatrix}
1 & -1 & -1 & -1 & 2 \\
0 & 1 & -2 & -6 & -2 \\
0 & -4 & -2 & 3 & -1 \\
0 & 2 & 1 & -2 & 1
\end{bmatrix}
$$

$$
\underset{\substack{R1 + 1R2 \\ R3 + 4R2 \\ R4 - 2R2}}{\longleftrightarrow}
\quad
\begin{bmatrix}
1 & 0 & -3 & -7 & 0 \\
0 & 1 & -2 & -6 & -2 \\
0 & 0 & -10 & -21 & -9 \\
0 & 0 & 5 & 10 & 5
\end{bmatrix}
\quad
\underset{R(3,4)}{\longleftrightarrow}
\quad
\begin{bmatrix}
1 & 0 & -3 & -7 & 0 \\
0 & 1 & -2 & -6 & -2 \\
0 & 0 & 5 & 10 & 5 \\
0 & 0 & -10 & -21 & -9
\end{bmatrix}
$$

$$
\underset{0.2R3}{\longleftrightarrow}
\quad
\begin{bmatrix}
1 & 0 & -3 & -7 & 0 \\
0 & 1 & -2 & -6 & -2 \\
0 & 0 & 1 & 2 & 1 \\
0 & 0 & -10 & -21 & -9
\end{bmatrix}
\quad
\underset{\substack{R1 + 3R3 \\ R2 + 2R3 \\ R4 + 10R3}}{\longleftrightarrow}
\quad
\begin{bmatrix}
1 & 0 & 0 & -1 & 3 \\
0 & 1 & 0 & -2 & 0 \\
0 & 0 & 1 & 2 & 1 \\
0 & 0 & 0 & -1 & 1
\end{bmatrix}
$$

$$
\underset{-1R4}{\longleftrightarrow}
\quad
\begin{bmatrix}
1 & 0 & 0 & -1 & 3 \\
0 & 1 & 0 & -2 & 0 \\
0 & 0 & 1 & 2 & 1 \\
0 & 0 & 0 & 1 & -1
\end{bmatrix}
\quad
\underset{\substack{R1 + 1R4 \\ R2 + 2R4 \\ R3 - 2R4}}{\longleftrightarrow}
\quad
\begin{bmatrix}
1 & 0 & 0 & 0 & 2 \\
0 & 1 & 0 & 0 & -2 \\
0 & 0 & 1 & 0 & 3 \\
0 & 0 & 0 & 1 & -1
\end{bmatrix}
$$

Again note that the final form has the identity matrix augmented by the solution vector.

Keeping in mind the final desired form of having the identity matrix augmented by the solution vector, the reduction process can be stated in words. For step one the first column vector is checked to find a nonzero element that could be easily changed to 1. The row vector to which the selected element belongs is then interchanged with the first row vector by an elementary operation of the first type. In the examples above this was the first component so no interchange of rows was necessary. The new first row vector is then multiplied by the reciprocal of its first component to make that component 1. This is an elementary operation of type two. For the examples this was not necessary. Using the third type of elementary operations, with the first row vector, the other row vectors are altered so that their first components are made 0. The process is then applied to the second column vector with the exception that the first row vector cannot be used in searching for the nonzero element. The row vector chosen this time is interchanged with the second row vector by a type one operation. Then the element placed in the second row is made 1 by an elementary operation of type two. One then uses type three operations to obtain zeros in the rest of the second column, including the first row. After the simplification of the second column, the process is repeated on the third column vector, with the first and second row vectors ruled out of consideration for the nonzero element. The row vector selected then becomes the new third row vector. At each succeeding step the modifications are made in a similar manner. Eventually, the process terminates, in many cases, with the desired identity matrix augmented by the solution vector.

It should be noted that in the technique outlined one moves from left to right across the columns of the matrix. This is not essential for it is possible to build up the identity matrix starting with the next to last column and working to the left. In this case, at the first step the chosen row vector is interchanged with the last one. At step two the row vector chosen is interchanged with the next to last one. This modification is then carried on through the reduction.

Other variations are possible but difficult to describe. Actually, any column vector with a convenient component could be used at any step so long as the row vector of that component is interchanged with the row vector of the same index as the column under consideration. Experience with the technique will lead to shortcuts that are valid for a particular example. The procedure outlined above is one that is systematic and will always work. It will have to be modified in the exceptional cases that will be discussed in the next sections.

2.4 Systems with Solutions Involving Arbitrary Parameters

A word of warning is needed at this point. It is not always possible to obtain the identity matrix augmented by the solution vector. It might happen that at the second step of the reduction, the only nonzero component of the second column vector belongs to the first row vector. There would be no way then of obtaining a nonzero element for the second column in the second row. In such a situation one goes on to the third column vector for the search for the nonzero element. The identity matrix cannot be obtained in such a case. This is illustrated by the following system.

$$x_1 + 2x_2 + x_3 = 2$$

$$2x_1 + 4x_2 + 3x_3 = 3$$

$$3x_1 + 6x_2 + 5x_3 = 4$$

Utilizing the reduced augmented matrix the solution is,

$$
\begin{bmatrix} 1 & 2 & 1 & 2 \\ 2 & 4 & 3 & 3 \\ 3 & 6 & 5 & 4 \end{bmatrix}
\begin{array}{c} \longleftrightarrow \\ R2-2R1 \\ R3-3R1 \end{array}
\begin{bmatrix} 1 & 2 & 1 & 2 \\ 0 & 0 & 1 & -1 \\ 0 & 0 & 2 & -2 \end{bmatrix}
\begin{array}{c} \longleftrightarrow \\ R1-1R2 \\ R3-2R2 \end{array}
\begin{bmatrix} 1 & 2 & 0 & 3 \\ 0 & 0 & 1 & -1 \\ 0 & 0 & 0 & 0 \end{bmatrix}
$$

It is possible that the third column also would have only zero elements outside the first row. In this event, attention is shifted on across the columns until one is found with a nonzero element below the first row vector. Then the row vector of this element is interchanged with the second row vector. The column vector is then simplified in the usual manner. There are also systems where this sort of trouble does not occur until after the second column is simplified. In any event, the procedure is to move on across the column vectors until one is found that can be used. Of course there is no reason why this sort of a situation may not occur more than once.

In case there is any column that has to be passed over for lack of a nonzero element, then the identity matrix cannot be obtained in the final form. What happens is that the ones, instead of appearing on the diagonal, are shifted to the right. In the final result, as one moves down the rows, the first nonzero element in each row is a one whereas the other elements in its column are all zeros. This element is always at least one more column to the right than in the preceding row. As soon as a zero row vector is found in the final form, all the remaining row vectors will also be zero.

To see what this does to the solution for a system of equations consider the equations defined in the reduced system above. They are

$$x_1 + 2x_2 = \quad 3$$

$$x_3 = -1$$

Solving the first equation for x_1 in terms of x_2 gives the system the form

$$x_1 = 3 - 2x_2$$

$$x_3 = -1$$

By assigning any value to x_2, a value for x_1 could be determined that would satisfy the first equation. For instance, if x_2 is given the value 2, then the equation is satisfied with $x_1 = -1$. Or, if x_2 is -3, and then x_1 is taken to be 9, the equation is again satisfied. In this example x_2 is said to be an *arbitrary parameter* since it can be assigned any value. (Actually, any value could be assigned to x_1 and a corresponding value for x_2 could be found. For convenience though, the x_2 is designated as being the arbitrary element since it was the second column where one could not obtain a nonzero element below the first row.) The final equations would usually be re-written as

$$x_1 = 3 - 2\lambda_1$$

$$x_2 = \lambda_1$$

$$x_3 = -1$$

The second equation emphasizes that x_2 is the arbitrary parameter of the system. This solution could also be given in the vector form

$$\begin{bmatrix} x_1 \\ x_2 \\ x_3 \end{bmatrix} = \begin{bmatrix} 3 - 2\lambda_1 \\ \lambda_1 \\ -1 \end{bmatrix}$$

For such a system there are an infinite number of solutions since λ_1 can be any real number. For each value assigned to λ_1 there will be a corresponding value determined for x_1 whereas x_3 will always be -1.

There may be situations where there is more than one arbitrary parameter involved. For instance, the following augmented matrix may contain the only nonzero row vectors left in a simplification of a system.

$$\begin{bmatrix} 1 & 3 & 0 & 2 & -1 & 0 & 1 & 2 \\ 0 & 0 & 1 & 2 & 4 & 0 & 3 & 1 \\ 0 & 0 & 0 & 0 & 0 & 1 & 2 & 3 \end{bmatrix}$$

Notice how the ones are the first nonzero elements in the rows. In the second and third rows they are shifted to the right of the diagonal position of the coefficient matrix. If one writes out the system of equations represented by this matrix, one can then solve each equation for the unknown of least subscript. This would give

$$x_1 = 2 - 3x_2 - 2x_4 + x_5 - x_7$$
$$x_3 = 1 - 2x_4 - 4x_5 - 3x_7$$
$$x_6 = 3 - 2x_7$$

Notice that the unknowns upon which the x_1, x_3, and x_6 depend, are just the other four unknowns in the system. Hence, each of these four could be chosen arbitrarily. Denoting them in order as λ_1, λ_2, λ_3, λ_4, the solution to the system can be written in the form

$$
\begin{bmatrix} x_1 \\ x_2 \\ x_3 \\ x_4 \\ x_5 \\ x_6 \\ x_7 \end{bmatrix}
=
\begin{bmatrix}
2 - 3\lambda_1 - 2\lambda_2 + \lambda_3 - \lambda_4 \\
\lambda_1 \\
1 \qquad - 2\lambda_2 - 4\lambda_3 - 3\lambda_4 \\
\lambda_2 \\
\lambda_3 \\
3 \qquad\qquad\qquad - 2\lambda_4 \\
\lambda_4
\end{bmatrix}
$$

There is another possibility that might arise in finding the solution to a system of equations. It might happen that at the final step there would be a row vector with only the last component nonzero. The equation represented by this vector would then be one with all coefficients of the unknowns equal to zero but whose constant is not zero. There can be no solution to such an equation so the system is said to be inconsistent. As an example of this, consider the equations with the augmented matrix

$$
\begin{bmatrix}
3 & -1 & -2 & 2 \\
0 & 2 & -1 & -1 \\
3 & -5 & 0 & 3
\end{bmatrix}
\xrightarrow[R3 - 1R1]{}
\begin{bmatrix}
3 & -1 & -1 & 2 \\
0 & 2 & -1 & -1 \\
0 & -4 & 2 & 1
\end{bmatrix}
$$

$$
\xrightarrow[0.5R2]{}
\begin{bmatrix}
3 & -1 & -2 & 2 \\
0 & 1 & -0.5 & -0.5 \\
0 & -4 & 2 & 1
\end{bmatrix}
\xrightarrow[\substack{R1 - 1R2 \\ R3 + 4R2}]{}
\begin{bmatrix}
3 & 0 & -2.5 & 1.5 \\
0 & 1 & -0.5 & -0.5 \\
0 & 0 & 0 & -1
\end{bmatrix}
$$

The equation determined by the last row is of the form

$$(0)x_1 + (0)x_2 + (0)x_3 = -1$$

Since there are no values of x for which this is true, this equation has no solution and hence the system has no solution.

2.5 Number of Equations and Unknowns not the Same

In all the systems considered so far, the number of equations and the number of unknowns have been the same. Only under such conditions is it possible to obtain the form with the identity matrix augmented by the solution vector. However, the methods used there are readily adapted to the following situations.

First of all, there may be more unknowns than equations. In this case, there could still be a solution but it would involve arbitrary parameters. There would be at least as many of these as the excess of unknowns over equations. As an example of this situation, consider the set of equations

$$5x_1 - 3x_2 - 7x_3 + x_4 = 10$$
$$-x_1 + 2x_2 + 6x_3 - 3x_4 = -3$$
$$x_1 + x_2 + 4x_3 - 5x_4 = 0$$

In this system there must be at least one arbitrary parameter in the solutions since there are four unknowns and only three equations. The reduction of the augmented matrix gives

$$\begin{bmatrix} 5 & -3 & -7 & 1 & 10 \\ -1 & 2 & 6 & -3 & -3 \\ 1 & 1 & 4 & -5 & 0 \end{bmatrix} \xleftrightarrow[R(1,3)]{} \begin{bmatrix} 1 & 1 & 4 & -5 & 0 \\ -1 & 2 & 6 & -3 & -3 \\ 5 & -3 & -7 & 1 & 10 \end{bmatrix}$$

$$\xleftrightarrow[\substack{R2+1R1 \\ R3-5R1}]{} \begin{bmatrix} 1 & 1 & 4 & -5 & 0 \\ 0 & 3 & 10 & -8 & 3 \\ 0 & -8 & -27 & 26 & 10 \end{bmatrix} \xleftrightarrow[\frac{1}{3}R2]{} \begin{bmatrix} 1 & 1 & 4 & -5 & 0 \\ 0 & 1 & \frac{10}{3} & -\frac{8}{3} & -1 \\ 0 & -8 & -27 & 26 & 10 \end{bmatrix}$$

$$\xleftrightarrow[\substack{R1-1R2 \\ R3+8R2}]{} \begin{bmatrix} 1 & 0 & \frac{2}{3} & -\frac{7}{3} & 1 \\ 0 & 1 & \frac{10}{3} & -\frac{8}{3} & -1 \\ 0 & 0 & -\frac{1}{3} & \frac{14}{3} & 2 \end{bmatrix} \xleftrightarrow[-3R3]{} \begin{bmatrix} 1 & 0 & \frac{2}{3} & -\frac{7}{3} & 1 \\ 0 & 1 & \frac{10}{3} & -\frac{8}{3} & -1 \\ 0 & 0 & 1 & -14 & -6 \end{bmatrix}$$

$$\xleftrightarrow[\substack{R1-\frac{2}{3}R3 \\ R2-\frac{10}{3}R3}]{} \begin{bmatrix} 1 & 0 & 0 & 7 & 5 \\ 0 & 1 & 0 & 44 & 19 \\ 0 & 0 & 1 & -14 & -6 \end{bmatrix}$$

If one solves each equation of the system for the unknown of least subscript, one would find the first three unknowns expressed in terms of x_4 and a constant. By letting $x_4 = \lambda_1$, the solution vector would be

$$\begin{bmatrix} x_1 \\ x_2 \\ x_3 \\ x_4 \end{bmatrix} = \begin{bmatrix} 5 - 7\lambda_1 \\ 19 - 44\lambda_1 \\ -6 + 14\lambda_1 \\ \lambda_1 \end{bmatrix}$$

It is possible that the number of equations might exceed the number of unknowns. To illustrate this, consider the system

$$x_1 + 2x_2 = 1$$

$$-3x_1 + 2x_2 = -2$$

$$-x_1 + 6x_2 = 0$$

The reduction of the augmented matrix gives

$$\begin{bmatrix} 1 & 2 & 1 \\ -3 & 2 & -2 \\ -1 & 6 & 0 \end{bmatrix} \xrightarrow[\substack{R2 + 3R1 \\ R3 + 1R1}]{} \begin{bmatrix} 1 & 2 & 1 \\ 0 & 8 & 1 \\ 0 & 8 & 1 \end{bmatrix} \xrightarrow[\frac{1}{8}R2]{} \begin{bmatrix} 1 & 2 & 1 \\ 0 & 1 & \frac{1}{8} \\ 0 & 8 & 1 \end{bmatrix}$$

$$\xrightarrow[\substack{R1 - 2R2 \\ R3 - 8R2}]{} \begin{bmatrix} 1 & 0 & \frac{3}{4} \\ 0 & 1 & \frac{1}{8} \\ 0 & 0 & 0 \end{bmatrix}$$

The solution for this system has the simple form

$$\begin{bmatrix} x_1 \\ x_2 \end{bmatrix} = \begin{bmatrix} \frac{3}{4} \\ \frac{1}{8} \end{bmatrix}$$

The set of equations above is an example of what is known as a dependent system. Such a system has the property that at least one of the equations can be expressed as a linear combination of the ones above it. This is shown by the fact that the last row turned out to be all zeros in the reduction.

In the set above, it can be verified that the last equation is the sum of the second equation and twice the first equation.

A system of linear equations in which all the constants are zero is said to be "homogeneous." All such systems are satisfied by letting all the unknowns have the value zero. This is known as the trivial solution for the homogeneous system. There may be solutions other than this one. To see this, consider the augmented matrix for such a system. The last column would be all zeros and so it would remain unaltered in the reduction. Furthermore, there could never be an inconsistent system since it would be impossible to have a nonzero element in the last column using row operations. There could be arbitrary parameters in the solution. This means that if there is a nontrivial solution to a homogeneous system, there is an infinite number of solutions.

In the procedure outlined for finding the solution for a given system of linear equations, it is apparent that one has some choice in the elementary operations that are used. The question arises then as to whether it is possible to obtain two different final forms for the augmented matrix. It is not; because the system of linear equations represented by the matrix at each step of the simplification has the same solution as the original system. In all cases, this solution is easily determined by the final form obtained for the augmented matrix.

2.6 Row Rank of a Matrix

Up to now, only the augmented matrix of a system of linear equations has been considered. One can discuss the elementary row operations on a rectangular matrix with no reference to a system of linear equations. The techniques above can be modified slightly to obtain a final, unique *simplest* or *canonical* form. The only change required in the final form for the augmented matrix would come in the case of the inconsistent system. For the general matrix, the last column is simplified like the others in case there is a nonzero element that can be used for this purpose. To illustrate this consider the following reduction.

$$
\begin{bmatrix}
1 & -1 & 2 & 2 \\
2 & -3 & 2 & 1 \\
5 & -8 & 4 & -2 \\
3 & 1 & 14 & 9
\end{bmatrix}
\begin{array}{c}
\longleftrightarrow \\
R2 - 2R1 \\
R3 - 5R1 \\
R4 - 3R1
\end{array}
\begin{bmatrix}
1 & -1 & 2 & 2 \\
0 & -1 & -2 & -3 \\
0 & -3 & -6 & -12 \\
0 & 4 & 8 & 3
\end{bmatrix}
$$

$$
\xleftrightarrow{-1R2}
\begin{bmatrix}
1 & -1 & 2 & 2 \\
0 & 1 & 2 & 3 \\
0 & -3 & -6 & -12 \\
0 & 4 & 8 & 3
\end{bmatrix}
\begin{matrix}
\\
\xleftrightarrow{} \\
R1 + 1R2 \\
R3 + 3R2 \\
R4 - 4R2
\end{matrix}
\begin{bmatrix}
1 & 0 & 4 & 5 \\
0 & 1 & 2 & 3 \\
0 & 0 & 0 & -3 \\
0 & 0 & 0 & -9
\end{bmatrix}
$$

$$
\xleftrightarrow{-\frac{1}{3}R3}
\begin{bmatrix}
1 & 0 & 4 & 5 \\
0 & 1 & 2 & 3 \\
0 & 0 & 0 & 1 \\
0 & 0 & 0 & -9
\end{bmatrix}
\begin{matrix}
\\
\xleftrightarrow{} \\
R1 - 5R3 \\
R2 - 3R3 \\
R4 + 9R3
\end{matrix}
\begin{bmatrix}
1 & 0 & 4 & 0 \\
0 & 1 & 2 & 0 \\
0 & 0 & 0 & 1 \\
0 & 0 & 0 & 0
\end{bmatrix}
$$

There are two new concepts that need to be defined. The first is based on the number of nonzero row vectors in the final form.

Definition 2.2. The row rank of a matrix is the number of nonzero row vectors in its canonical form.

The next definition is closely related to this one.

Definition 2.3. Two matrices are said to be row equivalent if one can be obtained from the other by a series of elementary row operations.

This definition implies that at each step of the reduction process, a matrix is obtained that is row equivalent to all the preceding matrices. It also implies that each of these matrices has the same rank since each has the same canonical form.

2.7 Elementary Matrices

In the discussion above, it was shown how to simplify matrices by elementary operations. It will now be shown that each of these operations can be performed by matrix multiplication. To do this consider the following case where the matrix A is subjected to an elementary row operation so that

$$
\begin{bmatrix}
2 & -4 & 3 & -3 \\
1 & -1 & 1 & -2 \\
0 & -2 & 3 & 7
\end{bmatrix}
\xleftrightarrow[R(1,2)]{}
\begin{bmatrix}
1 & -1 & 1 & -2 \\
2 & -4 & 3 & -3 \\
0 & -2 & 3 & 7
\end{bmatrix}
$$

Suppose that the same elementary row operation is performed on the 3×3 left identity matrix of A,

$$
\begin{bmatrix} 1 & 0 & 0 \\ 0 & 1 & 0 \\ 0 & 0 & 1 \end{bmatrix} \xleftrightarrow[R(1,2)]{} \begin{bmatrix} 0 & 1 & 0 \\ 1 & 0 & 0 \\ 0 & 0 & 1 \end{bmatrix}
$$

Denoting this new matrix as E_1,

$$
E_1 A = \begin{bmatrix} 0 & 1 & 0 \\ 1 & 0 & 0 \\ 0 & 0 & 1 \end{bmatrix} \begin{bmatrix} 2 & -4 & 3 & -3 \\ 1 & -1 & 1 & -2 \\ 0 & -2 & 3 & 7 \end{bmatrix} = \begin{bmatrix} 1 & -1 & 1 & -2 \\ 2 & -4 & 3 & -3 \\ 0 & -2 & 3 & 7 \end{bmatrix}
$$

The same matrix is obtained in both cases. This illustrates how to find a matrix that will perform an elementary row operation of type one when used as a left multiplier. The desired row operation is made on the left identity of the given matrix. The resulting matrix is then the one that is needed.

Using an elementary row operation of type three on $E_1 A$,

$$
\begin{bmatrix} 1 & -1 & 1 & -2 \\ 2 & -4 & 3 & -3 \\ 0 & -2 & 3 & 7 \end{bmatrix} \xleftrightarrow[R2 - 2R1]{} \begin{bmatrix} 1 & -1 & 1 & -2 \\ 0 & -2 & 1 & 1 \\ 0 & -2 & 3 & 7 \end{bmatrix}
$$

Doing this same operation on its left identity matrix gives,

$$
\begin{bmatrix} 1 & 0 & 0 \\ 0 & 1 & 0 \\ 0 & 0 & 1 \end{bmatrix} \xleftrightarrow[R2 - 2R1]{} \begin{bmatrix} 1 & 0 & 0 \\ -2 & 1 & 0 \\ 0 & 0 & 1 \end{bmatrix}
$$

Calling this matrix E_2, its product with the one simplified above gives

$$
E_2(E_1 A) = \begin{bmatrix} 1 & 0 & 0 \\ -2 & 1 & 0 \\ 0 & 0 & 1 \end{bmatrix} \begin{bmatrix} 1 & -1 & 1 & -2 \\ 2 & -4 & 3 & -3 \\ 0 & -2 & 3 & 7 \end{bmatrix} = \begin{bmatrix} 1 & -1 & 1 & -2 \\ 0 & -2 & 1 & 1 \\ 0 & -2 & 3 & 7 \end{bmatrix}
$$

In this case it was an elementary operation of type three that was performed on the identity matrix. This gave a left multiplier E_2 that effects the same row operation on the matrix.

Because of the associative property of matrix multiplication,

$$E_2(E_1A) = (E_2E_1)A = E_2E_1A$$

This shows that if the product of the two elementary matrices is used as a left multiplier on A, the same matrix will be obtained as when they are used successively. For the example above,

$$(E_2E_1)A = \begin{bmatrix} 0 & 1 & 0 \\ 1 & -2 & 0 \\ 0 & 0 & 1 \end{bmatrix} \begin{bmatrix} 2 & -4 & 3 & -3 \\ 1 & -1 & 1 & -2 \\ 0 & -2 & 3 & 7 \end{bmatrix} = \begin{bmatrix} 1 & -1 & 1 & -2 \\ 0 & -2 & 1 & 1 \\ 0 & -2 & 3 & 7 \end{bmatrix}$$

which is the same result as obtained when E_1 and E_2 were used successively as left multipliers for the matrix A.

The matrix E_2E_1A can be further simplified using a type two elementary row operation,

$$\begin{bmatrix} 1 & -1 & 1 & -2 \\ 0 & -2 & 1 & 1 \\ 0 & -2 & 3 & 7 \end{bmatrix} \xrightarrow[-0.5R2]{} \begin{bmatrix} 1 & -1 & 1 & -2 \\ 0 & 1 & -0.5 & -0.5 \\ 0 & -2 & 3 & 7 \end{bmatrix}$$

Performing this same operation on I_3 gives

$$\begin{bmatrix} 1 & 0 & 0 \\ 0 & 1 & 0 \\ 0 & 0 & 1 \end{bmatrix} \xrightarrow[-0.5R2]{} \begin{bmatrix} 1 & 0 & 0 \\ 0 & -0.5 & 0 \\ 0 & 0 & 1 \end{bmatrix}$$

If this matrix is designated as E_3,

$$E_3(E_2E_1A) = \begin{bmatrix} 1 & 0 & 0 \\ 0 & -0.5 & 0 \\ 0 & 0 & 1 \end{bmatrix} \begin{bmatrix} 1 & -1 & 1 & -2 \\ 0 & -2 & 1 & 1 \\ 0 & -2 & 3 & 7 \end{bmatrix}$$

$$= \begin{bmatrix} 1 & -1 & 1 & -2 \\ 0 & 1 & -0.5 & -0.5 \\ 0 & -2 & 3 & 7 \end{bmatrix}$$

Again because of the associativity property of matrix multiplication,

$$E_3[(E_2E_1)A] = (E_3E_2E_1)A = E_3E_2E_1A$$

Using the product $E_3E_2E_1$ as a left multiplier for A, one obtains

$$
\begin{bmatrix} 0 & 1 & 0 \\ -0.5 & 1 & 0 \\ 0 & 0 & 1 \end{bmatrix}
\begin{bmatrix} 2 & -4 & 3 & -3 \\ 1 & -1 & 1 & -2 \\ 0 & -2 & 3 & 7 \end{bmatrix}
=
\begin{bmatrix} 1 & -1 & 1 & -2 \\ 0 & 1 & -0.5 & -0.5 \\ 0 & -2 & 3 & 7 \end{bmatrix}
$$

The matrix on the right is the same as the one obtained after the three operations were performed on the original matrix A. The matrix $E_3E_2E_1$ can also be obtained by performing these operations in the same order on the identity matrix.

It can be shown that what has been illustrated above will always be true. In other words, the elementary row operations can be accomplished by matrix multiplication on the left. The multiplier is simply the matrix obtained by performing the operation on the left identity matrix. These matrices that are obtained from the identity matrix are called the "elementary matrices." Notice the forms of these matrices. Those that perform type two operations are diagonal with the scalar c as one of the nonzero elements. Those for type three are triangular with ones on the diagonal and k in some other position.

In the general situation, suppose one would like to find a matrix which, when used as a left multiplier, reduces a given rectangular matrix to canonical form. This can be done by performing the same row operations in the same order on the left identity matrix. If the resulting matrix is called P, then PA will be the canonical form for the matrix A under row equivalence. If the matrix A of this section is reduced to canonical form, the same operations applied in order on I_3 yield

$$
P = \begin{bmatrix} -0.25 & 1.5 & -0.25 \\ -0.75 & 1.5 & 0.25 \\ -0.50 & 1.0 & 0.50 \end{bmatrix}
$$

Forming the product of this matrix and the original matrix gives

$$
\begin{bmatrix} -0.25 & 1.5 & -0.25 \\ -0.75 & 1.5 & 0.25 \\ -0.50 & 1.0 & 0.50 \end{bmatrix}
\begin{bmatrix} 2 & -4 & 3 & -3 \\ 1 & -1 & 1 & -2 \\ 0 & -2 & 3 & 7 \end{bmatrix}
=
\begin{bmatrix} 1 & 0 & 0 & -4 \\ 0 & 1 & 0 & 1 \\ 0 & 0 & 1 & 3 \end{bmatrix}
$$

The matrix P is not unique unless the PA is the identity matrix. Its form depends upon the way the reduction is performed.

Before leaving these elementary matrices, it should be noted that they are nonsingular. This follows because every elementary row operation has an inverse. For instance, the elementary matrices of type one are their own inverses. In the case of the second type, the inverse would have the reciprocal of the multiplier c in the ith diagonal position. In the example above this would be

$$E_3^{-1} = \begin{bmatrix} 1 & 0 & 0 \\ 0 & -0.5 & 0 \\ 0 & 0 & 1 \end{bmatrix}^{-1} = \begin{bmatrix} 1 & 0 & 0 \\ 0 & -2 & 0 \\ 0 & 0 & 1 \end{bmatrix}$$

This can be easily verified. The inverse of the third type of elementary matrix is formed by replacing the off diagonal element by its negative. For the example,

$$E_2^{-1} = \begin{bmatrix} 1 & 0 & 0 \\ -2 & 1 & 0 \\ 0 & 0 & 1 \end{bmatrix}^{-1} = \begin{bmatrix} 1 & 0 & 0 \\ 2 & 1 & 0 \\ 0 & 0 & 1 \end{bmatrix}$$

Notice the use of the negative of the multiple used before. That this is the inverse can be readily checked.

Now what about the product of two elementary matrices, is this also nonsingular? The answer is yes, and this can be seen by noting how to obtain the inverse. Consider the first elementary operations performed above. The first and second row vectors were interchanged and then (-2) times the first was added to the second. To reverse this pair of operations, one would have to add 2 times the first row vector to the second and then interchange the two row vectors. Or, in terms of the matrices,

$$E_1^{-1}[E_2^{-1}(E_2 E_1)] = E_1^{-1}[(E_2^{-1} E_2) E_1] = E_1^{-1} E_1 = I$$

Using the explicit form of the matrices this gives,

$$\begin{bmatrix} 0 & 1 & 0 \\ 1 & 0 & 0 \\ 0 & 0 & 1 \end{bmatrix} \left(\begin{bmatrix} 1 & 0 & 0 \\ 2 & 1 & 0 \\ 0 & 0 & 1 \end{bmatrix} \begin{bmatrix} 0 & 1 & 0 \\ 1 & -2 & 0 \\ 0 & 0 & 1 \end{bmatrix} \right)$$

$$= \begin{bmatrix} 0 & 1 & 0 \\ 1 & 0 & 0 \\ 0 & 0 & 1 \end{bmatrix} \begin{bmatrix} 0 & 1 & 0 \\ 1 & 0 & 0 \\ 0 & 0 & 1 \end{bmatrix} = \begin{bmatrix} 1 & 0 & 0 \\ 0 & 1 & 0 \\ 0 & 0 & 1 \end{bmatrix}$$

This illustrates a remarkable property of the inverse of the product of two matrices. The inverse is equal to the product of the inverses of the two matrices, but with their order reversed. Put in the general form

$$(AB)^{-1} = B^{-1}A^{-1}$$

This is easy to verify for

$$(B^{-1}A^{-1})(AB) = B^{-1}(A^{-1}A)B = B^{-1}IB = B^{-1}B = I = (AB)^{-1}(AB)$$

It should be noted that the inverse factors must be reversed because matrix multiplication is not commutative.

2.8 Column Operations

The emphasis up to this point has all been on operations on the row vectors. A natural question to consider here would be: what about working with the column vectors? It turns out that essentially everything that has been done and said about row vectors can be done and said about the column vectors. This is not too surprising for, after all, by simply taking the transpose of a matrix, its column vectors become row vectors. It might be noted that if matrix multiplication were used, then on taking the transposes of the products, the elementary matrices would appear on the right. This will be brought out later.

The elementary column operations are defined as follows:

1. Interchange of the ith and jth column vectors, denoted by $C(i, j)$.

2. Multiplication of the ith column vector by the nonzero constant c, denoted by cCi.

3. Adding to the ith column vector, k times the jth column vector, denoted by $Ci + kCj$.

These operations are illustrated by simplifying the matrix used in Section 2.6.

$$
\begin{bmatrix}
1 & -1 & 2 & 2 \\
2 & -3 & 2 & 1 \\
5 & -8 & 4 & -2 \\
3 & 1 & 14 & 9
\end{bmatrix}
\xrightarrow[\substack{C2 + 1C1 \\ C3 - 2C1 \\ C4 - 2C1}]{\longleftrightarrow}
\begin{bmatrix}
1 & 0 & 0 & 0 \\
2 & -1 & -2 & -3 \\
5 & -3 & -6 & -12 \\
3 & 4 & 8 & 3
\end{bmatrix}
$$

$$\xleftrightarrow[-1C2]{} \begin{bmatrix} 1 & 0 & 0 & 0 \\ 2 & 1 & -2 & -3 \\ 5 & 3 & -6 & -12 \\ 3 & -4 & 8 & 3 \end{bmatrix} \qquad \xleftrightarrow[\substack{C1-2C2 \\ C3+2C2 \\ C4+3C2}]{} \begin{bmatrix} 1 & 0 & 0 & 0 \\ 0 & 1 & 0 & 0 \\ -1 & 3 & 0 & -3 \\ 11 & -4 & 0 & -9 \end{bmatrix}$$

$$\xleftrightarrow[C(3,4)]{} \begin{bmatrix} 1 & 0 & 0 & 0 \\ 0 & 1 & 0 & 0 \\ -1 & 3 & -3 & 0 \\ 11 & -4 & -9 & 0 \end{bmatrix} \qquad \xleftrightarrow[-\frac{1}{3}C3]{} \begin{bmatrix} 1 & 0 & 0 & 0 \\ 0 & 1 & 0 & 0 \\ -1 & 3 & 1 & 0 \\ 11 & -4 & 3 & 0 \end{bmatrix}$$

$$\xleftrightarrow[\substack{C1+1C3 \\ C2-3C3}]{} \begin{bmatrix} 1 & 0 & 0 & 0 \\ 0 & 1 & 0 & 0 \\ 0 & 0 & 1 & 0 \\ 14 & -13 & 3 & 0 \end{bmatrix}$$

Under the elementary column operations, a rectangular matrix may be reduced to a canonical form as shown in the example. The procedure is quite similar to that used for row operations. It involves interchanging the words "row" and "column" wherever they occur. The process is carried out by working down the rows instead of across the columns. This means that the first nonzero element in a column is 1. This element is at least one row lower than the one in the preceding column. All other elements are 0 in the row of this element 1. As soon as a zero column vector is found in the final form, all those of higher index will also be zero vectors. Finally, if these column operations are also carried out on the right identity matrix of A, then a matrix Q will be determined for which AQ is the canonical form for A.

For the example shown above this would give the matrix

$$Q = \begin{bmatrix} \frac{14}{3} & -6 & \frac{5}{3} & -4 \\ 3 & -4 & 1 & -2 \\ 0 & 0 & 0 & 1 \\ -\frac{1}{3} & 1 & -\frac{1}{3} & 0 \end{bmatrix}$$

This could be verified easily as well as the fact that the product of this matrix and the original matrix gives the canonical form for that matrix. The matrix Q depends on how the reduction is performed, so is not unique except when the canonical form is the identity matrix.

With the concept above, the following two definitions can be made. They are the column analogues of Definitions 2.2 and 2.3.

Definition 2.4. The column rank of a matrix is the number of nonzero column vectors in its canonical form.

Definition 2.5. Two matrices are said to be column equivalent if one can be obtained from the other by a series of elementary column operations.

From these definitions it follows that two matrices that are column equivalent have the same column rank.

Closely connected with the question of elementary column operations is the concept of change of variable in a system of linear equations. Suppose that in the general system of equations each x_i is to be replaced by a linear combination of new unknowns y_j. On substituting these expressions for the x_i, there will result a new system of linear equations in the new variables y_j. To illustrate, consider the system of equations

$$x_1 + 2x_2 + 2x_3 = -1$$
$$2x_1 + 2x_2 + x_3 = -3$$
$$5x_1 + 4x_2 - 2x_3 = -8$$

For this system suppose the following change of variable is to be made,

$$x_1 = -\tfrac{4}{3}y_1 + 2y_2 - \tfrac{1}{3}y_3$$
$$x_2 = \tfrac{3}{2}y_1 - 2y_2 + \tfrac{1}{2}y_3$$
$$x_3 = -\tfrac{1}{3}y_1 + y_2 - \tfrac{1}{3}y_3$$

On substitution of these expressions for the x_i, the system becomes

$$(-\tfrac{4}{3}y_1 + 2y_2 - \tfrac{1}{3}y_3) + 2(\tfrac{3}{2}y_1 - 2y_2 + \tfrac{1}{2}y_3) + 2(-\tfrac{1}{3}y_1 + y_2 - \tfrac{1}{3}y_3) = -1$$
$$2(-\tfrac{4}{3}y_1 + 2y_2 - \tfrac{1}{3}y_3) + 2(\tfrac{3}{2}y_1 - 2y_2 + \tfrac{1}{2}y_3) + (-\tfrac{1}{3}y_1 + y_2 - \tfrac{1}{3}y_3) = -3$$
$$5(-\tfrac{4}{3}y_1 + 2y_2 - \tfrac{1}{3}y_3) + 4(\tfrac{3}{2}y_1 - 2y_2 + \tfrac{1}{2}y_3) - 2(-\tfrac{1}{3}y_1 + y_2 - \tfrac{1}{3}y_3) = -8$$

When like terms are collected, the system has the form

$$(-\tfrac{4}{3} + 3 - \tfrac{2}{3})y_1 + (2 - 4 + 2)y_2 + (-\tfrac{1}{3} + 1 - \tfrac{2}{3})y_3 = -1$$
$$(-\tfrac{8}{3} + 3 - \tfrac{1}{3})y_1 + (4 - 4 + 1)y_2 + (-\tfrac{2}{3} + 1 - \tfrac{1}{3})y_3 = -3$$
$$(-\tfrac{20}{3} + 6 + \tfrac{2}{3})y_1 + (10 - 8 - 2)y_2 + (-\tfrac{5}{3} + 2 + \tfrac{2}{3})y_3 = -8$$

Combining the coefficients leads to the system in the y_j of

$$y_1 + 0y_2 + 0y_3 = -1$$
$$0y_1 + y_2 + 0y_3 = -3$$
$$0y_1 + 0y_2 + y_3 = -8$$

This can now be written in matrix form as

$$\begin{bmatrix} 1 & 0 & 0 \\ 0 & 1 & 0 \\ 0 & 0 & 1 \end{bmatrix} \begin{bmatrix} y_1 \\ y_2 \\ y_3 \end{bmatrix} = \begin{bmatrix} -1 \\ -3 \\ -8 \end{bmatrix}$$

The system of equations and the change of variable equations could also be written in matrix form as

$$\begin{bmatrix} 1 & 2 & 2 \\ 2 & 2 & 1 \\ 5 & 4 & -2 \end{bmatrix} \begin{bmatrix} x_1 \\ x_2 \\ x_3 \end{bmatrix} = \begin{bmatrix} -1 \\ -3 \\ -8 \end{bmatrix} \qquad \begin{bmatrix} x_1 \\ x_2 \\ x_3 \end{bmatrix} = \begin{bmatrix} -\frac{4}{3} & 2 & -\frac{1}{3} \\ \frac{3}{2} & -2 & \frac{1}{2} \\ -\frac{1}{3} & 1 & -\frac{1}{3} \end{bmatrix} \begin{bmatrix} y_1 \\ y_2 \\ y_3 \end{bmatrix}$$

If this matrix product is substituted for the vector of unknowns, there would result the matrix equation

$$\begin{bmatrix} 1 & 2 & 2 \\ 2 & 2 & 1 \\ 5 & 4 & -2 \end{bmatrix} \begin{bmatrix} -\frac{4}{3} & 2 & -\frac{1}{3} \\ \frac{3}{2} & -2 & \frac{1}{2} \\ -\frac{1}{3} & 1 & -\frac{1}{3} \end{bmatrix} \begin{bmatrix} y_1 \\ y_2 \\ y_3 \end{bmatrix} = \begin{bmatrix} -1 \\ -3 \\ -8 \end{bmatrix}$$

Using the definition of matrix multiplication, the left side can be simplified to give

$$\begin{bmatrix} 1 & 0 & 0 \\ 0 & 1 & 0 \\ 0 & 0 & 1 \end{bmatrix} \begin{bmatrix} y_1 \\ y_2 \\ y_3 \end{bmatrix} = \begin{bmatrix} -1 \\ -3 \\ -8 \end{bmatrix}$$

Notice this is precisely the result obtained above. This is often given as the justification for the definition of multiplication that is used. In order to obtain the desired result for the problem of change of variable, multiplication must be defined as row by column multiplication.

In the change of variable, the coefficient matrix is multiplied on the right by the coefficient matrix of the change of variable. This is the same thing that is done in applying elementary column operations, using matrix multiplication. This means that the elementary column operations are associated with changing the variables in the system whereas the elementary row operations are associated with changing the equations.

In the example given, the number of variables in the original system is the same as the number in the new system. This is not always the case, the new system could have more variables or fewer variables than the original system.

2.9 Equivalence of Matrices

So far only row operations or only column operations have been used to reduce a rectangular matrix to a canonical form. If both operations are permitted, then a very simple canonical form is possible. To illustrate this consider the matrix used in Section 2.6, and the simplification

$$
\begin{bmatrix} 1 & -1 & 2 & 2 \\ 2 & -3 & 2 & 1 \\ 5 & -8 & 4 & -2 \\ 3 & 1 & 14 & 9 \end{bmatrix}
\xrightarrow[\substack{R2-2R1 \\ R3-5R1 \\ R4-3R1}]{}
\begin{bmatrix} 1 & -1 & 2 & -2 \\ 0 & -1 & -2 & -3 \\ 0 & -3 & -6 & -12 \\ 0 & 4 & 8 & 3 \end{bmatrix}
$$

$$
\xrightarrow[\substack{C2+1C1 \\ C3-2C1 \\ C4-2C1}]{}
\begin{bmatrix} 1 & 0 & 0 & 0 \\ 0 & -1 & -2 & -3 \\ 0 & -3 & -6 & -12 \\ 0 & 4 & 8 & 3 \end{bmatrix}
\xrightarrow[-1R2]{}
\begin{bmatrix} 1 & 0 & 0 & 0 \\ 0 & 1 & 2 & 3 \\ 0 & -3 & -6 & -12 \\ 0 & 4 & 8 & 3 \end{bmatrix}
$$

$$
\xrightarrow[\substack{C3-2C2 \\ C4-3C2}]{}
\begin{bmatrix} 1 & 0 & 0 & 0 \\ 0 & 1 & 0 & 0 \\ 0 & -3 & 0 & -3 \\ 0 & 4 & 0 & -9 \end{bmatrix}
\xrightarrow[\substack{R3+3R2 \\ R4-4R2}]{}
\begin{bmatrix} 1 & 0 & 0 & 0 \\ 0 & 1 & 0 & 0 \\ 0 & 0 & 0 & -3 \\ 0 & 0 & 0 & -9 \end{bmatrix}
$$

$$
C(3,4) \xleftrightarrow{\quad}
\begin{bmatrix}
1 & 0 & 0 & 0 \\
0 & 1 & 0 & 0 \\
0 & 0 & -3 & 0 \\
0 & 0 & -9 & 0
\end{bmatrix}
\xleftrightarrow{-\frac{1}{3}R3}
\begin{bmatrix}
1 & 0 & 0 & 0 \\
0 & 1 & 0 & 0 \\
0 & 0 & 1 & 0 \\
0 & 0 & -9 & 0
\end{bmatrix}
$$

$$
\xleftrightarrow{R4 + 9R3}
\begin{bmatrix}
1 & 0 & 0 & 0 \\
0 & 1 & 0 & 0 \\
0 & 0 & 1 & 0 \\
0 & 0 & 0 & 0
\end{bmatrix}
$$

At each step only one type of elementary operation is used. It may be either a row or a column operation but not both.

For this example, it was found before that its row rank and its column rank were both three. This is also the number of ones in this canonical form. For any matrix, its row rank and its column rank are equal to the number of ones in the canonical form for the matrix under both types of operations. The following definition gives a name to this.

Definition 2.6. The rank of a matrix is the number of ones in the canonical form under both row and column operations.

The rank of a matrix can actually be determined from any of the three canonical forms already given. This is a consequence of the equality of row rank, column rank, and rank of a matrix. A later chapter will have an older definition of rank in terms of determinants.

As before, if the row operations used in the reduction are applied to the left identity matrix, a left multiplier will be obtained that will perform these operations. Similarly, if the column operations are used on the right identity, a right multiplier will be obtained that will perform the column operations. If the matrix obtained by the row operations is called P, and if the matrix obtained by the column operations is called Q, then it will be true that

$$
PAQ =
\begin{bmatrix}
I_r & 0 \\
0 & 0
\end{bmatrix}
$$

where r is the rank of the matrix A. Again the matrices P and Q are not unique.

One more definition can be made now.

Definition 2.7. Two matrices are said to be equivalent if one can be obtained from the other by combinations of row and/or column operations.

This definition implies that equivalent matrices are obtained at each step in the reduction to canonical form using both types of operations.

In the row reduction process, all the matrices formed at each step were row equivalent while in the column reduction they were all column equivalent. Under this broader definition, each of these sets contains matrices that are also equivalent, since it is not required that both kinds of operations have to be used.

PROBLEMS

1. Write the following systems of equations in the standard form and in the form of a matrix equation.

(a) $3x_1 - x_2 + 6x_3 \qquad = 1$

$\qquad x_1 + 2x_2 - 3x_3 \qquad = 0$

$\qquad 2x_1 - 3x_2 - x_3 + 9 = 0$

(b) $2x_1 - x_2 - 2x_3 \qquad = 5$

$\qquad 2x_3 + x_2 + 4x_1 - 1 = 0$

$\qquad 8x_1 + x_3 - x_2 - 5 = 0$

(c) $\quad x_1 - x_2 + 4x_3 - 2x_4 = 3$

$\qquad 4x_4 - x_1 - x_2 - 2x_3 = 1$

$\qquad 2x_2 - 4x_3 + 3x_4 + 5 \quad = 0$

$\qquad 3x_3 + x_4 - x_1 \qquad = 2$

2. Solve the systems of 1 by the triangular method of Section 2.2.

3. Solve the systems of 1 by using elementary row operations.

4. By using elementary row operations, find the solution or solutions, if they exist, for the following systems of equations.

(a) $2x_1 + 3x_2 - 4x_3 = 2$

$\quad x_1 - 3x_2 + x_3 = 1$

$\quad 3x_1 - 5x_3 - 4 \quad = 0$

(b) $\quad x_1 - x_2 - x_3 - x_4 = 2$

$\quad 2x_1 + 4x_2 - 3x_3 \qquad = 6$

$\quad 3x_2 - 4x_3 - 2x_4 + 1 = 0$

$\quad 4x_3 + 3x_4 - 2x_1 + 3 = 0$

(c) $2x_1 + x_3 - 3x_5 = 1$

$\quad x_2 + 2x_3 + 3x_4 + 2x_5 = 0$

$\quad x_1 - x_2 + x_3 + x_4 - x_5 = -1$

$\quad 2x_1 + 3x_2 - x_3 - 3x_5 = 0$

$\quad 3x_3 + 4x_4 - x_5 - 3 = 0$

(d) $x_1 + x_2 - x_3 \qquad = 0$

$\quad 5x_2 - x_1 + x_3 + 6 = 0$

$\quad 2x_3 - x_2 - 2x_1 + 1 = 0$

(e) $\quad x_1 - 2x_2 - 3x_3 = 2$

$\quad x_1 - 4x_2 + 3x_3 = 14$

$\quad -3x_1 + 5x_2 + 4x_3 = 0$

(f) $4x_1 + 5x_3 = 6$

$\quad x_2 - 6x_3 = -2$

$\quad 3x_1 + 4x_3 = 3$

(g) $\quad x_1 + 2x_2 + 3x_3 + 4x_4 = 10$

$\quad 2x_1 - x_2 + x_3 - x_4 = 1$

$\quad 3x_1 + x_2 + 4x_3 + 3x_4 = 11$

$\quad -2x_1 + 6x_2 + 4x_3 + 10x_4 = 18$

(h) $-4x_1 + 3x_2 + 2x_3 = -2$

$\quad 5x_1 - 4x_2 + x_3 = 3$

(i) $\quad x_1 - 2x_2 + x_3 - x_4 + 1 = 0$

$\quad 3x_1 - 2x_3 + 3x_4 + 4 = 0$

$\quad 5x_1 - 4x_2 + x_4 + 3 = 0$

(j) $-4x_1 + 3x_2 = 2$

$\quad 5x_1 - 4x_2 = 0$

$\quad 2x_1 - x_2 = 5$

(k) $\quad x_1 - 2x_2 - 3x_3 = 0$

$\quad x_1 - 4x_2 - 13x_3 = 0$

$\quad -3x_1 + 5x_2 + 4x_3 = 0$

(m) $x_1 + x_2 + x_3 = 0$

$\quad 2x_1 + 4x_2 + 3x_3 = 0$

$\quad 4x_2 + 4x_3 = 0$

5. Reduce the following matrices to canonical form using only elementary row operations. What are the row ranks of the matrices? Find matrices that will reduce the given matrices to canonical form.

(a) $\begin{bmatrix} 1 & -1 & 1 \\ 2 & -4 & 3 \\ 0 & -2 & 3 \end{bmatrix}$

(b) $\begin{bmatrix} 1 & 1 & 1 & -2 \\ 2 & 4 & 3 & 3 \\ 0 & 4 & 2 & 2 \end{bmatrix}$

(c) $\begin{bmatrix} 2 & -1 & 1 & 2 \\ 4 & -2 & -1 & 16 \\ -2 & 1 & -3 & 6 \\ 6 & -3 & 5 & -2 \end{bmatrix}$

6. What are the inverses of the following matrices?

(a)
$$\begin{bmatrix} 1 & 0 & 0 & 0 \\ 0 & 0 & 1 & 0 \\ 0 & 1 & 0 & 0 \\ 0 & 0 & 0 & 1 \end{bmatrix}$$

(b)
$$\begin{bmatrix} 1 & 0 & 0 & 0 \\ 0 & 1 & 0 & 0 \\ 0 & 0 & 1 & 0 \\ 0 & 0 & 0 & 3 \end{bmatrix}$$

(c)
$$\begin{bmatrix} 1 & 0 & 0 & 0 \\ -5 & 1 & 0 & 0 \\ 0 & 0 & 1 & 0 \\ 0 & 0 & 0 & 1 \end{bmatrix}$$

(d) The product of the matrices of a and b in that order?

7. Find the product of the matrices of 6(a) and 6(b), of 6(b) and 6(c), and of 6(a), 6(b), and 6(c). What are the inverses of these products?

8. Reduce the matrices in Problem 5 to canonical form using only column operations. What are the column ranks? Find matrices that will reduce the given matrices to canonical form.

9. Using 5(a) as the matrix for a change of variable, find the new system of equations in the y_i for the system of 1(a). Do by direct substitution and verify by matrix multiplication.

10. In the following system make the indicated change of variable.

$$x_1 - 2x_2 - x_3 = 5 \qquad\qquad x_1 = -7y_1 + 3y_2 + 5y_3$$

$$4x_1 - 3x_2 + x_3 = 10 \qquad\qquad x_2 = -11y_1 - y_2 + 5y_3$$

$$3x_1 - x_2 - 2x_3 = 8 \qquad\qquad x_3 = y_1 - y_2 + y_3$$

Solve the resulting system for the y's. Use these results to solve for the x's.

11. Do the same things as in Problem 10 for the system given in 1(c) and the change of variables

$$x_1 = 41y_1 + 7y_2 + 6y_3 - 9y_4$$

$$x_2 = -3y_1 - 17y_2 + 4y_3 + 7y_4$$

$$x_3 = 9y_1 - y_2 + y_3 + 5y_4$$

$$x_4 = 14y_1 + 10y_2 + 3y_3 + 2y_4$$

Compare the final solution with that obtained in 1(c).

12. Reduce the matrix in 5(c) to canonical form using both row and column operations.

3

Vector Spaces and
Linear Transformations

3.1 Vector Spaces

In Section 1.2, vectors were defined as special types of matrices with only one row or one column. They were then used in the definition for multiplication of matrices. It is the purpose of this section to consider sets of vectors of the same size and to discuss some of their properties. The term vector will again apply to either a row or a column vector.

In Section 1.7, addition of matrices was defined and discussed. It was indicated that in order to add two matrices, they had to be of the same dimension. The resulting matrix is again of the same size. It was shown that the operation of addition is commutative and associative. The zero matrix is the identity of addition and there is an inverse of addition for all matrices. Since vectors are matrices with only one row or column, those of the same size can be added. The sum is again a matrix of the same dimension. Furthermore, the addition of vectors will have the properties noted for the addition of matrices.

In the definition of matrix multiplication in section 1.8, it was necessary that the number of columns of the first matrix be the same as the number of rows of the second matrix. For vectors all of the same size, this condition is not met except for the trivial vectors with a single component. This means that vectors of the same size cannot be multiplied in the usual manner.

Recall that scalar multiplication was defined in section 1.9 without any restrictions on the matrices involved. This means that it can be applied to vectors. The properties of this operation were given in that same section. With these properties of addition and scalar multiplication in mind, the following definition can be made.

Definition 3.1. A set of vectors forms a vector space if:

(1) The sum of any two vectors in the set is also in the set.

(2) All scalar multiples of any vector in the set are also in the set.

This definition leads to some important conclusions. If A_1 and A_2 are any two vectors in a vector space V, then by the first part of the definition, $A_1 + A_2$ is also in V. By the second part of the definition, k_1A_1 and k_2A_2 are in V for all scalars k_1 and k_2. Again by part one, $k_1A_1 + k_2A_2$ is a vector in V for all k_1 and k_2. The next definition describes this last vector in general terms.

Definition 3.2. A linear combination of a set of vectors A_1, A_2, $\cdots$, A_t is the vector $k_1A_1 + k_2A_2 + \cdots + k_tA_t$, where k_1, k_2, $\cdots$, k_t are scalars.

The definition indicates that a linear combination of a set of vectors is a sum of scalar multiples of the vectors.

3.2 Basis for a Vector Space

It is actually true that all linear combinations of two vectors A_1 and A_2 of the same size will themselves form a vector space U. According to Definition 3.1, this is true if two conditions are satisfied. First, the sum of any two vectors of this type must be of this type. Second, all scalar multiples of the vectors must also be of this form. Consider the sum of the two vectors,

$$(a_1A_1 + a_2A_2) + (b_1A_1 + b_2A_2) = (a_1A_1 + b_1A_1) + (a_2A_2 + b_2A_2)$$

$$= (a_1 + b_1)A_1 + (a_2 + b_2)A_2$$

$$= c_1A_1 + c_2A_2$$

The sequence of steps follows by using the associative and commutative laws of addition as well as the distributive law for scalars. The result is again a linear combination of the vectors A_1 and A_2 so is in the set. Finally,

$$c(a_1A_1 + a_2A_2) = c(a_1A_1) + c(a_2A_2)$$
$$= (ca_1)A_1 + (ca_2)A_2$$
$$= d_1A_1 + d_2A_2$$

This means that any scalar multiple is again a linear combination of A_1 and A_2. Since both parts of the definition are satisfied, all the linear combinations of these two vectors form a vector space U.

As an example, let

$$A_1 = \begin{bmatrix} 1 & 1 & 1 \end{bmatrix}, \quad A_2 = \begin{bmatrix} 1 & 1 & 0 \end{bmatrix}$$

Then for the sum of two linear combinations take

$$(3A_1 + 4A_2) + (5A_1 - 11A_2) = \begin{bmatrix} 7 & 7 & 3 \end{bmatrix} + \begin{bmatrix} -6 & -6 & 5 \end{bmatrix}$$
$$= \begin{bmatrix} 1 & 1 & 8 \end{bmatrix} = 8A_1 - 7A_2$$

which is again a linear combination of A_1 and A_2.

Taking a scalar multiple of the first vector

$$7(3A_1 + 4A_2) = 7\begin{bmatrix} 7 & 7 & 3 \end{bmatrix} = \begin{bmatrix} 49 & 49 & 21 \end{bmatrix}$$
$$= 21A_1 + 28A_2 = 7 \cdot 3A_1 + 7 \cdot 4A_2$$

This vector is also in the set.

Actually one can describe this vector space quite readily. It will consist of those 1×3 vectors whose first two components are equal for

$$k_1A_1 + k_2A_2 = \begin{bmatrix} k_1 + k_2 & k_1 + k_2 & k_1 \end{bmatrix}$$

The concept of a vector space determined by linear combinations of vectors of the same dimension can be generalized to involve more than two vectors. One can take any set of t vectors of the same size and consider the sums of scalar multiples of these vectors. In other words, one can speak of the linear combination

$$a_1A_1 + a_2A_2 + \cdots + a_tA_t$$

of the vectors $A_1, A_2, \cdots, A_t$. The sum of two linear combinations of these vectors is again of the same form for

$$(a_1A_1 + a_2A_2 + \cdots + a_tA_t) + (b_1A_1 + b_2A_2 + \cdots + b_tA_t)$$
$$= (a_1A_1 + b_1A_1) + (a_2A_2 + b_2A_2) + \cdots + (a_tA_t + b_tA_t)$$
$$= (a_1 + b_1)A_1 + (a_2 + b_2)A_2 + \cdots + (a_t + b_t)A_t$$
$$= c_1A_1 + c_2A_2 + \cdots + c_tA_t$$

The associative and commutative laws of addition of vectors are used as well as the distributive law for scalars. For the scalar product,

$$c(a_1A_1 + a_2A_2 + \cdots + a_tA_t) = c(a_1A_1) + c(a_2A_2) + \cdots + c(a_tA_t)$$
$$= (ca_1)A_1 + (ca_2)A_2 + \cdots + (ca_t)A_t$$
$$= d_1A_1 + d_2A_2 + \cdots + d_tA_t$$

The final vector is again a linear combination of the $A_1, A_2, \cdots, A_t$. This says the set of all linear combinations of these vectors forms a vector space.

As an example, consider the following vectors from the set of 3×1 column vectors.

$$A_1 = \begin{bmatrix} 1 \\ 1 \\ 1 \end{bmatrix} \qquad A_2 = \begin{bmatrix} 1 \\ 1 \\ 0 \end{bmatrix} \qquad A_3 = \begin{bmatrix} 1 \\ 0 \\ 0 \end{bmatrix} \qquad A_4 = \begin{bmatrix} 0 \\ 1 \\ 0 \end{bmatrix}$$

A linear combination of these vectors would be

$$2A_1 + 3A_2 - A_3 + 5A_4 = 2\begin{bmatrix} 1 \\ 1 \\ 1 \end{bmatrix} + 3\begin{bmatrix} 1 \\ 1 \\ 0 \end{bmatrix} + (-1)\begin{bmatrix} 1 \\ 0 \\ 0 \end{bmatrix} + 5\begin{bmatrix} 0 \\ 1 \\ 0 \end{bmatrix}$$

$$= \begin{bmatrix} 2 \\ 2 \\ 2 \end{bmatrix} + \begin{bmatrix} 3 \\ 3 \\ 0 \end{bmatrix} + \begin{bmatrix} -1 \\ 0 \\ 0 \end{bmatrix} + \begin{bmatrix} 0 \\ 5 \\ 0 \end{bmatrix} = \begin{bmatrix} 4 \\ 10 \\ 2 \end{bmatrix}$$

A second linear combination would be

$$5A_1 - 4A_2 + 2A_3 - 7A_4 = \begin{bmatrix} 3 \\ -6 \\ 5 \end{bmatrix}$$

Their sum is a vector of the same form for it is

$$\begin{bmatrix} 7 \\ 4 \\ 7 \end{bmatrix} = 7A_1 - A_2 + A_3 - 2A_4$$

For a scalar multiple of the first vector, consider

$$-3(2A_1 + 3A_2 - A_3 + 5A_4) = \begin{bmatrix} -12 \\ -30 \\ -6 \end{bmatrix} = -6A_1 - 9A_2 + 3A_3 - 15A_4$$

The result is again a vector in the system.

The vector space here also turns out to have a simple description, it is the vector space of all 3×1 column vectors. To show this, one must be able to express any 3×1 vector as a linear combination of these four vectors. To do this the vector equation

$$k_1A_1 + k_2A_2 + k_3A_3 + k_4A_4 = k_1\begin{bmatrix} 1 \\ 1 \\ 1 \end{bmatrix} + k_2\begin{bmatrix} 1 \\ 1 \\ 0 \end{bmatrix} + k_3\begin{bmatrix} 1 \\ 0 \\ 0 \end{bmatrix} + k_4\begin{bmatrix} 0 \\ 1 \\ 0 \end{bmatrix}$$

$$= \begin{bmatrix} a \\ b \\ c \end{bmatrix}$$

must be solved for the k_i where the last vector represents any 3×1 column vector. Combining the left side of the last equality into a single vector gives the vector equation

$$\begin{bmatrix} k_1 + k_2 + k_3 \\ k_1 + k_2 + k_4 \\ k_1 \end{bmatrix} = \begin{bmatrix} a \\ b \\ c \end{bmatrix}$$

In order for these two vectors to be equal, corresponding components must be equal so that

$$k_1 + k_2 + k_3 = a$$
$$k_1 + k_2 + k_4 = b$$
$$k_1 \quad\quad = c$$

Since there are four k_i and only three equations, the solution for this system of equations involves an arbitrary parameter. By choosing k_2 as this arbitrary parameter d, one solution for this system of equations indicates that the linear combination

$$cA_1 + dA_2 + (a - c - d)A_3 + (b - c - d)A_4$$

$$= \begin{bmatrix} c \\ c \\ c \end{bmatrix} + \begin{bmatrix} d \\ d \\ 0 \end{bmatrix} + \begin{bmatrix} a - c - d \\ 0 \\ 0 \end{bmatrix} + \begin{bmatrix} 0 \\ b - c - d \\ 0 \end{bmatrix} = \begin{bmatrix} a \\ b \\ c \end{bmatrix}$$

for any value of d. This illustrates the next definition.

Definition 3.3. A set of vectors $A_1, A_2, \cdots, A_t$ is said to span a vector space V if they are in V and every vector in V can be expressed as a linear combination of the $A_1, A_2, \cdots, A_t$.

It is customary to exclude the zero vector in a set of spanning vectors for it really contributes nothing. Any scalar multiple of the zero vector is again the zero vector. If the zero vector is added to any vector, one obtains this second vector. From here on it will be assumed that the zero vector is not in any spanning set considered.

While the second set illustrated will span the space of all 3×1 vectors, so will the vectors A_1, A_2, and A_3. For these, the general vector can be formed by letting $d = b - c$ so that

$$cA_1 + (b - c)A_2 + (a - b)A_3 = \begin{bmatrix} c \\ c \\ c \end{bmatrix} + \begin{bmatrix} b - c \\ b - c \\ 0 \end{bmatrix} + \begin{bmatrix} a - b \\ 0 \\ 0 \end{bmatrix}$$

$$= \begin{bmatrix} a \\ b \\ c \end{bmatrix}$$

If an attempt is made to use fewer than three vectors, then the vector space formed will no longer contain all of the 3×1 vectors. This minimal number of three is unique for the given vector space, but the vectors in the spanning set are not unique. By letting $d = a - c$, the coefficient of the third vector would be zero so the other three vectors would also span the same vector space.

In any vector space, one can always obtain the zero vector as a linear combination of any set of vectors. For

$$0A_1 + 0A_2 + \cdots + 0A_t = 0$$

for any set of vectors. This is called a trivial linear combination since all coefficients are zero. It is not always possible to find a nontrivial linear combination of a given set of vectors that will give the zero vector. The next definition is concerned with sets of vectors from which one can obtain the zero vector as a nontrivial linear combination.

Definition 3.4. The set of vectors A_1, A_2, $\cdots$, A_t is said to be linearly dependent if there is a set of k_i not all zero such that

$$k_1A_1 + k_2A_2 + \cdots + k_tA_t = 0$$

If the set of vectors is not linearly dependent it is said to be *linearly independent*. This definition implies that the set of vectors is linearly independent if all the k_i have to be zero to obtain the zero vector.

For the numerical example above,

$$0A_1 + kA_2 - kA_3 - kA_4 = 0$$

for any k as can be easily verified. This means the vectors A_1, A_2, A_3, A_4 are linearly dependent. It also says the vectors A_2, A_3, and A_4 are linearly dependent for

$$kA_2 - kA_3 - kA_4 = 0$$

for any k. In contrast, if one tried to get a nontrivial linear combination of the A_1, A_2, and A_3 that was equal to the zero vector, it would be found to be impossible. To see this consider,

$$k_1A_1 + k_2A_2 + k_3A_3 = \begin{bmatrix} k_1 \\ k_1 \\ k_1 \end{bmatrix} + \begin{bmatrix} k_2 \\ k_2 \\ 0 \end{bmatrix} + \begin{bmatrix} k_3 \\ 0 \\ 0 \end{bmatrix}$$

$$= \begin{bmatrix} k_1 + k_2 + k_3 \\ k_1 + k_2 \\ k_1 \end{bmatrix} = \begin{bmatrix} 0 \\ 0 \\ 0 \end{bmatrix}$$

In order for these last two vectors to be equal, corresponding components must be equal. This means $k_1 = 0$ and, hence, since $k_1 + k_2 = 0$, it follows that $k_2 = 0$. Then, because $k_1 + k_2 + k_3 = 0$ in the first component,

$k_3 = 0$. In this case, the set of vectors is linearly independent. With these concepts it is now possible to make another definition.

Definition 3.5. A basis for a vector space is a set of linearly independent vectors that span the space.

A simple basis for the space of all 3×1 column vectors is the set

$$\begin{bmatrix} 1 \\ 0 \\ 0 \end{bmatrix} \quad \begin{bmatrix} 0 \\ 1 \\ 0 \end{bmatrix} \quad \text{and} \quad \begin{bmatrix} 0 \\ 0 \\ 1 \end{bmatrix}$$

since

$$a\begin{bmatrix} 1 \\ 0 \\ 0 \end{bmatrix} + b\begin{bmatrix} 0 \\ 1 \\ 0 \end{bmatrix} + c\begin{bmatrix} 0 \\ 0 \\ 1 \end{bmatrix} = \begin{bmatrix} a \\ b \\ c \end{bmatrix}$$

for any scalars a, b, and c. These are called the *unit vectors* of the space. For the vector space given in the example above, another basis would consist of the three vectors A_1, A_2, and A_3 since they span the space and were just shown to be linearly independent.

Definition 3.6. The dimension of a vector space is the number of vectors in a basis.

Recall that any matrix A can be thought of as being composed of a set of row vectors or a set of column vectors. The set of row vectors would span a vector space that is designated as the *row space* of the matrix A. Similarly, the column vectors can be taken as a set of spanning vectors. The space so determined is called the *column space* of the matrix.

It can be shown that the row space of a matrix is unchanged under elementary row operations. This means the same space is spanned by both the row vectors of the row canonical form of a matrix and the row vectors of the matrix. There is an important difference between the two sets of spanning vectors. It is true that the nonzero row vectors in the canonical form are r in number and linearly independent so they constitute a basis for the row space of the matrix. Since the row vectors of the original matrix may be linearly dependent, this suggests a way to find a basis for a vector space spanned by a given set of row vectors. One forms a matrix with the vectors and reduces it to row canonical form. The nonzero row vectors of the reduced form will constitute a basis for the given vector space, so the rank of the matrix is also the dimension of its row space.

If the vectors were column vectors, a similar thing could be done. One forms a matrix with the given set of vectors as its column vectors. This matrix is then reduced to column canonical form. The nonzero column vectors in this form will constitute a basis for the column space spanned by the original vectors.

In case the vectors are $1 \times n$ or $n \times 1$, and n in number, the matrix formed is square. The canonical form could then be the identity matrix. In this situation, the unit vectors would be the basis obtained. This tells one that the space spanned by the original vectors consists of all vectors of that size. It also implies that the original vectors also form a basis.

To illustrate the discussion above, consider the vectors A_1, A_2, A_3, A_4 that were used before. Forming the matrix with these as column vectors and reducing to canonical form gives

$$\begin{bmatrix} 1 & 1 & 1 & 0 \\ 1 & 1 & 0 & 1 \\ 1 & 0 & 0 & 0 \end{bmatrix} \quad \underset{\substack{C(1,3) \\ C(2,4)}}{\longleftrightarrow} \quad \begin{bmatrix} 1 & 0 & 1 & 1 \\ 0 & 1 & 1 & 1 \\ 0 & 0 & 1 & 0 \end{bmatrix} \quad \underset{\substack{C3 - 1C1 \\ C4 - 1C1}}{\longleftrightarrow} \quad \begin{bmatrix} 1 & 0 & 0 & 0 \\ 0 & 1 & 1 & 1 \\ 0 & 0 & 1 & 0 \end{bmatrix}$$

$$\underset{\substack{C3 - 1C2 \\ C4 - 1C2}}{\longleftrightarrow} \quad \begin{bmatrix} 1 & 0 & 0 & 0 \\ 0 & 1 & 0 & 0 \\ 0 & 0 & 1 & 0 \end{bmatrix}$$

This shows that the three unit vectors will form a basis for the space so it must consist of all 3×1 column vectors.

As another example take the row vectors

$$\begin{bmatrix} 1 & 3 & 2 \end{bmatrix}, \quad \begin{bmatrix} -1 & 6 & -2 \end{bmatrix}, \quad \text{and} \quad \begin{bmatrix} 6 & 0 & 12 \end{bmatrix}$$

Forming a matrix with these vectors and simplifying gives,

$$\begin{bmatrix} 1 & 3 & 2 \\ -1 & 6 & -2 \\ 6 & 0 & 12 \end{bmatrix} \quad \underset{\substack{R2 + 1R1 \\ R3 - 6R1}}{\longleftrightarrow} \quad \begin{bmatrix} 1 & 3 & 2 \\ 0 & 9 & 0 \\ 0 & -18 & 0 \end{bmatrix} \quad \underset{\substack{R1 - \frac{1}{3}R2 \\ R3 + 2R2}}{\longleftrightarrow} \quad \begin{bmatrix} 1 & 0 & 2 \\ 0 & 9 & 0 \\ 0 & 0 & 0 \end{bmatrix}$$

This means the vectors $\begin{bmatrix} 1 & 0 & 2 \end{bmatrix}$ and $\begin{bmatrix} 0 & 1 & 0 \end{bmatrix}$ are a basis for the space spanned by the given vectors. (Notice that one more step would be required to finish the reduction but the final result can be seen without doing this. Actually, [0 9 0] could be used in place of [0 1 0].) This space is not the entire space of 1 × 3 row vectors, for the vector [1 0 0] cannot be expressed as a linear combination of these two vectors.

3.3 Geometric Interpretation of a Vector Space

The vector space composed of all 1 × 2 row vectors has an interesting geometric interpretation. To see this, consider the usual two-dimensional rectangular coordinate system. This enables one to associate a pair of real numbers with every point in a plane and vice versa. For example, pairs of numbers in Figure 3.1 are associated with the corresponding points in the plane.

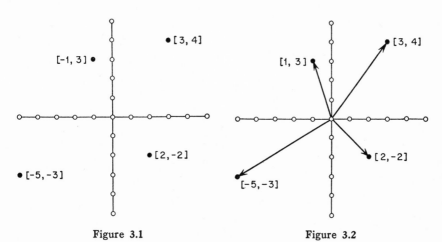

Figure 3.1   Figure 3.2

If each of these points is connected to the origin and an arrow head put on the line segment at the given point, one obtains Figure 3.2.

Each of these line segments then can be considered as determining a direction from the origin.

If the coordinates of the point are written without the comma, then the notation is exactly what is used for 1 × 2 row vectors. Therefore, one can think of the 1 × 2 row vectors as "directed line segments" joining the origin to a point in a plane coordinate system. These line segments have length and direction. The length of each can be found by dropping a perpendicular from the point that determines the vector, to the horizontal axis. The lengths of the sides of the right triangle that is formed are given by the coordinates of the point. The length of the vector is the length of the hypotenuse of this right triangle and therefore is equal to the square root of the sum of the squares of the sides. It can be shown that the lengths of the vectors determined by the points $[3, 4]$, $[-1, 3]$, and $[-5, -3]$ are 5, $\sqrt{10}$, and $\sqrt{34}$ respectively.

With this geometric interpretation of a vector, one can consider the meaning of vector addition. By the definition of addition of vectors,

$$[3 \quad 1] + [1 \quad 2] = [4 \quad 3]$$

These three vectors plotted in a plane coordinate system give Figure 3.3.

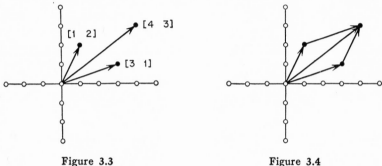

Figure 3.3   Figure 3.4

Suppose one were to connect the points $[1 \quad 2]$ and $[3 \quad 1]$ to $[4 \quad 3]$, the resulting figure, Figure 3.4, looks very much like a parallelogram. It can be easily shown that this is true. In other words, to add two vectors geometrically, one forms a parallelogram with the given vectors as two sides. Then the vector drawn to the vertex opposite the origin is the sum of the vectors.

The next question to consider is the geometric interpretation of a scalar multiple of a given vector. For instance, if the vector is $[3 \quad 4]$, what about

$$2[3 \quad 4] = [6 \quad 8]?$$

If the point with these coordinates is plotted and connected with the origin, the connecting line will pass through the point with coordinates $[3 \quad 4]$. Furthermore, the length of the second vector is 10, which is twice the length of the first vector. In general, the positive scalar multiple of a vector is a vector with the same direction but with its length multiplied by the scalar. Now what about the negative scalar multiples? Consider

$$(-3)[3 \quad 4] = [-9 \quad -12]$$

This vector and the original one will lie on the same straight line again but will have opposite directions! The length of this vector is 15. The negative scalar multiple reverses the direction of the vector as well as multiplying its length. In other words, all scalar multiples of a vector will lie along a line going through the origin in both directions.

The geometric interpretation of the 1×2 row vectors above could be applied to the 2×1 column vectors equally well. The interpretation can also be extended to the three-dimensional rectangular coordinate system. The vectors now would be either 1×3 row vectors or 3×1 column vectors. The concept of scalar multiplication would be the same. Multiplication of a vector by a positive scalar leaves the direction of the vector unchanged and influences its length only, whereas the multiplication by a negative scalar reverses the direction of the vector as well as affecting its length. Two vectors can again be added using the parallelogram rule. Any two vectors will determine a plane and in that plane one forms the parallelogram with these vectors as sides. The diagonal from the origin is the sum of the two vectors.

3.4 Inner Product of Vectors

For any two row or column vectors of the same size one can form a special product using matrix multiplication. This is given in the next definition.

Definition 3.7. The inner product of two row vectors A and B is the scalar AB'.

In the exercises, the reader is asked to show that $AB' = BA'$ and to make the corresponding definition for column vectors. In case the inner product of two vectors is zero, they are said to be *mutually orthogonal*.

The next definition is concerned with the inner product of a vector with itself.

Definition 3.8. The square of the length of a row vector A is given by the scalar AA'.

This definition gives the same length for a 1×2 row vector as was obtained in the previous section. For example, the square of the length of the vector $[3 \quad 4]$ is

$$[3 \quad 4]\begin{bmatrix} 3 \\ 4 \end{bmatrix} = 9 + 16 = 25$$

For the $1 \times n$ row vector $A = [a_1 \quad a_2 \quad \cdots \quad a_n]$, the square of its length is

$$[a_1 \quad a_2 \quad \cdots \quad a_n] \begin{bmatrix} a_1 \\ a_2 \\ \cdot \\ \cdot \\ \cdot \\ a_n \end{bmatrix} = a_1^2 + a_2^2 + \cdots + a_n^2$$

Notice that the square of the length of the vector is always a nonnegative number so it has a real square root. The positive root can then be taken as the measure of the length of the vector. In case the vector is of length 1, it is said to be a *normal vector*.

In Chapter 1, an orthogonal matrix was defined as a nonsingular matrix whose transpose is also its inverse. For this reason, the set of row vectors and the set of column vectors of an orthogonal matrix are mutually orthogonal and normal. To show this for the general 3×3 case, write the orthogonal matrix A in terms of its row vectors as

$$A = \begin{bmatrix} A_1 \\ A_2 \\ A_3 \end{bmatrix} \quad \text{so that} \quad A' = [A_1' \quad A_2' \quad A_3']$$

Then

$$AA^{-1} = AA' = \begin{bmatrix} A_1 \\ A_2 \\ A_3 \end{bmatrix} [A_1' \quad A_2' \quad A_3'] = \begin{bmatrix} A_1A_1' & A_1A_2' & A_1A_3' \\ A_2A_1' & A_2A_2' & A_2A_3' \\ A_3A_1' & A_3A_2' & A_3A_3' \end{bmatrix}$$

$$= \begin{bmatrix} 1 & 0 & 0 \\ 0 & 1 & 0 \\ 0 & 0 & 1 \end{bmatrix}$$

By the definition of equality of matrices, corresponding components of these last two matrices must be equal. Those on the diagonal give the equations $A_iA_i' = 1$ for $i = 1, 2, 3$. This shows that the row vectors of A are normal. The other equations imply that $A_iA_j' = 0$ for $i \neq j$, so the **row** vectors are mutually orthogonal.

The argument for the general $n \times n$ orthogonal matrix is quite similar to the one just given for the 3×3 matrix. A corresponding argument can be used to show that the column vectors of an orthogonal matrix are also normal and mutually orthogonal.

3.5 Linear Transformations

An important concept in mathematics is that of a mapping of the elements of one system into the elements of another. This means that one has a way of associating an element of the second system with every element of the first system. Or, put another way, one starts with a given system, then for each of its elements there is a corresponding element in the second system called the *image element*. The second system may be the same as the first, it may be just a part of the first, or it may be a different system altogether.

For vector spaces some mappings are called linear transformations. The image vectors are often referred to then as "transform vectors." In order to have a linear transformation the vector space and its map must have the same scalars; that is, the elements of the vectors must belong to the same algebraic system. The following definition indicates when a mapping is a linear transformation of a vector space.

Definition 3.9. A linear transformation T of a vector space V is a mapping of V onto a set of vectors U such that

(1) $T(X + Y) = T(X) + T(Y)$,

(2) $T(kX) = kT(X)$.

The X and Y refer to vectors in V and the k is a scalar of both V and U. The $T(X)$, $T(Y)$, $T(X + Y)$, and $T(kX)$ are used to indicate the corresponding transform vectors in U where capital T is an abbreviation for "transform of." The first condition says that the transform vector of a sum of two vectors in V is the sum of their transform vectors. The second condition says that the transform vector of a scalar multiple of a vector in V is the scalar multiple of the transform of the vector. The first property also indicates how to find the sum of two elements in U so that the system U is closed under addition. The second property implies that the system U is closed under scalar multiplication. Thus, by Definition 3.1, the set of vectors U must also be a vector space. In other words, the set of transforms of all the vectors of a given vector space also form a vector space. It can be shown that if a set of vectors span V, then their transforms will span U.

In the discussion on mappings, it was pointed out that one has some way of finding an image element for every element in a given system. For linear transformations this can be done by matrix multiplication. Recall that if a column vector is multiplied on the left by a matrix, a column vector will be obtained. Similarly, multiplication on the right of a row vector gives a row vector. In particular, if the matrix is square, the resulting vector is of the same dimension as the original vector.

In Section 2.8 there was a discussion of a change of variable using the product of matrices. There the vector X was replaced by the product AY, where A was a square matrix and Y was a column vector. In terms of the concept of linear transformations, the vector X can be thought of as the transform vector of Y. The matrix used to effect this mapping can be used as a multiplier for all vectors in the space to which Y belongs. The product vector would be the transform vector. To find the transform of any vector under this linear transformation, one simply multiplies the vector by the matrix of the linear transformation. It is easy to see that this is a linear transformation for

$$A(X + Y) = AX + AY \quad \text{and} \quad A(kX) = kAX$$

using the properties of matrices and vectors.

Another example of the concept of linear transformations is found in the matrix equation for a system of linear equations. The system was written as $AX = G$. This can be interpreted as meaning the vector X is transformed into the vector G by the matrix A. In this problem, one is trying to find a vector knowing what its image vector is under a given linear transformation. From what was discussed previously in Chapter 2, it is seen that usually there is only one column vector X that is transformed into the vector G. However, there are situations where there is no solution to the problem, or there may be an infinite number of solutions.

A system of homogeneous equations requires that the column vector X be transformed into the zero column vector by a given matrix. It is true that the zero column vector will always be transformed into itself under any linear transformation. This is the trivial solution for the homogeneous system. However, in case there is a nonzero column vector that is transformed into the zero column by a given matrix A, there will be an infinite number of such vectors. This is a consequence of the fact that there would be an infinite number of solutions to the homogeneous system if there is one nontrivial solution.

3.6 The Algebra of Linear Transformations

Thus far, the discussion has been concerned with the concept of a single linear transformation. The next question to be considered is whether one can talk about combining linear transformations, as was done for matrices in Chapter 1. One can simply define these operations in general terms, or one can be specific and use the matrix multiplication notation. If this latter system is used, all the properties of the operations with matrices can be used.

Assume that the vector space V consists of $m \times 1$ column vectors. These vectors can be multiplied on the left by any $n \times m$ matrix where n is any positive integer. This means each $n \times m$ matrix will determine a linear transformation of V. Furthermore, the transform spaces will consist of $n \times 1$ column vectors. In other words, the transform vectors may not be of the same size as the vectors of V. However, in this discussion let the matrices of the linear transformations be square so that the transform vectors are of the same size as the original vectors.

The first operation to be defined is that of "addition of linear transformations." For this operation one considers the linear transformation with matrix $(A + B)$ as the sum of the linear transformations determined by each of the matrices A and B. For any vector X of V, the transform vector determined by $A + B$ would be given by

$$(A + B)X = AX + BX$$

In other words, the transform vector of the sum $A + B$ is determined by adding the two transform vectors. This is the way the sum of two linear transformations is defined. It is fairly obvious that, since vector addition is commutative and associative, the addition of linear transformations is also commutative and associative. The zero linear transformation would be the one determined by the zero matrix. Under this linear transformation, all vectors would go into the zero vector so this is the identity of addition in the set of linear transformations. The additive inverse of a linear transformation would be the one whose matrix is the negative of the matrix of the original linear transformation. This operation of addition is rarely used in practice.

The concept of multiplication of linear transformations is of far greater importance. Suppose that one has the matrix product

$$(AB)X = Y$$

where X and Y are column vectors, and A and B are square matrices. What is meant by this in terms of linear transformations? By the associative law of matrices, this can be written as

$$(AB)X = A(BX) = Y$$

In terms of linear transformations, this would say that the transform of the product AB is the transform vector by A, of the transform vector by B of the vector X. In other words, the vector is first transformed by B into a new vector. Then this vector is transformed by A to give the final transform vector Y. The product of two linear transformations implies that two successive transformations are to be performed, and the resulting transformation is the product. This operation of multiplication of linear transformations is not commutative, but it is associative since matrix multiplication has these properties. The identity matrix I_n would transform all $n \times 1$ vectors into themselves as can be easily shown. The inverse of a linear transformation with respect to multiplication does not always exist. When it does, it would be the linear transformation that would reverse the roles of the vector and its transform. A linear transformation which has an inverse is said to be nonsingular. Such a transformation has the same transform space as the original space.

An important subclass of the nonsingular linear transformations are the orthogonal linear transformations. These are represented by orthogonal matrices. They have the property of leaving the lengths of the vectors unchanged. To see this, consider the column vector G and the orthogonal matrix A. The square of the length of the transform vector AG is

$$(AG)'(AG) = (G'A')(AG)$$

$$= G'(A^{-1}A)G$$

$$= G'G$$

However, $G'G$ is the square of the length of the vector G. Therefore, the two vectors are of the same length.

The interpretation of the distributive law as applied to linear transformations is a little involved. It would say that the linear transformation determined by the product of a sum of two linear transformations by a third one, is the same as the sum of each of the products of the two linear transformations by the third. A check of what is involved can be made by the use of the matrix notation for linear transformations

$$[A(B + C)]X = A[(B + C)X]$$

$$= A(BX + CX)$$

$$= (AB)X + (AC)X$$

Scalar multiplication as applied to linear transformations is quite simple for

$$(kA)X = k(AX)$$

This means that the scalar multiple by k of the linear transformation determined by A is the linear transformation that multiplies by k the transform vector by A; or put another way, a scalar k multiplies the transform vector by k.

PROBLEMS

1. Find a basis for the vector space spanned by the following sets of vectors. What is the dimension of each space?

  (a) $[1 \quad 1 \quad 0 \quad 0]$, $[1 \quad 0 \quad 1 \quad 1]$, $[1 \quad 1 \quad 1 \quad 1]$, and $[1 \quad -1 \quad 0 \quad 0]$.

  (b) $[1 \quad 0 \quad 1]$, $[0 \quad 2 \quad 3]$, $[1 \quad 0 \quad 0]$, and $[2 \quad 3 \quad 5]$.

  (c)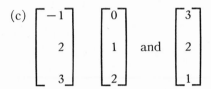

  (d)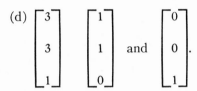

2. What are the lengths of each of the vectors given in Problem 1?

3. In each of the four sets of spanning vectors of Problem 1, are there any vectors that are mutually orthogonal? Are there any mutually orthogonal vectors in the sets of basis vectors?

4. Verify that if $A = [a_1 \quad a_2 \quad \cdots \quad a_n]$ and $B = [b_1 \quad b_2 \quad \cdots \quad b_n]$, then $AB' = BA'$.

5. State the definition of the inner product of two column vectors. Also state the definition of the length of a column vector.

6. Show that the column vectors of a general 3×3 orthogonal matrix are normal and mutually orthogonal.

7. Let the matrix

$$A = \begin{bmatrix} 1 & -1 & 2 \\ 2 & -3 & 1 \\ 5 & -8 & -2 \end{bmatrix}$$

define a linear transformation of the vector space spanned by the vectors in Problem 1(c). Determine the transform vectors for each of these spanning vectors and find a basis for the transform space.

8. Repeat Problem 7 using in place of the matrix A:

(a) The matrix

$$B = \begin{bmatrix} 1 & 1 & -3 \\ -1 & -2 & -4 \\ 3 & 4 & -2 \end{bmatrix}$$

(b) The matrix $A + B$

(c) The matrix AB

(d) The matrix BA

4

Determinants

4.1 Evaluation of Determinants

A number of the system to which the elements belong can be associated with any square matrix. This number is called the *determinant* of the matrix. If the elements are real numbers, then the determinant will be a real number. If the elements are rational numbers, then the determinant will also be a rational number. To indicate that one is referring to this number for a given matrix A, the following notations are in general use.

$$
\begin{vmatrix}
a_{11} & a_{12} & \cdots & a_{1n} \\
a_{21} & a_{22} & \cdots & a_{2n} \\
\cdot & \cdot & \cdots & \cdot \\
\cdot & \cdot & \cdots & \cdot \\
\cdot & \cdot & \cdots & \cdot \\
a_{n1} & a_{n2} & \cdots & a_{nn}
\end{vmatrix} = |\,A\,|
$$

This does not give the number but shows that the determinant of the matrix indicated is the number that is desired.

This chapter will be concerned with how to find the determinant of a given matrix. Two methods will be given, the first will rely on the techniques of Chapter 2 whereas the second will be developed using some properties of determinants. This second method will be taken up in a later chapter.

The first technique is based on the following series of three properties of determinants.

Property 4.1. The determinant of a triangular matrix is the product of the diagonal elements.

This property says that the determinant of the matrix

$$\begin{bmatrix} 3 & 1 & 2 & 4 \\ 0 & 2 & -1 & 3 \\ 0 & 0 & -1 & 2 \\ 0 & 0 & 0 & 2 \end{bmatrix}$$

is

$$3 \cdot 2 \cdot -1 \cdot 2 = -12$$

Since diagonal matrices are also triangular, the determinant of a diagonal matrix would be the product of the diagonal elements. In particular, the determinant of the identity matrix is one. Also, since a 1×1 matrix is trivially triangular with only one diagonal element, its determinant is that diagonal element.

In Section 2.7 it was found that elementary matrices of type two were diagonal. The nonzero elements are all ones except for the single constant c. This means that the determinant of a type two elementary matrix is c. The elementary matrices of type three are triangular with only ones on the diagonal. Their determinants will always be equal to one. The scalar k will have no effect on the value of the determinant. The elementary matrices of type one are not triangular so the following property is needed. It will then enable one to write the determinant for any elementary matrix.

Property 4.2. The determinant of an elementary matrix of type one is -1.

The reason why this value is -1 can be partially justified. First of all, an elementary matrix of type one is its own inverse. In other words, its square is equal to the identity matrix. The next property says the determinant of a product of two matrices is the product of their determinants. This means that the determinant of the square of an elementary matrix of type one is equal to the square of its determinant. Since the determinant of the identity matrix is one, then the determinant of the type one matrix is a square root of 1. The root -1 does distinguish it from the identity matrix.

The next property will play a key role in the technique to be developed.

Property 4.3. The determinant of the product of two matrices is the product of the determinants of the two matrices.

For example, the determinant of the following product,

$$
\begin{bmatrix}
3 & 1 & 2 & 4 \\
0 & 2 & -1 & 3 \\
0 & 0 & -1 & 2 \\
0 & 0 & 0 & 2
\end{bmatrix}
\begin{bmatrix}
-1 & -1 & 2 & -4 \\
0 & 2 & 1 & 3 \\
0 & 0 & 1 & 2 \\
0 & 0 & 0 & 1
\end{bmatrix}
=
\begin{bmatrix}
-3 & -1 & 9 & -1 \\
0 & 4 & 1 & 7 \\
0 & 0 & -1 & 0 \\
0 & 0 & 0 & 2
\end{bmatrix}
$$

is easily seen to be 24. The determinants of the two matrices on the left are -12 and -2, respectively, so their product is also 24.

With these properties, a procedure for finding the determinant of a given matrix can now be outlined. First of all, suppose a matrix A could be reduced to a triangular matrix B by a single elementary row operation. There would be an elementary matrix E such that $EA = B$. If one takes the determinant of B in the form EA then, by Property 4.3,

$$ |EA| = |E||A| = |B| $$

Of the three determinants indicated in the last equality, two of them can be evaluated. Since E is an elementary matrix, its determinant is known, and since B is a triangular matrix, its determinant is computed using Property 4.1. Solving the above equation for $|A|$ gives,

$$ |A| = \frac{|B|}{|E|} $$

If E were a matrix of type one, the determinant of the matrix A would be the negative of that of the matrix B. If E were a matrix of type two, the determinant of the matrix A would be $|B|/c$. Finally, if E were of type three, then the determinant of the matrix A would be the same as that of the matrix B since $|E| = 1$. In other words, $|A| = -|B|$ for type one, $|A| = |B|/c$ for type two, and $|A| = |B|$ for type three.

Suppose that it takes two elementary operations to reduce a matrix A to triangular form B. If these were column operations, then

$$ A E_1 E_2 = B $$

By Property 4.3, applied twice,

$$ |A E_1 E_2| = |A E_1||E_2| = |A||E_1||E_2| = |B| $$

Solving for $|A|$ gives

$$ |A| = \frac{|B|}{|E_1||E_2|} $$

Since B is assumed to be triangular its determinant can be evaluated. Also, the E_1 and E_2 are elementary matrices and their determinants are known. This means then, that $|A|$ can be found.

These are but special examples of the general situation. If a matrix A is reduced to triangular form by a series of elementary operations, its determinant can be evaluated. It would be the determinant of the triangular matrix divided by the product of the determinants of the elementary matrices used in reducing the matrix A. It is possible to obtain a different triangular form for the matrix A using other elementary operations; yet, when one evaluates the determinant of A by this method, the same result will always be obtained. In case the final matrix has a zero on the diagonal, the product of the diagonal elements would be zero. This matrix then has value zero for its determinant. However, it also means that the original matrix has zero for its determinant.

It is not necessary to actually form the elementary matrices in order to know what their determinants are. All that is necessary is to note the type of elementary operation involved. If two rows or columns are interchanged, then the determinant of the corresponding elementary matrix is equal to -1. If a row or column is multiplied by c, the determinant of the corresponding elementary matrix has a value of c. In the first case, the value obtained for $|B|$ must be divided by -1, or, what is equivalent, $|B|$ is multiplied by -1. In the second case, the $|B|$ must be divided by c. Finally, if there are any type three operations, there will be no change in the determinant. The following simple example illustrates this last statement. Suppose that the matrix A is simplified

$$
\begin{bmatrix}
3 & -1 & -2 & 2 \\
0 & 2 & -1 & -1 \\
3 & -5 & 1 & 3 \\
-3 & -1 & 4 & 0
\end{bmatrix}
\begin{matrix}
\\
\\
\xleftarrow{\;\;\;\longrightarrow\;\;\;} \\
R3 - 1R1 \\
R4 + 1R1
\end{matrix}
\begin{bmatrix}
3 & -1 & -2 & 2 \\
0 & 2 & -1 & -1 \\
0 & -4 & 3 & 1 \\
0 & -2 & 2 & 2
\end{bmatrix}
$$

$$
\begin{matrix}
\xleftarrow{\;\;\;\longrightarrow\;\;\;} \\
R3 + 2R2 \\
R4 + 1R2
\end{matrix}
\begin{bmatrix}
3 & -1 & -2 & 2 \\
0 & 2 & -1 & -1 \\
0 & 0 & 1 & -1 \\
0 & 0 & 1 & 1
\end{bmatrix}
\begin{matrix}
\xleftarrow{\;\;\;\longrightarrow\;\;\;} \\
R4 - 1R3
\end{matrix}
\begin{bmatrix}
3 & -1 & -2 & 2 \\
0 & 2 & -1 & -1 \\
0 & 0 & 1 & -1 \\
0 & 0 & 0 & 2
\end{bmatrix}
$$

From the notation used at each step, notice that only type three operations are used. Since the determinant of the corresponding elementary matrices are all 1, the determinant of the starting matrix is the same as that of the resulting triangular form matrix. Here that would be

$$|A| = 3 \cdot 2 \cdot 1 \cdot 2 = 12$$

In any evaluation of a determinant by this technique, one can ignore the operations of type three since they will not change the value of the determinant. The operations of type one change only the sign. If there are any of these, the final determinant will have either the same or the opposite sign as the original one. If there is an odd number of these operations, the sign will be changed. If there is an even number, the sign of the result is the same as that for the determinant of the original matrix. The operations of type two are the only ones that change the numerical value of the result. Here one divides the determinant of the final triangular matrix by each of the various constants that are used.

Another example might help bring out these points. Consider the reduction of the following matrix.

$$
\begin{bmatrix}
2 & -1 & 2 & -1 \\
1 & 1 & -1 & 2 \\
1 & 2 & 1 & -3 \\
1 & 3 & 4 & 7
\end{bmatrix}
\xrightarrow{\underset{R(1,2)}{\longleftrightarrow}}
\begin{bmatrix}
1 & 1 & -1 & 2 \\
2 & -1 & 2 & -1 \\
1 & 2 & 1 & -3 \\
1 & 3 & 4 & 7
\end{bmatrix}
$$

$$
\underset{\substack{R2-2R1 \\ R3-1R1 \\ R4-1R1}}{\longleftrightarrow}
\begin{bmatrix}
1 & 1 & -1 & 2 \\
0 & -3 & 4 & -5 \\
0 & 1 & 2 & -5 \\
0 & 2 & 5 & 5
\end{bmatrix}
\xrightarrow{\underset{R(2,3)}{\longleftrightarrow}}
\begin{bmatrix}
1 & 1 & -1 & 2 \\
0 & 1 & 2 & -5 \\
0 & -3 & 4 & -5 \\
0 & 2 & 5 & 5
\end{bmatrix}
$$

$$
\underset{\substack{R3+3R2 \\ R4-2R2}}{\longleftrightarrow}
\begin{bmatrix}
1 & 1 & -1 & 2 \\
0 & 1 & 2 & 5 \\
0 & 0 & 10 & -20 \\
0 & 0 & 1 & 15
\end{bmatrix}
\xrightarrow{\underset{R(3,4)}{\longleftrightarrow}}
\begin{bmatrix}
1 & 1 & -1 & 2 \\
0 & 1 & 2 & -5 \\
0 & 0 & 1 & 15 \\
0 & 0 & 10 & -20
\end{bmatrix}
$$

$$
\underset{R4-10R3}{\longleftrightarrow}
\begin{bmatrix}
1 & 1 & -1 & 2 \\
0 & 1 & 2 & -5 \\
0 & 0 & 1 & 15 \\
0 & 0 & 0 & -170
\end{bmatrix}
$$

The evaluation here gives

$$|A| = (-1)^3(1)(1)(1)(-170) = 170$$

Since there are no operations of type two, and three of type one, only the sign is changed. If this same matrix is reduced using column operations then

$$
\begin{bmatrix}
2 & -1 & 2 & -1 \\
1 & 1 & -1 & 2 \\
1 & 2 & 1 & -3 \\
1 & 3 & 4 & 7
\end{bmatrix}
\xrightarrow[\;C(1,2)\;]{\longleftrightarrow}
\begin{bmatrix}
-1 & 2 & 2 & -1 \\
1 & 1 & -1 & 2 \\
2 & 1 & 1 & -3 \\
3 & 1 & 4 & 7
\end{bmatrix}
$$

$$
\xrightarrow[\substack{C2+2C1 \\ C3+2C1 \\ C4-1C1}]{\longleftrightarrow}
\begin{bmatrix}
-1 & 0 & 0 & 0 \\
1 & 3 & 1 & 1 \\
2 & 5 & 5 & -5 \\
3 & 7 & 10 & 4
\end{bmatrix}
\xrightarrow[\;C(2,4)\;]{\longleftrightarrow}
\begin{bmatrix}
-1 & 0 & 0 & 0 \\
1 & 1 & 1 & 3 \\
2 & -5 & 5 & 5 \\
3 & 4 & 10 & 7
\end{bmatrix}
$$

$$
\xrightarrow[\substack{C3-1C2 \\ C4-3C2}]{\longleftrightarrow}
\begin{bmatrix}
-1 & 0 & 0 & 0 \\
1 & 1 & 0 & 0 \\
2 & -5 & 10 & 20 \\
3 & 4 & 6 & -5
\end{bmatrix}
\xrightarrow[\;C4-2C3\;]{\longleftrightarrow}
\begin{bmatrix}
-1 & 0 & 0 & 0 \\
1 & 1 & 0 & 0 \\
2 & -5 & 10 & 0 \\
3 & 4 & 6 & -17
\end{bmatrix}
$$

For this reduction since there are two elementary operations of type one and none of type two, the determinants of the matrices are equal and

$$|A| = (-1)^2(-1)(1)(10)(-17) = 170$$

4.2 Further Properties of Determinants

Using the technique of Section 4.1, one can note when certain matrices will have a zero determinant without actually completing the reduction. The following three properties indicate these cases.

Property 4.4. The determinant of a matrix with a zero vector is zero.

If a matrix with a zero vector is reduced to triangular form in the usual manner, the zero vector will never be changed. In the final form of the matrix, there would be one of its diagonal elements equal to zero. Then, as noted in Section 4.1, the determinant of the original matrix must have zero for the value of its determinant.

Property 4.5. The determinant of a matrix with two row or two column vectors which are identical, is zero.

If one of these vectors is subtracted from the other by an elementary operation of type three, the resulting matrix will have a zero vector. Then, by Property 4.4, this matrix has determinant zero. Since the determinant of the original matrix is the same as the determinant of the reduced matrix, its value must also be zero.

Property 4.6. The determinant of a matrix with one row (or column) vector a multiple of another row (or column) vector, is zero.

An elementary operation of type three can be used again to obtain a zero vector. Thus, by Property 4.4, the matrices must have determinants of zero value.

In a previous chapter it was noted that the transpose of an elementary matrix was also an elementary matrix of the same type. This means that the determinant of elementary matrices of type one are the same as the determinant of their transposes. Further, the transpose of a triangular matrix B is also triangular. The diagonal elements of B and B' would be the same and therefore, $|B| = |B'|$. This means that an elementary matrix of type two will have this property. In other words, the determinants of all elementary matrices and all triangular matrices are equal to the determinants of their transposes. The next property extends this result to all matrices.

Property 4.7. The determinant of a matrix and its transpose are equal; that is, $|A| = |A'|$.

Any matrix can be reduced to triangular form by a series of t elementary row operations so that

$$E_1 E_2 \cdots E_t A = B$$

By taking transposes of both sides,

$$A'E_t' \cdots E_2'E_1' = B'$$

If B is triangular then $|B| = |B'|$. Since the E_i are all elementary matrices, $|E_i'| = |E_i|$ so it must follow that $|A| = |A'|$.

The next three properties are direct results of the properties given in Section 4.1. They are given in the usual discussion of determinants as an aid in the computation.

Property 4.8. If a matrix B is formed from a matrix A by the interchange of two rows or columns, then $|B| = -|A|$.

This follows at once by Properties 4.2 and 4.3 since the interchange can be made by an operation of type one.

Property 4.9. If a matrix B is obtained from a matrix A by removing a common factor c from any row or column, then $|A| = c|B|$.

The "factoring out" of the constant c can be done by an elementary operation of type two using $1/c$ as the multiplier. The determinant of the corresponding elementary matrix is $1/c$ so that

$$|A| = \frac{|B|}{1/c} = c|B|$$

Property 4.10. If a matrix B is obtained from a matrix A by adding a multiple of a row (or column) to another row (or column), then

$$|B| = |A|.$$

This simplification can be done using an elementary matrix of type three. Hence, the result follows at once, since this elementary matrix has a determinant whose value is 1.

The next property is a generalization of Property 4.1 to a triangular matrix whose elements are matrices. It requires only that the matrices on the diagonal be square.

Property 4.11. If the matrix A can be partitioned to form a triangular matrix with square matrices $A_{11}, A_{22}, \cdots, A_{tt}$, on the diagonal, then

$$|A| = |A_{11}||A_{22}| \cdots |A_{tt}|$$

This property can be best shown for a numerical example where the reduction is first carried out in the usual way:

$$
\begin{bmatrix}
1 & 3 & -1 & 2 & 3 \\
4 & 2 & 3 & -1 & 5 \\
0 & 0 & 1 & 3 & 2 \\
0 & 0 & -1 & 4 & 2 \\
0 & 0 & 2 & -1 & 5
\end{bmatrix}
\quad
\xleftarrow[R2-4R1]{}
\quad
\begin{bmatrix}
1 & 3 & -1 & 2 & 3 \\
0 & -10 & 7 & -9 & -7 \\
0 & 0 & 1 & 3 & 2 \\
0 & 0 & -1 & 4 & 2 \\
0 & 0 & 2 & -1 & 5
\end{bmatrix}
$$

$$
\xleftarrow[\substack{R4+1R3 \\ R5-2R3}]{}
\quad
\begin{bmatrix}
1 & 3 & -1 & 2 & 3 \\
0 & -10 & 7 & -9 & -7 \\
0 & 0 & 1 & 3 & 2 \\
0 & 0 & 0 & 7 & 4 \\
0 & 0 & 0 & -7 & 1
\end{bmatrix}
$$

$$
\xleftarrow[R5+1R4]{}
\quad
\begin{bmatrix}
1 & 3 & -1 & 2 & 3 \\
0 & -10 & 7 & -9 & -7 \\
0 & 0 & 1 & 3 & 2 \\
0 & 0 & 0 & 7 & 4 \\
0 & 0 & 0 & 0 & 5
\end{bmatrix}
$$

[handwritten annotations in left margin:]

$2-12$

$\begin{vmatrix} 1 & 3 \\ 4 & 2 \end{vmatrix} = \begin{bmatrix} 1 & 3 \\ 0 & -10 \end{bmatrix} = -10$

$\begin{vmatrix} 1 & 3 & 2 \\ -1 & 4 & 2 \\ 2 & -1 & 5 \end{vmatrix} = \begin{vmatrix} 1 & 3 & 2 \\ 0 & 7 & 4 \\ 0 & -7 & 1 \end{vmatrix}$

$= \begin{vmatrix} 1 & 3 & 2 \\ 0 & 7 & 4 \\ 0 & 0 & 5 \end{vmatrix} = 35 = -350$

It is easily seen that $|A| = 1 \cdot -10 \cdot 1 \cdot 7 \cdot 5 = -350$. In the reduction, note that at the first step only the first two row vectors were involved. The last two steps dealt with just the last three row vectors of the matrix. These are precisely the operations that could have been used to simplify the 2×2 matrix in the upper left-hand corner and the 3×3 matrix in the lower right-hand corner. Thus the same diagonal elements are obtained as would be if the matrix were partitioned between the second and third row and column vectors and each diagonal matrix were reduced. Since the determinants of the matrices would be equal to the product of the diagonal elements, the same value is obtained with the partitioning as without it.

In general, if a matrix can be partitioned in the manner prescribed, the operations used to simplify without partitioning could be used to simplify the diagonal matrices of the partitioned form. The diagonal elements of the resulting triangular matrices of the partitioned form then constitute the diagonal elements of the original matrix in its reduced triangular form. This would mean the determinant is the same in both cases.

4.3 Expansion by Cofactors

A second way to evaluate the determinant of a matrix is an expansion type technique. The determinant of a square matrix of a given size is expressed in terms of a set of determinants of square matrices of smaller dimension. The same thing is then done to the determinants of each of these smaller matrices to obtain determinants of still smaller matrices. By repeated use of the technique, the finding of the determinant of the original matrix is reduced to the evaluation of the determinants of 2×2 matrices. The determinant of this size matrix can be evaluated using the next property.

Property 4.12. The determinant of a 2×2 matrix A is given by

$$\begin{vmatrix} a_{11} & a_{12} \\ a_{21} & a_{22} \end{vmatrix} = a_{11}a_{22} - a_{12}a_{21}$$

When one reduces this matrix to triangular form using elementary row operations,

$$\begin{bmatrix} a_{11} & a_{12} \\ a_{21} & a_{22} \end{bmatrix} \xrightarrow[a_{11}R2]{} \begin{bmatrix} a_{11} & a_{12} \\ a_{11}a_{21} & a_{11}a_{22} \end{bmatrix} \xrightarrow[R2 - a_{21}R1]{} \begin{bmatrix} a_{11} & a_{12} \\ 0 & a_{11}a_{22} - a_{12}a_{21} \end{bmatrix}$$

Then, it follows that

$$\begin{vmatrix} a_{11} & a_{12} \\ a_{21} & a_{22} \end{vmatrix} = (1/a_{11})(a_{11})(a_{11}a_{22} - a_{12}a_{21})$$

$$= a_{11}a_{22} - a_{12}a_{21}$$

This result can be stated in words as follows: "the determinant of a 2×2 matrix is equal to the product of the diagonal elements minus the product of the other elements."

The following definitions will be found to be useful not only for this section but for later work as well.

Definition 4.1. The determinant of a square submatrix of a matrix A is called a minor of A.

In case only the rth row and the sth column are deleted to form the submatrix, the minor is denoted as m_{rs}.

Definition 4.2. A principal minor of a matrix is the determinant of a square submatrix formed by deleting corresponding row and column vectors.

Included in this set are the m_{rs}, where $s = r$.

For instance, the principal minors of the general 3×3 matrix are

$$|a_{11}| \qquad |a_{22}| \qquad |a_{33}| \qquad \begin{vmatrix} a_{11} & a_{12} \\ a_{21} & a_{22} \end{vmatrix} \qquad \begin{vmatrix} a_{11} & a_{13} \\ a_{31} & a_{33} \end{vmatrix} \qquad \begin{vmatrix} a_{22} & a_{23} \\ a_{32} & a_{33} \end{vmatrix}$$

For the first minor the second and third row and column vectors are deleted, for the second minor the first and third vectors are deleted, and in the third minor it is the first and second vectors that are deleted. The next group are the minors m_{33}, m_{22}, and m_{11}.

Definition 4.3. The cofactor c_{rs} of the element a_{rs} is given by

$$(-1)^{r+s} m_{rs}.$$

In case the r and s are both even or both odd, the cofactor is equal to the minor. If either r or s is odd and the other is even, the cofactor is the negative of the minor. The cofactor is often called the signed minor for this reason. In other words, it is a minor with a possible sign changed.

With Definition 4.3, the second technique for evaluating a determinant can now be given. This is contained in the next property.

Property 4.13. For any square matrix A, and any choice of r and s,

$$|A| = \sum_{i=1}^{n} a_{ri} c_{ri} = \sum_{j=1}^{n} a_{js} c_{js}$$

where the c_{ri} and the c_{js} are cofactors of the matrix A.

The first expression is said to be an "expansion by cofactors" along the rth row vector of A while the second is an "expansion by cofactors" along the sth column vector of A.

This expansion by cofactors can be illustrated by a simple example for the general 3×3 matrix. After the expansion along the second row vector, the problem is reduced to the evaluation of the determinants of three 2×2 matrices. By the use of Property 4.12, the determinants for these matrices can then be found. The expansion and simplification gives, for the determinant of the matrix A,

$$|A| = \begin{vmatrix} a_{11} & a_{12} & a_{13} \\ a_{21} & a_{22} & a_{23} \\ a_{31} & a_{32} & a_{33} \end{vmatrix} = a_{21}C_{21} + a_{22}C_{22} + a_{23}C_{23}$$

$$= a_{21}(-1)^{2+1}\begin{vmatrix} a_{12} & a_{13} \\ a_{32} & a_{33} \end{vmatrix} + a_{22}(-1)^{2+2}\begin{vmatrix} a_{11} & a_{13} \\ a_{31} & a_{33} \end{vmatrix} + a_{23}(-1)^{2+3}\begin{vmatrix} a_{11} & a_{12} \\ a_{31} & a_{32} \end{vmatrix}$$

$$= -a_{21}(a_{12}a_{33} - a_{13}a_{32}) + a_{22}(a_{11}a_{33} - a_{13}a_{31}) - a_{23}(a_{11}a_{32} - a_{12}a_{31})$$

$$= -a_{21}a_{12}a_{33} + a_{21}a_{13}a_{32} + a_{22}a_{11}a_{33} - a_{22}a_{13}a_{31} - a_{23}a_{11}a_{32} + a_{23}a_{12}a_{31}$$

$$= -a_{12}a_{21}a_{33} + a_{13}a_{21}a_{32} + a_{11}a_{22}a_{33} - a_{13}a_{22}a_{31} - a_{11}a_{23}a_{32} + a_{12}a_{23}a_{31}$$

Consider the expansion and simplification along the third column vector

$$|A| = a_{13}C_{13} + a_{23}C_{23} + a_{33}C_{33}$$

$$= a_{13}(-1)^{1+3}\begin{vmatrix} a_{21} & a_{22} \\ a_{31} & a_{32} \end{vmatrix} + a_{23}(-1)^{2+3}\begin{vmatrix} a_{11} & a_{12} \\ a_{31} & a_{32} \end{vmatrix} + a_{33}(-1)^{3+3}\begin{vmatrix} a_{11} & a_{12} \\ a_{21} & a_{22} \end{vmatrix}$$

$$= a_{13}(a_{21}a_{32} - a_{22}a_{31}) - a_{23}(a_{11}a_{32} - a_{12}a_{31}) + a_{33}(a_{11}a_{22} - a_{12}a_{21})$$

$$= a_{13}a_{21}a_{32} - a_{13}a_{22}a_{31} - a_{23}a_{11}a_{32} + a_{23}a_{12}a_{31} + a_{33}a_{11}a_{22} - a_{33}a_{12}a_{21}$$

$$= a_{13}a_{21}a_{32} - a_{13}a_{22}a_{31} - a_{11}a_{23}a_{32} + a_{12}a_{23}a_{31} + a_{11}a_{22}a_{33} - a_{12}a_{21}a_{33}$$

It is easily seen that these two results are the same.

To illustrate this with a numerical example, consider the matrix evaluated near the beginning of this chapter. Expanding by cofactors along the second row vector gives

$$
\begin{vmatrix}
3 & -1 & -2 & 2 \\
0 & 2 & -1 & -1 \\
3 & -5 & 1 & 3 \\
-3 & -1 & 4 & 0
\end{vmatrix}
= 0(-1)^{2+1}
\begin{vmatrix}
-1 & -2 & 2 \\
-5 & 1 & 3 \\
-1 & 4 & 0
\end{vmatrix}
$$

$$
+ 2(-1)^{2+2}
\begin{vmatrix}
3 & -2 & 2 \\
3 & 1 & 3 \\
-3 & 4 & 0
\end{vmatrix}
+ (-1)(-1)^{2+3}
\begin{vmatrix}
3 & -1 & 2 \\
3 & -5 & 3 \\
-3 & -1 & 0
\end{vmatrix}
$$

$$
+ (-1)(-1)^{2+4}
\begin{vmatrix}
3 & -1 & -2 \\
3 & -5 & 1 \\
-3 & -1 & 4
\end{vmatrix}
$$

Noting that the first term is zero, it can be omitted from further discussion. The problem is now reduced to finding determinants of 3×3 matrices. Each of these can be expanded in terms of determinants of 2×2 matrices. To do this, the first is expanded along the third column vector, the second along the third row vector, and the last one along the first row vector. The selection of these vectors is completely arbitrary. This particular choice gives, for $|A|$,

$$
2\left(2(-1)^{1+3}
\begin{vmatrix}
3 & 1 \\
-3 & 4
\end{vmatrix}
+ 3(-1)^{2+3}
\begin{vmatrix}
3 & -2 \\
-3 & 4
\end{vmatrix}
\right)
$$

$$
+ \left((-3)(-1)^{3+1}
\begin{vmatrix}
-1 & 2 \\
-5 & 3
\end{vmatrix}
+ (-1)(-1)^{3+2}
\begin{vmatrix}
3 & 2 \\
3 & 3
\end{vmatrix}
\right)
$$

$$
+ (-1)\left(3(-1)^{1+1}
\begin{vmatrix}
-5 & 1 \\
-1 & 4
\end{vmatrix}
+ (-1)(-1)^{1+2}
\begin{vmatrix}
3 & 1 \\
-3 & 4
\end{vmatrix}
+ (-2)(-1)^{1+3}
\begin{vmatrix}
3 & -5 \\
-3 & -1
\end{vmatrix}
\right)
$$

Notice that the indices used at this step are those of the 3×3 matrix without any reference to the original indices in A. This is true at each step of the reduction, the indices used to determine the sign are those of the particular matrix whose determinant is being sought. With the problem reduced to the form above, the determinant can now be evaluated. This gives

$$|A| = 2[2(12 + 3) - 3(12 - 6)] + [-3(-3 + 10) + (9 - 6)]$$

$$- [3(-20 + 1) + (12 + 3) - 2(-3 - 15)] = 2(30 - 18)$$

$$+ (-21 + 3) - (-57 + 15 + 36) = 24 - 18 + 6 = 12$$

This result agrees with the value determined in Section 4.1.

The determinant of a triangular matrix can be found using expansion by cofactors. Consider the first example in the chapter,

$$\begin{vmatrix} 3 & 1 & 2 & 4 \\ 0 & 2 & -1 & 3 \\ 0 & 0 & -1 & 2 \\ 0 & 0 & 0 & 2 \end{vmatrix} = 3(-1)^{1+1} \begin{vmatrix} 2 & -1 & 3 \\ 0 & -1 & 2 \\ 0 & 0 & 2 \end{vmatrix} = 3 \cdot 2(-1)^{1+1} \begin{vmatrix} -1 & 2 \\ 0 & 2 \end{vmatrix}$$

$$= 3 \cdot 2 \cdot (-2) = -12$$

By successive expansions along the first column vector there is only one determinant of a matrix to evaluate at each step. Also, at each step an additional diagonal element becomes a factor in the final result. At the final step, the last two diagonal elements become factors by applying Property 4.12 to find the determinant of the 2×2 matrix. In the final result, the determinant is always equal to the product of the diagonal elements.

This technique of expansion by cofactors can be simplified. By using elementary operations of type three, some vector of the matrix can be reduced to a form where it has only one nonzero component. This will not change the value of the determinant of the matrix as was noted in Section 4.1. The expansion by cofactors is then made along this vector with the one nonzero component. This would mean that there would be the determinant of only one matrix of smaller size to consider because all others would be multiplied by zero. This new matrix is modified in a similar manner. The vector to be simplified does not have to be of the same type as the vector used in the first step. Expansion along this new simplified vector again reduces the problem to a constant times the determinant of a smaller matrix. The process can be repeated until the problem is reduced to evaluating a constant times the determinant of a 2×2 matrix.

4.4 The Adjoint Matrix

There is an important generalization of finding the determinant of a matrix by expansion along some vector. Consider the following sum:

$$a_{i1}c_{j1} + a_{i2}c_{j2} + \cdots + a_{in}c_{jn}$$

If $i = j$, this would give $|A|$ by Property 4.13. However, what is its value if $i \neq j$? First of all notice that the cofactors of the elements of the jth row of a matrix do not depend upon the elements in the jth row. One could change the elements in the jth row and not alter the cofactors of the elements of that row. If, in particular, one would replace the jth row of the matrix A by its ith row, the cofactors of the elements of the jth row would be unchanged. If the determinant of this new matrix is found by expansion along its jth row, the expression given above would be obtained. However, by a property of determinants mentioned before, this new matrix would have zero for its determinant since it has two row vectors that are equal, its ith and jth. Therefore,

$$(1) \qquad a_{i1}c_{j1} + a_{i2}c_{j2} + \cdots + a_{in}c_{jn} = \sum_{k=1}^{n} a_{ik}c_{jk} = |A|\, \delta_{ij}$$

where δ_{ij} has the value one if the subscripts are equal, and zero otherwise. This can be illustrated using the following matrix where the last row is replaced by one of the three rows of A. The expansion along the third row then gives

$$|B| = \begin{vmatrix} a_{11} & a_{12} & a_{13} \\ a_{21} & a_{22} & a_{23} \\ a_{i1} & a_{i2} & a_{i3} \end{vmatrix}$$

$$= a_{i1}(-1)^{3+1}\begin{vmatrix} a_{12} & a_{13} \\ a_{22} & a_{23} \end{vmatrix} + a_{i2}(-1)^{3+2}\begin{vmatrix} a_{11} & a_{13} \\ a_{21} & a_{23} \end{vmatrix}$$

$$+ a_{i3}(-1)^{3+3}\begin{vmatrix} a_{11} & a_{12} \\ a_{21} & a_{22} \end{vmatrix}$$

Note that

$$c_{31} = (-1)^{3+1}\begin{vmatrix} a_{12} & a_{13} \\ a_{22} & a_{23} \end{vmatrix} \qquad c_{32} = (-1)^{3+2}\begin{vmatrix} a_{11} & a_{13} \\ a_{21} & a_{23} \end{vmatrix}$$

$$c_{33} = (-1)^{3+3}\begin{vmatrix} a_{11} & a_{12} \\ a_{21} & a_{22} \end{vmatrix}$$

In other words, the cofactors of the third row of B are the same as those for the third row of A. Consequently,

$$| B | = a_{i1}c_{31} + a_{i2}c_{32} + a_{i3}c_{33}$$

In case $i = 3$, then $B = A$, and they would have the same determinant. If $i = 1$ or 2, the matrix B would have two rows the same, and hence, would have a determinant equal to zero. In other words,

$$| B | = \sum_{k=1}^{3} a_{ik}c_{3k} = | A | \delta_{i3}$$

By similar reasoning it can be shown that

$$(2) \qquad a_{1i}c_{1j} + a_{2i}c_{2j} + \cdots + a_{ni}c_{nj} = \sum_{k=1}^{n} a_{ki}c_{kj} = | A | \delta_{ij}$$

These two results will be used after the next concept is discussed.

With the set of cofactors c_{rs} of a matrix A, one can form a matrix related to A. This new matrix is called the "cofactor" matrix of A; that is, the cofactor matrix of A is (c_{rs}). The elements of the new matrix are from the same field as those of the matrix A. The transpose of the cofactor matrix is the one that is needed in the next definition.

Definition 4.4. The adjoint of a matrix A is given by

$$\operatorname{adj} A = C' = (c_{sr}) = \begin{bmatrix} c_{11} & c_{21} & \cdots & c_{n1} \\ c_{12} & c_{22} & \cdots & c_{n2} \\ \cdot & \cdot & \cdots & \cdot \\ \cdot & \cdot & \cdots & \cdot \\ \cdot & \cdot & \cdots & \cdot \\ c_{1n} & c_{2n} & \cdots & c_{nn} \end{bmatrix}$$

As an illustration of this concept consider the following matrix A that has been used before.

$$A = \begin{bmatrix} 3 & -1 & -2 & 2 \\ 0 & 2 & -1 & -1 \\ 3 & -5 & 1 & 3 \\ -3 & -1 & 4 & 0 \end{bmatrix}$$

The computations for the cofactors give the following results:

$$c_{11} = \begin{vmatrix} 2 & -1 & -1 \\ -5 & 1 & 3 \\ -1 & 4 & 0 \end{vmatrix} = -2 \qquad c_{12} = -1 \begin{vmatrix} 0 & -1 & -1 \\ 3 & 1 & 3 \\ -3 & 4 & 0 \end{vmatrix} = 6$$

$$c_{13} = \begin{vmatrix} 0 & 2 & -1 \\ 3 & -5 & 3 \\ -3 & -1 & 0 \end{vmatrix} = 0 \qquad c_{14} = -1 \begin{vmatrix} 0 & 2 & -1 \\ 3 & -5 & 1 \\ -3 & -1 & 4 \end{vmatrix} = 12$$

$$c_{21} = -1 \begin{vmatrix} -1 & -2 & 2 \\ -5 & 1 & 3 \\ -1 & 4 & 0 \end{vmatrix} = 20 \qquad c_{22} = \begin{vmatrix} 3 & -2 & 2 \\ 3 & 1 & 3 \\ -3 & 4 & 0 \end{vmatrix} = 12$$

$$c_{23} = -1 \begin{vmatrix} 3 & -1 & 2 \\ 3 & -5 & 3 \\ -3 & -1 & 0 \end{vmatrix} = 18 \qquad c_{24} = \begin{vmatrix} 3 & -1 & -2 \\ 3 & -5 & 1 \\ -3 & -1 & 4 \end{vmatrix} = -6$$

$$c_{31} = \begin{vmatrix} -1 & -2 & 2 \\ 2 & -1 & -1 \\ -1 & 4 & 0 \end{vmatrix} = 8 \qquad c_{32} = -1 \begin{vmatrix} 3 & -2 & 2 \\ 0 & -1 & -1 \\ -3 & 4 & 0 \end{vmatrix} = 0$$

$$c_{33} = \begin{vmatrix} 3 & -1 & 2 \\ 0 & 2 & -1 \\ -3 & -1 & 0 \end{vmatrix} = 6 \qquad c_{34} = -1 \begin{vmatrix} 3 & -1 & -2 \\ 0 & 2 & -1 \\ -3 & -1 & 4 \end{vmatrix} = -6$$

$$c_{41} = -1 \begin{vmatrix} -1 & -2 & 2 \\ 2 & -1 & -1 \\ -5 & 1 & 3 \end{vmatrix} = 2 \qquad c_{42} = \begin{vmatrix} 3 & -2 & 2 \\ 0 & -1 & -1 \\ 3 & 1 & 3 \end{vmatrix} = 6$$

$$c_{43} = -1 \begin{vmatrix} 3 & -1 & 2 \\ 0 & 2 & -1 \\ 3 & -5 & 3 \end{vmatrix} = 6 \qquad c_{44} = \begin{vmatrix} 3 & -1 & -2 \\ 0 & 2 & -1 \\ 3 & -5 & 1 \end{vmatrix} = 6$$

This means that

$$\text{adj } A = \begin{bmatrix} -2 & 20 & 8 & 2 \\ 6 & 12 & 0 & 6 \\ 0 & 18 & 6 & 6 \\ 12 & -6 & -6 & 6 \end{bmatrix}$$

If one forms the product of this matrix with A in both orders, then

$$\begin{bmatrix} 3 & -1 & -2 & 2 \\ 0 & 2 & -1 & -1 \\ 3 & -5 & 1 & 3 \\ -3 & -1 & 4 & 0 \end{bmatrix} \begin{bmatrix} -2 & 20 & 8 & 2 \\ 6 & 12 & 0 & 6 \\ 0 & 18 & 6 & 6 \\ 12 & -6 & -6 & 6 \end{bmatrix} = \begin{bmatrix} 12 & 0 & 0 & 0 \\ 0 & 12 & 0 & 0 \\ 0 & 0 & 12 & 0 \\ 0 & 0 & 0 & 12 \end{bmatrix}$$

$$= 12I_4 = |A| I_4$$

and

$$\begin{bmatrix} -2 & 20 & 8 & 2 \\ 6 & 12 & 0 & 6 \\ 0 & 18 & 6 & 6 \\ 12 & -6 & -6 & 6 \end{bmatrix} \begin{bmatrix} 3 & -1 & -1 & 2 \\ 0 & 2 & -1 & -1 \\ 3 & -5 & 1 & 3 \\ -3 & -1 & 4 & 0 \end{bmatrix} = \begin{bmatrix} 12 & 0 & 0 & 0 \\ 0 & 12 & 0 & 0 \\ 0 & 0 & 12 & 0 \\ 0 & 0 & 0 & 12 \end{bmatrix}$$

$$= 12I_4 = |A| I_4$$

This illustrates a very important relationship between a matrix and its adjoint that will now be considered for general matrices.

Suppose one considers now the product of the general 3×3 matrix A with its adjoint. This will give

$$A \cdot \text{adj } A = \begin{bmatrix} a_{11} & a_{12} & a_{13} \\ a_{21} & a_{22} & a_{23} \\ a_{31} & a_{32} & a_{33} \end{bmatrix} \begin{bmatrix} c_{11} & c_{21} & c_{31} \\ c_{12} & c_{22} & c_{32} \\ c_{13} & c_{23} & c_{33} \end{bmatrix}$$

$$= \begin{bmatrix} a_{11}c_{11} + a_{12}c_{12} + a_{13}c_{13} & a_{11}c_{21} + a_{12}c_{22} + a_{13}c_{23} & a_{11}c_{31} + a_{12}c_{32} + a_{13}c_{33} \\ a_{21}c_{11} + a_{22}c_{12} + a_{23}c_{13} & a_{21}c_{21} + a_{22}c_{22} + a_{23}c_{23} & a_{21}c_{31} + a_{22}c_{32} + a_{23}c_{33} \\ a_{31}c_{11} + a_{32}c_{12} + a_{33}c_{13} & a_{31}c_{21} + a_{32}c_{22} + a_{33}c_{23} & a_{31}c_{31} + a_{32}c_{32} + a_{33}c_{33} \end{bmatrix}$$

$$= \begin{bmatrix} \sum_{k=1}^{3} a_{1k}c_{1k} & \sum_{k=1}^{3} a_{1k}c_{2k} & \sum_{k=1}^{3} a_{1k}c_{3k} \\ \sum_{k=1}^{3} a_{2k}c_{1k} & \sum_{k=1}^{3} a_{2k}c_{2k} & \sum_{k=1}^{3} a_{2k}c_{3k} \\ \sum_{k=1}^{3} a_{3k}c_{1k} & \sum_{k=1}^{3} a_{3k}c_{2k} & \sum_{k=1}^{3} a_{3k}c_{3k} \end{bmatrix}$$

By the use of relation (1), $\sum_{k=1}^{3} a_{ik}c_{jk} = |A|\,\delta_{ij}$ and, hence,

$$A \cdot \mathrm{adj}\, A = \begin{bmatrix} |A| & 0 & 0 \\ 0 & |A| & 0 \\ 0 & 0 & |A| \end{bmatrix} = |A|\, I_3$$

What about the product in reverse order? Here that would give

$$(\mathrm{adj}\, A)A = \begin{bmatrix} c_{11} & c_{21} & c_{31} \\ c_{12} & c_{22} & c_{32} \\ c_{13} & c_{23} & c_{33} \end{bmatrix} \begin{bmatrix} a_{11} & a_{12} & a_{13} \\ a_{21} & a_{22} & a_{23} \\ a_{31} & a_{32} & a_{33} \end{bmatrix}$$

$$= \begin{bmatrix} c_{11}a_{11} + c_{21}a_{21} + c_{31}a_{31} & c_{11}a_{12} + c_{21}a_{22} + c_{31}a_{32} & c_{11}a_{13} + c_{21}a_{23} + c_{31}a_{33} \\ c_{12}a_{11} + c_{22}a_{21} + c_{32}a_{31} & c_{12}a_{12} + c_{22}a_{22} + c_{32}a_{32} & c_{12}a_{13} + c_{22}a_{23} + c_{32}a_{33} \\ c_{13}a_{11} + c_{23}a_{21} + c_{33}a_{31} & c_{13}a_{12} + c_{23}a_{22} + c_{33}a_{32} & c_{13}a_{13} + c_{23}a_{23} + c_{33}a_{33} \end{bmatrix}$$

$$= \begin{bmatrix} \sum_{k=1}^{3} c_{k1}a_{k1} & \sum_{k=1}^{3} c_{k1}a_{k2} & \sum_{k=1}^{3} c_{k1}a_{k3} \\ \sum_{k=1}^{3} c_{k2}a_{k1} & \sum_{k=1}^{3} c_{k2}a_{k2} & \sum_{k=1}^{3} c_{k2}a_{k3} \\ \sum_{k=1}^{3} c_{k3}a_{k1} & \sum_{k=1}^{3} c_{k3}a_{k2} & \sum_{k=1}^{3} c_{k3}a_{k3} \end{bmatrix}$$

By the use of relation (2), $\sum_{k=1}^{3} a_{ki}c_{kj} = \sum_{k=1}^{3} c_{kj}a_{ki} = |A| \delta_{ij}$ and, hence,

$$(\text{adj } A)A = \begin{bmatrix} |A| & 0 & 0 \\ 0 & |A| & 0 \\ 0 & 0 & |A| \end{bmatrix} = |A| I_3$$

This illustrates the general situation that

$$A \cdot \text{adj } A = (\text{adj } A)A = |A| I_n$$

This follows by simply writing out

$$A \cdot \text{adj } A = (a_{rs})(c_{sr}) = \left(\sum_{k=1}^{n} a_{rk}c_{sk} \right) = (|A| \delta_{rs}) = |A| I_n$$

In contrast,

$$(\text{adj } A)A = (c_{sr})(a_{rs}) = \left(\sum_{k=1}^{n} c_{kr}a_{ks} \right) = (|A| \delta_{rs}) = |A| I_n$$

In case $|A| \neq 0$, the matrix equations can be written

$$\frac{A \cdot \text{adj } A}{|A|} = \frac{(\text{adj } A)A}{|A|} = I_n$$

However, by the definition of the inverse of a matrix,

$$AA^{-1} = A^{-1}A = I_n \quad \text{so} \quad A^{-1} = \frac{\text{adj } A}{|A|}$$

if $|A| \neq 0$. This is another way of finding the inverse of a matrix.
For the matrix used as an example

$$A^{-1} = \begin{bmatrix} -\frac{1}{6} & \frac{5}{3} & \frac{2}{3} & \frac{1}{6} \\ \frac{1}{2} & 1 & 0 & \frac{1}{2} \\ 0 & \frac{3}{2} & \frac{1}{2} & \frac{1}{2} \\ 1 & -\frac{1}{2} & -\frac{1}{2} & \frac{1}{2} \end{bmatrix}$$

The result above also gives another criterion for a matrix to have an inverse. Note that it was necessary for the determinant of A to be nonzero. It is true then, that to say a matrix is nonsingular is the same as saying it has a nonzero determinant as well as saying it has an inverse. Or, put another way, a singular matrix is one that has no inverse and whose determinant is equal to zero.

4.5 Solving Systems of Equations Using Determinants

One of the older applications of determinants is in the solution of systems of linear equations. Consider the system of n equations in n unknowns written in matrix form

$$AX = G$$

If both sides of this equation are multiplied by adj A, then

$$(\text{adj } A)AX = (\text{adj } A)G$$

However, $(\text{adj } A)A = |A| I_n$ so that

$$|A| I_n X = |A| X = (\text{adj } A)G$$

If this vector equation is written out,

$$
\begin{bmatrix}
|A| x_1 \\
|A| x_2 \\
\cdot \\
\cdot \\
\cdot \\
|A| x_n
\end{bmatrix}
=
\begin{bmatrix}
c_{11} & c_{21} & \cdots & c_{n1} \\
c_{12} & c_{22} & \cdots & c_{n2} \\
\cdot & \cdot & \cdots & \cdot \\
\cdot & \cdot & \cdots & \cdot \\
\cdot & \cdot & \cdots & \cdot \\
c_{1n} & c_{2n} & \cdots & c_{nn}
\end{bmatrix}
\begin{bmatrix}
g_1 \\
g_2 \\
\cdot \\
\cdot \\
\cdot \\
g_n
\end{bmatrix}
=
\begin{bmatrix}
\sum_{k=1}^{n} c_{k1} g_k \\
\sum_{k=1}^{n} c_{k2} g_k \\
\cdot \\
\cdot \\
\cdot \\
\sum_{k=1}^{n} c_{kn} g_k
\end{bmatrix}
$$

In other words, for the general component,

$$|A| x_i = \sum_{k=1}^{n} c_{ki} g_k$$

Note the similarity between what is on the right and

$$\sum_{k=1}^{n} c_{ki} a_{ki} = |A|$$

The sum above is the same as this one except that the a_{ki} are replaced by the g_k. Suppose a new matrix A_i is formed from A by replacing its ith column vector by the column vector G. Evaluating the determinant of A_i by expansion along the ith column vector would give

$$|A_i| = \sum_{k=1}^{n} c_{ki} g_k$$

With this new matrix defined it follows that

$$|A| x_i = |A_i|$$

In case A is nonsingular so that $|A| \neq 0$, one can solve this equation for

$$x_i = \frac{|A_i|}{|A|}$$

This result is known as Cramer's rule. It says that to solve for x_i a system of n linear equations in n unknowns, form a new matrix from the coefficient matrix by replacing the coefficients of x_i by the constants. Then x_i is the quotient of the determinant of this new matrix by the determinant of the coefficient matrix provided this matrix is nonsingular.

As an example of this technique, consider the following system of equations and its solution.

$$2x_1 - x_2 - 2x_3 = 5$$
$$4x_1 + x_2 + 2x_3 = 1$$
$$8x_1 - x_2 + x_3 = 5$$

The determinants needed for the solution are

$$|A| = \begin{vmatrix} 2 & -1 & -2 \\ 4 & 1 & 2 \\ 8 & -1 & 1 \end{vmatrix} = 18 \qquad |A_1| = \begin{vmatrix} 5 & -1 & -2 \\ 1 & 1 & 2 \\ 5 & -1 & 1 \end{vmatrix} = 18$$

$$|A_2| = \begin{vmatrix} 2 & 5 & -2 \\ 4 & 1 & 2 \\ 8 & 5 & 1 \end{vmatrix} = 18 \qquad |A_3| = \begin{vmatrix} 2 & -1 & 5 \\ 4 & 1 & 1 \\ 8 & -1 & 5 \end{vmatrix} = -36$$

From these results, it follows that

$$x_1 = \frac{|A_1|}{|A|} = \frac{18}{18} = 1$$

$$x_2 = \frac{|A_2|}{|A|} = \frac{18}{18} = 1$$

$$x_3 = \frac{|A_3|}{|A|} = -\frac{36}{18} = -2$$

In case $|A| = 0$, one could not solve for any of the x_i by this method. If any of the $|A_i|$ were not zero, the system would actually be inconsistent, for one would have

$$0x_i = |A_i| \neq 0$$

If the solution exists and all the $|A_i| = 0$ when $|A| = 0$, then there would be arbitrary parameters in the solution. However, Cramer's rule could not be used to find the parametric solution in this case.

If the rule is applied to a homogeneous system, then $|A_i| = 0$ for all i since the constant vector for such a system is the zero vector. This means that there would be only the trivial solution for all the x_i if $|A| \neq 0$. Or, put another way, there is a nontrivial solution only when $|A| = 0$. In case $|A| = 0$, there would be an arbitrary parameter in the solution and one could not find it by this method. So in any event, Cramer's rule is not applicable to a homogeneous system.

4.6 Rank of a Matrix

In the previous chapter, the rank of a matrix was defined in terms of the number of nonzero vectors of its canonical form. There is an older definition of rank in terms of determinants.

Definition 4.5. The rank of a matrix A is the order of its largest nonzero minor.

In this definition, all minors of this size may be nonzero, only some may be nonzero, or only the one may be nonzero.

In order to use this definition, one must have a way to find the largest nonzero minor. There are two ways to do this. One is to start with the largest minor which would be $|A|$, and then consider successively smaller minors. The other way is to start with the smallest minors and then consider successively larger minors. In the procedure, one notes that the rank is at least one if there is any nonzero element in the matrix, that is, if it is a nonzero matrix. Next, the 2×2 submatrices could be checked at sight to see if there is one with nonzero determinant; if so, the rank is at least two. The next step requires checking to see if any 3×3 submatrix has a nonzero determinant. The definition requires all of these determinants to be zero when the rank is two, but only one has to be nonzero if the rank is at least three. However, for the simple 4×4 there are sixteen 3×3 submatrices to be checked when the rank is two. Fortunately, not all of these will have to be evaluated. It can be proved that if some $t \times t$ submatrix has a nonzero determinant and all $(t + 1) \times (t + 1)$ submatrices that contain this $t \times t$ submatrix have a zero determinant, all $(t + 1) \times (t + 1)$ submatrices have zero determinant. This means that the matrix must be of rank t by the definition.

This can be illustrated better using a numerical example. Consider the following matrix A whose rank is to be found.

$$A = \begin{bmatrix} 1 & -1 & 0 & 2 \\ 2 & 0 & 1 & 3 \\ 2 & 4 & 3 & 1 \\ 3 & 5 & 4 & 2 \end{bmatrix}$$

To determine its rank by the definition above, notice that it is at least one since it is not the zero matrix. The principal 2×2 minor in the upper left-hand corner is nonzero as can be easily seen. This means then that the rank is at least two. Now consider the 3×3 submatrices that contain this 2×2 submatrix and the one step column simplifications:

$$\begin{bmatrix} 1 & -1 & 2 \\ 2 & 0 & 3 \\ 3 & 5 & 2 \end{bmatrix} \begin{matrix} \longleftrightarrow \\ C2 + 1C1 \\ C3 - 2C1 \end{matrix} \begin{bmatrix} 1 & 0 & 0 \\ 2 & 2 & -1 \\ 3 & 8 & -4 \end{bmatrix}$$

$$\begin{bmatrix} 1 & -1 & 2 \\ 2 & 0 & 3 \\ 2 & 4 & 1 \end{bmatrix} \begin{matrix} \longleftrightarrow \\ C2 + 1C1 \\ C3 - 2C1 \end{matrix} \begin{bmatrix} 1 & 0 & 0 \\ 2 & 2 & -1 \\ 2 & 6 & -3 \end{bmatrix}$$

$$\begin{bmatrix} 1 & -1 & 0 \\ 2 & 0 & 1 \\ 3 & 5 & 4 \end{bmatrix} \begin{matrix} \longleftrightarrow \\ C2 + 1C1 \end{matrix} \begin{bmatrix} 1 & 0 & 0 \\ 2 & 2 & 1 \\ 3 & 8 & 4 \end{bmatrix} \quad \begin{bmatrix} 1 & -1 & 0 \\ 2 & 0 & 1 \\ 2 & 4 & 3 \end{bmatrix} \begin{matrix} \longleftrightarrow \\ C2 + 1C1 \end{matrix} \begin{bmatrix} 1 & 0 & 0 \\ 2 & 2 & 1 \\ 2 & 6 & 3 \end{bmatrix}$$

In all four cases, after the simplification a matrix is obtained where the second column vector is a multiple of the third. Hence, by Property 4.6 of Section 4.2, the determinants of all of these 3×3 matrices are zero. This means that the rank of the original matrix is two. This can be readily verified using the technique of column reduction,

$$\begin{bmatrix} 1 & -1 & 0 & 2 \\ 2 & 0 & 1 & 3 \\ 2 & 4 & 3 & 1 \\ 3 & 5 & 4 & 2 \end{bmatrix} \begin{matrix} \longleftrightarrow \\ C2 + 1C1 \\ C4 - 2C1 \end{matrix} \begin{bmatrix} 1 & 0 & 0 & 0 \\ 2 & 2 & 1 & -1 \\ 2 & 6 & 3 & -3 \\ 3 & 8 & 4 & -4 \end{bmatrix} \begin{matrix} \longleftrightarrow \\ C3 - 0.5C2 \\ C4 + 0.5C2 \end{matrix} \begin{bmatrix} 1 & 0 & 0 & 0 \\ 2 & 2 & 0 & 0 \\ 2 & 6 & 0 & 0 \\ 3 & 8 & 0 & 0 \end{bmatrix}$$

In this form the rank is easily seen to be two. This is in agreement then with the result obtained using determinants. It is generally simpler to use the elementary operations rather than the determinant technique.

PROBLEMS

1. Find the determinant of each of the following matrices

(a) $\begin{bmatrix} 1 & -1 & 3 & 2 \\ 0 & 3 & -8 & 7 \\ 0 & 0 & -2 & 5 \\ 0 & 0 & 0 & 4 \end{bmatrix}$

(b) $\begin{bmatrix} -7 & 0 & 0 & 0 \\ 4 & 10 & 0 & 0 \\ -8 & 9 & 11 & 0 \\ 14 & 21 & 32 & 2 \end{bmatrix}$

(c) $\begin{bmatrix} 2+i & 1-2i & 7-2i \\ 0 & 3i & 4+3i \\ 0 & 0 & 4 \end{bmatrix}$

(d) $\begin{bmatrix} 1 & -1 & 2 & 3 \\ 2 & -3 & 2 & 1 \\ 5 & -5 & 4 & 3 \\ 3 & -2 & 1 & 4 \end{bmatrix}$

(e) $\begin{bmatrix} 2 & -1 & 0 & 1 \\ -3 & 0 & 1 & -2 \\ 1 & 1 & -1 & 1 \\ 2 & -1 & 5 & 0 \end{bmatrix}$

(f) $\begin{bmatrix} 1 & 0 & -1 & 2 \\ 2 & 1 & -2 & 3 \\ 4 & 3 & 0 & 6 \\ -1 & 1 & 4 & 3 \end{bmatrix}$

(g) $\begin{bmatrix} -4 & 1 & 0 & 1 \\ -2 & 0 & 2 & 1 \\ -1 & 2 & -3 & 0 \\ -7 & 2 & 0 & 2 \end{bmatrix}$

(h) $\begin{bmatrix} -1 & 2 & 3 & -4 \\ 4 & 2 & 0 & 1 \\ -1 & 2 & 2 & 3 \\ -5 & 10 & 6 & 2 \end{bmatrix}$

(i) $\begin{bmatrix} 1 & -3 & -1 & 5 & 6 \\ 2 & 0 & -1 & 2 & 3 \\ -1 & 0 & 2 & -1 & 3 \\ 3 & 1 & 3 & 2 & 1 \\ -2 & -1 & 0 & 1 & 2 \end{bmatrix}$

2. Evaluate the determinant of the transposes of each of the matrices of 1(a) and 1(f) and show that each is equal to the determinant of the original matrix.

3. Evaluate the determinants of the matrices of 1(b) and 1(e) by the method of expansion by cofactors.

4. Find the adjoint matrix of each of the matrices of 1(d) and 1(g). Form the product $A \cdot \text{adj } A$ and $(\text{adj } A)A$ for these two matrices. Do either of these matrices have an inverse? If so, what is it?

5. Solve the following systems of equations using Cramer's rule.

(a) $3x_1 - x_2 + 6x_3 = 1$ (b) $2x_1 - x_2 - 2x_3 = 5$

    $x_1 + 2x_2 - 3x_3 = 0$ $3x_3 + x_2 + 4x_1 - 1 = 0$

    $2x_1 - 3x_2 - x_3 + 9 = 0$ $8x_1 + x_3 - x_2 - 5 = 0$

6. Find the rank of the following matrix using the Definition 4.5. Verify by elementary operations.

$$\begin{bmatrix} 4 & -2 & -4 & 6 \\ -4 & 1 & 0 & -1 \\ 2 & 1 & 6 & -7 \\ 1 & 0 & 1 & -1 \end{bmatrix}$$

5

Characteristic Roots and Vectors

5.1 Introduction

In the last sections of Chapter 3 on linear transformations a square matrix was used to transform a given vector into a second vector. The matrix equation for a system of linear equations was then interpreted as a linear transformation. In this case, one was seeking a vector X that would be transformed into a given vector G by the matrix A. It is conceivable that the unknown vector X might turn out to be equal to the vector G. In other words, the matrix might be one that transforms a given vector into itself. The identity matrix will always do this for all vectors. This was the reason for the choice of the canonical form for the augmented matrix of a system of equations. If an equivalent system of equations with the identity matrix as the coefficient matrix can be obtained, then the vector of constants for the new system is the solution vector for the system.

While the identity matrix is the only one which will transform every vector into itself, there are matrices that will transform some but not all vectors into themselves. For instance, consider the linear transformation

$$\begin{bmatrix} 1 & 0 & 2 \\ 0 & 1 & 3 \\ 0 & 0 & -2 \end{bmatrix} \begin{bmatrix} c_1 \\ c_2 \\ 0 \end{bmatrix} = \begin{bmatrix} c_1 \\ c_2 \\ 0 \end{bmatrix}$$

Any vector with a zero third component will be transformed into itself by this matrix. However, any vector with a nonzero third component will not be its own transform.

If the matrix of another linear transformation is the same as the matrix used above except that the ones on the diagonal are replaced by threes, then the resulting matrix would transform 3×1 vectors with zero third components by simply multiplying them by the scalar 3. This is easily verified since

$$\begin{bmatrix} 3 & 0 & 2 \\ 0 & 3 & 3 \\ 0 & 0 & -2 \end{bmatrix} \begin{bmatrix} c_1 \\ c_2 \\ 0 \end{bmatrix} = \begin{bmatrix} 3c_1 \\ 3c_2 \\ 0 \end{bmatrix} = 3 \begin{bmatrix} c_1 \\ c_2 \\ 0 \end{bmatrix}$$

This brings up the more general problem of whether it is possible to find vectors whose transforms by a given matrix are scalar multiples of the given vectors; that is, for a given A does there exist a nonzero vector X such that $AX = rX$? It is true that any scalar matrix would transform all vectors in this manner, but they are the only ones that will do this for all vectors. For a general matrix this question gives rise to the very important concept of characteristic roots and vectors.

It is true that for any $n \times n$ matrix A, with real elements, there does exist a scalar r and a nonzero vector X such that $AX = rX$. Actually, there will be n scalars associated with the matrix A, not all necessarily distinct. Some of them may be complex numbers. For these, the vector X has complex elements. It will be shown in the next section that if for a given scalar r there exists a nonzero vector X that satisfies the relation $AX = rX$, then there are infinitely many such vectors.

5.2 A Numerical Example

Before investigating the general situation, it might be helpful to consider a simple numerical example. Suppose that

$$A = \begin{bmatrix} 2 & 2 & 0 \\ 2 & 1 & 1 \\ -7 & 2 & -3 \end{bmatrix}$$

The problem then is to find a scalar r and a nonzero vector X such that

$AX = rX$. If this equation is written out, it becomes

$$\begin{bmatrix} 2 & 2 & 0 \\ 2 & 1 & 1 \\ -7 & 2 & -3 \end{bmatrix} \begin{bmatrix} x_1 \\ x_2 \\ x_3 \end{bmatrix} = \begin{bmatrix} r & 0 & 0 \\ 0 & r & 0 \\ 0 & 0 & r \end{bmatrix} \begin{bmatrix} x_1 \\ x_2 \\ x_3 \end{bmatrix}$$

On both sides of this equality there is a product of a matrix with the same column vector. If the left side is subtracted from both sides, one obtains

$$(1) \quad \begin{bmatrix} r & 0 & 0 \\ 0 & r & 0 \\ 0 & 0 & r \end{bmatrix} \begin{bmatrix} x_1 \\ x_2 \\ x_3 \end{bmatrix} - \begin{bmatrix} 2 & 2 & 0 \\ 2 & 1 & 1 \\ -7 & 2 & -3 \end{bmatrix} \begin{bmatrix} x_1 \\ x_2 \\ x_3 \end{bmatrix}$$

$$= \left(\begin{bmatrix} r & 0 & 0 \\ 0 & r & 0 \\ 0 & 0 & r \end{bmatrix} - \begin{bmatrix} 2 & 2 & 0 \\ 2 & 1 & 1 \\ -7 & 2 & -3 \end{bmatrix} \right) \begin{bmatrix} x_1 \\ x_2 \\ x_3 \end{bmatrix}$$

$$= \begin{bmatrix} r-2 & -2 & 0 \\ -2 & r-1 & -1 \\ 7 & -2 & r+3 \end{bmatrix} \begin{bmatrix} x_1 \\ x_2 \\ x_3 \end{bmatrix} = \begin{bmatrix} 0 \\ 0 \\ 0 \end{bmatrix}$$

This last equality is the matrix form for a system of homogeneous equations whose solution vector is the one that is desired. Of course the zero vector will satisfy the requirement, but the original problem calls for a nonzero vector X. This means the homogeneous system must have a nontrivial solution. In the previous chapter, it was noted that this can happen if and only if the determinant of the coefficient matrix is zero. This would mean, for this example, that there will be a nonzero solution for X if and only if

$$\begin{vmatrix} r-2 & -2 & 0 \\ -2 & r-1 & -1 \\ 7 & -2 & r+3 \end{vmatrix} = 0$$

Evaluating this determinant by expansion along the first row gives

$$\begin{vmatrix} r-2 & -2 & 0 \\ -2 & r-1 & -1 \\ 7 & -2 & r+3 \end{vmatrix} = (r-2)(-1)^{1+1} \begin{vmatrix} r-1 & -1 \\ -2 & r+3 \end{vmatrix}$$

$$+ (-2)(-1)^{1+2} \begin{vmatrix} -2 & -1 \\ 7 & r+3 \end{vmatrix}$$

$$= (r-2)[(r-1)(r+3) - 2] + 2[-2(r+3) + 7]$$

$$= (r-2)[r^2 + 2r - 3 - 2] + 2[-2r - 6 + 7]$$

$$= r^3 - 9r + 10 - 4r + 2$$

$$= r^3 - 13r + 12 = 0$$

This is a cubic polynomial in r that must be zero in order for the X to be nonzero. A cubic polynomial equation has three numbers called its roots, each of which will make the polynomial zero when substituted for the variable. This means that if the r is one of these, then there will be a non-trivial solution for the vector X. These numbers that satisfy the equation are called *characteristic roots* of the given matrix. Sometimes they are also called *eigenvalues* or *latent roots* of the matrix.

For this example, the roots of the cubic polynomial equation can be obtained from its factored form. Since

$$r^3 - 13r + 12 = (r+4)(r-3)(r-1) = 0$$

the roots are -4, 3, and 1. It is easy to see that each of these numbers makes the cubic polynomial zero.

For each value of r there will be a nontrivial solution for the corresponding homogeneous system of equations. Any such solution vector for a given r is called a *characteristic vector* of the matrix corresponding to the characteristic root r. When the term eigenvalue is used, these are called eigenvectors. To find the characteristic vector corresponding to a given characteristic root r, one substitutes that value of r into the coefficient matrix of the homogeneous system. A solution vector is then found in terms of arbitrary parameters. For this example, the matrix form of the homogeneous system corresponding to the root $r_1 = -4$ is

$$\begin{bmatrix} -6 & -2 & 0 \\ -2 & -5 & -1 \\ 7 & -2 & -1 \end{bmatrix} \begin{bmatrix} x_1 \\ x_2 \\ x_3 \end{bmatrix} = \begin{bmatrix} 0 \\ 0 \\ 0 \end{bmatrix}$$

To solve this system, the coefficient matrix is reduced to canonical form. The steps in the process are as follows:

$$\begin{bmatrix} -6 & -2 & 0 \\ -2 & -5 & -1 \\ 7 & -2 & -1 \end{bmatrix} \underset{-\frac{1}{6}R1}{\longleftrightarrow} \begin{bmatrix} 1 & \frac{1}{3} & 0 \\ -2 & -5 & -1 \\ 7 & -2 & -1 \end{bmatrix} \underset{\substack{R2+2R1 \\ R3-7R1}}{\longleftrightarrow} \begin{bmatrix} 1 & \frac{1}{3} & 0 \\ 0 & -\frac{13}{3} & -1 \\ 0 & -\frac{13}{3} & -1 \end{bmatrix}$$

$$\underset{-\frac{3}{13}R2}{\longleftrightarrow} \begin{bmatrix} 1 & \frac{1}{3} & 0 \\ 0 & 1 & \frac{3}{13} \\ 0 & -\frac{13}{3} & -1 \end{bmatrix} \underset{\substack{R1-\frac{1}{3}R2 \\ R2+\frac{13}{3}R2}}{\longleftrightarrow} \begin{bmatrix} 1 & 0 & -\frac{1}{13} \\ 0 & 1 & \frac{3}{13} \\ 0 & 0 & 0 \end{bmatrix}$$

The equivalent homogeneous system is

$$\begin{bmatrix} 1 & 0 & -\frac{1}{13} \\ 0 & 1 & \frac{3}{13} \\ 0 & 0 & 0 \end{bmatrix} \begin{bmatrix} x_1 \\ x_2 \\ x_3 \end{bmatrix} = \begin{bmatrix} 0 \\ 0 \\ 0 \end{bmatrix}$$

By choosing $x_3 = \lambda_1$, the solution vector becomes

$$P_1 = \begin{bmatrix} \lambda_1/13 \\ -3\lambda_1/13 \\ \lambda_1 \end{bmatrix}$$

To verify that for all values of λ_1 this is a characteristic vector corresponding to $r_1 = -4$, consider the following product

$$AP_1 = \begin{bmatrix} 2 & 2 & 0 \\ 2 & 1 & 1 \\ -7 & 2 & -3 \end{bmatrix} \begin{bmatrix} \lambda_1/13 \\ -3\lambda_1/13 \\ \lambda_1 \end{bmatrix} = \begin{bmatrix} -4\lambda_1/13 \\ 12\lambda_1/13 \\ -4\lambda_1 \end{bmatrix} = -4 \begin{bmatrix} \lambda_1/13 \\ -3\lambda_1/13 \\ \lambda_1 \end{bmatrix}$$

$$= -4P_1$$

To find the characteristic vectors corresponding to $r_2 = 3$, this value is substituted into (1) of this section to obtain

$$\begin{bmatrix} 1 & -2 & 0 \\ -2 & 2 & -1 \\ 7 & -2 & 6 \end{bmatrix} \begin{bmatrix} x_1 \\ x_2 \\ x_3 \end{bmatrix} = \begin{bmatrix} 0 \\ 0 \\ 0 \end{bmatrix}$$

By elementary row operations the homogeneous system can be reduced to the form

$$\begin{bmatrix} 1 & 0 & 1 \\ 0 & 1 & \frac{1}{2} \\ 0 & 0 & 0 \end{bmatrix} \begin{bmatrix} x_1 \\ x_2 \\ x_3 \end{bmatrix} = \begin{bmatrix} 0 \\ 0 \\ 0 \end{bmatrix}$$

By choosing $x_3 = \lambda_2$, the solution vectors become

$$P_2 = \begin{bmatrix} -\lambda_2 \\ -\lambda_2/2 \\ \lambda_2 \end{bmatrix}$$

Multiplying this vector on the left with the original matrix gives

$$AP_2 = \begin{bmatrix} 2 & 2 & 0 \\ 2 & 1 & 1 \\ -7 & 2 & -3 \end{bmatrix} \begin{bmatrix} -\lambda_2 \\ -\lambda_2/2 \\ \lambda_2 \end{bmatrix} = \begin{bmatrix} -3\lambda_2 \\ -3\lambda_2/2 \\ 3\lambda_2 \end{bmatrix} = 3 \begin{bmatrix} -\lambda_2 \\ -\lambda_2/2 \\ \lambda_2 \end{bmatrix} = 3P_2$$

so the P_2 is a characteristic vector corresponding to $r_2 = 3$.

Finally, to determine the characteristic vectors corresponding to $r_3 = 1$, this value is substituted into (1) to obtain

$$\begin{bmatrix} -1 & -2 & 0 \\ -2 & 0 & -1 \\ 7 & -2 & 4 \end{bmatrix} \begin{bmatrix} x_1 \\ x_2 \\ x_3 \end{bmatrix} = \begin{bmatrix} 0 \\ 0 \\ 0 \end{bmatrix}$$

The coefficient matrix can be reduced by elementary row operations so that the system becomes

$$\begin{bmatrix} 1 & 0 & \frac{1}{2} \\ 0 & 1 & -\frac{1}{4} \\ 0 & 0 & 0 \end{bmatrix} \begin{bmatrix} x_1 \\ x_2 \\ x_3 \end{bmatrix} = \begin{bmatrix} 0 \\ 0 \\ 0 \end{bmatrix}$$

By choosing $x_3 = \lambda_3$, the solution vectors can be written as

$$P_3 = \begin{bmatrix} -\lambda_3/2 \\ \lambda_3/4 \\ \lambda_3 \end{bmatrix}$$

The product of this vector with the original matrix

$$A P_3 = \begin{bmatrix} 2 & 2 & 0 \\ 2 & 1 & 1 \\ -7 & 2 & -3 \end{bmatrix} \begin{bmatrix} -\lambda_3/2 \\ \lambda_3/4 \\ \lambda_3 \end{bmatrix} = \begin{bmatrix} -\lambda_3/2 \\ \lambda_3/4 \\ \lambda_3 \end{bmatrix} = 1 P_3$$

shows that P_3 is a characteristic vector corresponding to $r_3 = 1$. Note that for all three permissible values of r there is an arbitrary parameter involved in the corresponding characteristic vectors. This is why there is an infinite set of characteristic vectors corresponding to a given r. By assigning different values to the parameter one obtains various characteristic vectors in the particular set.

5.3 The General Concept of Characteristic Vectors

For a general matrix A one seeks a scalar r and a nonzero vector X such that $AX = rX$. As in the example of the previous section, this matrix equation can be written in the form

$$\begin{bmatrix} a_{11} & a_{12} & \cdots & a_{1n} \\ a_{21} & a_{22} & \cdots & a_{2n} \\ \cdot & \cdot & \cdots & \cdot \\ \cdot & \cdot & \cdots & \cdot \\ \cdot & \cdot & \cdots & \cdot \\ a_{n1} & a_{n2} & \cdots & a_{nn} \end{bmatrix} \begin{bmatrix} x_1 \\ x_2 \\ \cdot \\ \cdot \\ \cdot \\ x_n \end{bmatrix} = \begin{bmatrix} r & 0 & \cdots & 0 \\ 0 & r & \cdots & 0 \\ \cdot & \cdot & \cdots & \cdot \\ \cdot & \cdot & \cdots & \cdot \\ \cdot & \cdot & \cdots & \cdot \\ 0 & 0 & \cdots & r \end{bmatrix} \begin{bmatrix} x_1 \\ x_2 \\ \cdot \\ \cdot \\ \cdot \\ x_n \end{bmatrix}$$

As before, both sides are products of a matrix with the same vector. If the left side is subtracted from both sides and the result simplified, the matrix equation becomes

$$\begin{bmatrix} r - a_{11} & -a_{12} & \cdots & -a_{1n} \\ -a_{21} & r - a_{22} & \cdots & -a_{2n} \\ \cdot & \cdot & \cdots & \cdot \\ \cdot & \cdot & \cdots & \cdot \\ \cdot & \cdot & \cdots & \cdot \\ -a_{n1} & -a_{n2} & \cdots & r - a_{nn} \end{bmatrix} \begin{bmatrix} x_1 \\ x_2 \\ \cdot \\ \cdot \\ \cdot \\ x_n \end{bmatrix} = \begin{bmatrix} 0 \\ 0 \\ \cdot \\ \cdot \\ \cdot \\ 0 \end{bmatrix}$$

If one uses the shorter form for the matrices, this equation can be written

$$AX = rX = (rI)X$$

or

$$(rI - A)X = 0$$

This is a homogeneous system whose coefficient matrix is $(rI - A)$. Since a nonzero vector X is required, it is necessary for this coefficient matrix to have a determinant equal to zero, that is, $|\, rI - A\, | = 0$. It can be shown that this determinant is a polynomial equation in r of degree n so there are n possible values of r that will lead to sets of vectors satisfying the required condition. They may not all be distinct; they may not all be real.

The next definitions are needed to describe the concepts of the discussion above.

Definition 5.1. The characteristic matrix of A is the matrix $rI - A$.

Definition 5.2. The characteristic equation of the matrix A is the polynomial equation $|\, rI - A\, | = 0$.

The polynomial $|\, rI - A\, |$ of degree n is called the *characteristic polynomial*. An important property of a matrix is that its transpose matrix has the same characteristic polynomial. Recall that the determinant of a matrix and its transpose are equal and the transpose of a scalar matrix is that matrix. From these properties of matrices it follows that

$$|\, rI - A'\, | = |\, rI' - A'\, | = |\, (rI - A)'\, | = |\, rI - A\, |$$

Since these two determinants are equal, A and A' have the same characteristic polynomials.

Definition 5.3. The characteristic roots of A are the roots of the characteristic equation.

As noted before, these are also called latent roots or eigenvalues.

For each characteristic root there will be a set of vectors that satisfy the homogeneous system determined by that particular root. In the numerical example the three roots determined three different homogeneous systems, each one of which had an arbitrary parameter in its solution. There are matrices whose characteristic roots are not all distinct. For some of these, the multiple roots may give characteristic vectors with multiple parameters. There are matrices with real elements that have pairs of conjugate complex characteristic roots. These pairs of roots have corresponding characteristic vectors that are complex conjugates.

Definition 5.4. A characteristic vector of a matrix A corresponding to a characteristic root r is any nonzero vector X satisfying the condition that $AX = rX$.

The definitions above have some very simple interpretations for a diagonal matrix D. First of all, the characteristic matrix $rI - D$ is also diagonal with the nonzero elements

$$r - d_{11}, \quad r - d_{22}, \quad \cdots, \quad r - d_{nn}$$

Its determinant would be equal to the product of these elements. However, this is the factored form of the characteristic equation so that the

$$d_{11}, \quad d_{22}, \quad \cdots, \quad d_{nn}$$

are the characteristic roots, for each makes one factor in this product zero. The characteristic vectors are also quite easy to find, for consider

$$
\begin{bmatrix}
d_{11} & 0 & \cdots & 0 \\
0 & d_{22} & \cdots & 0 \\
\cdot & \cdot & \cdots & \cdot \\
\cdot & \cdot & \cdots & \cdot \\
\cdot & \cdot & \cdots & \cdot \\
0 & 0 & \cdots & d_{nn}
\end{bmatrix}
\begin{bmatrix}
\lambda_1 \\ 0 \\ \cdot \\ \cdot \\ \cdot \\ 0
\end{bmatrix}
=
\begin{bmatrix}
d_{11}\lambda_1 \\ 0 \\ \cdot \\ \cdot \\ \cdot \\ 0
\end{bmatrix}
= d_{11}
\begin{bmatrix}
\lambda_1 \\ 0 \\ \cdot \\ \cdot \\ \cdot \\ 0
\end{bmatrix}
$$

In other words, for $r_i = d_{ii}$, the characteristic vectors have all components zero except for the ith one and that one can have any arbitrary value.

5.4 Relationship of a Matrix to its Characteristic Equation

There are two useful relationships between the matrix A and the characteristic roots. It can be shown that the sum of the elements on the diagonal of A is the same as the sum of its characteristic roots. This sum is known as the "trace of A," and is written $T(A)$ so that

$$T(A) = \sum_{i=1}^{n} a_{ii}$$

For the numerical example of Section 5.2, this sum is zero.

In case the matrix A is the product of a column vector and a row vector, the trace is easy to determine. Consider the simple example where

$$A = BC = \begin{bmatrix} b_{11} \\ b_{21} \\ b_{31} \end{bmatrix} \begin{bmatrix} c_{11} & c_{12} & c_{13} \end{bmatrix} = \begin{bmatrix} b_{11}c_{11} & b_{11}c_{12} & b_{11}c_{13} \\ b_{21}c_{11} & b_{21}c_{12} & b_{21}c_{13} \\ b_{31}c_{11} & b_{31}c_{12} & b_{31}c_{13} \end{bmatrix}$$

Then

$$T(A) = b_{11}c_{11} + b_{21}c_{12} + b_{31}c_{13}$$

$$= \sum_{k=1}^{3} b_{k1}c_{1k}$$

$$= \sum_{k=1}^{3} c_{1k}b_{k1}$$

Now, note that

$$CB = \begin{bmatrix} c_{11} & c_{12} & c_{13} \end{bmatrix} \begin{bmatrix} b_{11} \\ b_{21} \\ b_{31} \end{bmatrix} = \sum_{k=1}^{3} c_{1k}b_{k1}$$

In other words, for this example $T(BC) = CB$.

It can easily be seen that in general, if C is a $1 \times n$ row vector and B is an $n \times 1$ column vector, then $T(BC) = CB$. Since the kth diagonal element of BC is $b_{k1}c_{1k}$, the sum of all the diagonal elements of BC is

$$T(BC) = \sum_{k=1}^{n} b_{k1}c_{1k}$$

$$= \sum_{k=1}^{n} c_{1k}b_{k1}$$

$$= CB$$

The second relationship is that the determinant of the matrix A is equal to the product of the characteristic roots. This in turn is numerically equal to the constant term of the characteristic equation. For the example, the constant term of the characteristic equation is 12, the product of the roots is -12, and the value of the determinant of the matrix is -12.

There is an important connection between the matrix A and its characteristic equation. In the matrix of the illustration, it was found that its characteristic equation was $r^3 - 13r + 12 = 0$. It can be verified that, $A^3 - 13A + 12I$ is equal to zero since

$$\begin{bmatrix} 14 & 26 & 0 \\ 26 & 1 & 13 \\ -91 & 26 & -51 \end{bmatrix} - \begin{bmatrix} 26 & 26 & 0 \\ 26 & 13 & 13 \\ -91 & 26 & -39 \end{bmatrix} + \begin{bmatrix} 12 & 0 & 0 \\ 0 & 12 & 0 \\ 0 & 0 & 12 \end{bmatrix}$$

$$= \begin{bmatrix} 0 & 0 & 0 \\ 0 & 0 & 0 \\ 0 & 0 & 0 \end{bmatrix}$$

This illustrates the well-known Cayley-Hamilton theorem that every matrix "satisfies" its characteristic equation. This statement needs to be explained. First of all, the characteristic equation of a matrix A can be considered as a linear combination of powers of r that is equal to zero. The Cayley-Hamilton theorem says this same linear combination of corresponding powers of the matrix A will give the zero matrix if one lets $A^0 = I$. In this context, the matrix is said to satisfy its characteristic equation. This idea can be generalized so that one can speak of a matrix satisfying a given polynomial equation. Again one considers the equation as a linear combination of powers of the unknown that equals zero. Then the matrix A satisfies the given equation if the same linear combination of corresponding powers of A gives the zero matrix.

This leads to the question, does a matrix ever satisfy an equation of lower degree than n? The answer is yes, there are some matrices that do. The following definition is concerned with this.

Definition 5.5. The minimum equation of a matrix A is the equation of least degree satisfied by the matrix A.

As an example of a matrix where the minimum equation is not the same as the characteristic equation, consider the following matrix.

$$B = \begin{bmatrix} 1 & 0 & -2 \\ 2 & 2 & 4 \\ 0 & 0 & 2 \end{bmatrix}$$

It is true that $B^2 - 3B + 2I = 0$ for

$$B = \begin{bmatrix} 1 & 0 & -2 \\ 2 & 2 & 4 \\ 0 & 0 & 2 \end{bmatrix}$$

$$\begin{bmatrix} 1 & 0 & -6 \\ 6 & 4 & 12 \\ 0 & 0 & 4 \end{bmatrix} - \begin{bmatrix} 3 & 0 & -6 \\ 6 & 6 & 12 \\ 0 & 0 & 6 \end{bmatrix} + \begin{bmatrix} 2 & 0 & 0 \\ 0 & 2 & 0 \\ 0 & 0 & 2 \end{bmatrix} = \begin{bmatrix} 0 & 0 & 0 \\ 0 & 0 & 0 \\ 0 & 0 & 0 \end{bmatrix}$$

Since B cannot satisfy any linear equation of the form $B - kI$, its minimum equation is

$$r^2 - 3r + 2 = (r - 2)(r - 1) = 0$$

Its characteristic equation is

$$\begin{vmatrix} r - 1 & 0 & 2 \\ -2 & r - 2 & -4 \\ 0 & 0 & r - 2 \end{vmatrix} = (r - 2)(r - 2)(r - 1) = 0$$

It is easy to show that B also satisfies its characteristic equation. Notice that the root two appears twice in the characteristic equation but only once in the minimum equation. However, the distinct roots of the characteristic equation are the same as those of the minimum equation. It can be shown that the characteristic equation always has the same distinct roots as the minimum equation, but it may have some roots with greater multiplicity than in the minimum equation. In case the roots of the characteristic equation are all distinct, then it would necessarily follow that the minimum equation must be the same as the characteristic equation. This is true of the example of Section 5.2.

5.5 Finding the Inverse of a Matrix

From the concept of the minimum equation comes another technique for finding the inverse of a matrix. For the matrix A, of Section 5.2, the minimum equation is the same as the characteristic equation,

$$A^3 - 13A + 12I = 0$$

This equation could be solved for the matrix I by first subtracting $A^3 - 13A$ from both sides. This gives

$$12I = 13A - A^3$$
$$= (13I - A^2)A$$

so that

$$I = \tfrac{1}{12}(13I - A^2)A$$

This means that the first two factors on the right constitute the inverse of A since their product with A gives the identity matrix. In other words,

$$A^{-1} = \tfrac{13}{12}I - \tfrac{1}{12}A^2 = \begin{bmatrix} \frac{13}{12} & 0 & 0 \\ 0 & \frac{13}{12} & 0 \\ 0 & 0 & \frac{13}{12} \end{bmatrix} - \begin{bmatrix} \frac{8}{12} & \frac{1}{2} & \frac{1}{6} \\ -\frac{1}{12} & \frac{7}{12} & -\frac{1}{6} \\ \frac{11}{12} & -\frac{3}{2} & \frac{11}{12} \end{bmatrix}$$

$$= \begin{bmatrix} \frac{5}{12} & -\frac{1}{2} & -\frac{1}{6} \\ \frac{1}{12} & \frac{1}{2} & \frac{1}{6} \\ -\frac{11}{12} & \frac{3}{2} & \frac{1}{6} \end{bmatrix}$$

To show that this is the inverse of A, note that

$$AA^{-1} = \begin{bmatrix} 2 & 2 & 0 \\ 2 & 1 & 1 \\ -7 & 2 & -3 \end{bmatrix} \begin{bmatrix} \frac{5}{12} & -\frac{1}{2} & -\frac{1}{6} \\ \frac{1}{12} & \frac{1}{2} & \frac{1}{6} \\ -\frac{11}{12} & \frac{3}{2} & \frac{1}{6} \end{bmatrix} = \begin{bmatrix} 1 & 0 & 0 \\ 0 & 1 & 0 \\ 0 & 0 & 1 \end{bmatrix}$$

For the matrix B of the last section,

$$B^2 - 3B + 2I = 0$$

so

$$I = \tfrac{1}{2}(3I - B)B$$

or

$$B^{-1} = \begin{bmatrix} \frac{3}{2} & 0 & 0 \\ 0 & \frac{3}{2} & 0 \\ 0 & 0 & \frac{3}{2} \end{bmatrix} - \begin{bmatrix} \frac{1}{2} & 0 & -1 \\ 1 & 1 & 2 \\ 0 & 0 & 1 \end{bmatrix} = \begin{bmatrix} 1 & 0 & 1 \\ -1 & \frac{1}{2} & -2 \\ 0 & 0 & \frac{1}{2} \end{bmatrix}$$

To show that this is the inverse, consider the product

$$BB^{-1} = \begin{bmatrix} 1 & 0 & -2 \\ 2 & 2 & 4 \\ 0 & 0 & 2 \end{bmatrix} \begin{bmatrix} 1 & 0 & 1 \\ -1 & \frac{1}{2} & -2 \\ 0 & 0 & \frac{1}{2} \end{bmatrix} = \begin{bmatrix} 1 & 0 & 0 \\ 0 & 1 & 0 \\ 0 & 0 & 1 \end{bmatrix}$$

In this process for finding the inverse of a matrix one can also use the characteristic equation. The minimum equation is preferred since it may be of lower degree than the characteristic equation and is never of higher degree.

When the coefficient of I is zero, the technique of the last paragraph breaks down. In this event, the constant term of the characteristic equation must be zero. Since this term is numerically equal to the product of the characteristic roots, at least one of these roots must be zero. This also means that the determinant of the matrix must be zero since the product of all the characteristic roots is zero. At the end of Section 3.4, it was noted that the determinant of a matrix being zero is equivalent to the matrix being singular. This means the matrix has no inverse when the determinant is zero. All of this implies that the only time the process fails is when the matrix has no inverse. Thus, if a matrix has an inverse, the technique above will give it.

5.6 Similarity of Matrices

From the discussion in Sections 5.2 and 5.3, comes another important relationship between matrices. To illustrate this, consider the numerical example of Section 5.2. Using the characteristic vectors P_1, P_2, and P_3 corresponding to the characteristic roots -4, 3, and 1, one can form a matrix P. It can be seen that

$$
\begin{aligned}
AP &= A[P_1 \quad P_2 \quad P_3] \\
&= [AP_1 \quad AP_2 \quad AP_3] \\
&= [-4P_1 \quad 3P_2 \quad 1P_3] \\
&= [P_1 \quad P_2 \quad P_3] \begin{bmatrix} -4 & 0 & 0 \\ 0 & 3 & 0 \\ 0 & 0 & 1 \end{bmatrix} \\
&= PD
\end{aligned}
$$

where D is the diagonal matrix with the characteristic roots of A for its nonzero elements. The order of the diagonal elements of D depends upon the order in which the characteristic vectors are taken to form the matrix P. If

$$ P = [P_3 \quad P_1 \quad P_2] $$

then the diagonal elements of D would be 1, -4, and 3 in that order.

To illustrate this with numerical values, let P_1, P_2, and P_3 be determined by assigning $\lambda_1 = 13$, $\lambda_2 = 2$, and $\lambda_3 = 4$. Then

$$P = \begin{bmatrix} 1 & -2 & -2 \\ -3 & -1 & 1 \\ 13 & 2 & 4 \end{bmatrix}$$

so that

$$AP = \begin{bmatrix} 2 & 2 & 0 \\ 2 & 1 & 1 \\ -7 & 2 & -3 \end{bmatrix} \begin{bmatrix} 1 & -2 & -2 \\ -3 & -1 & 1 \\ 13 & 2 & 4 \end{bmatrix} = \begin{bmatrix} -4 & -6 & -2 \\ 12 & -3 & 1 \\ -52 & 6 & 4 \end{bmatrix}$$

$$= \begin{bmatrix} 1 & -2 & -2 \\ -3 & -1 & 1 \\ 13 & 2 & 4 \end{bmatrix} \begin{bmatrix} -4 & 0 & 0 \\ 0 & 3 & 0 \\ 0 & 0 & 1 \end{bmatrix} = PD$$

In this particular example, P is nonsingular and has an inverse

$$P^{-1} = \begin{bmatrix} \frac{3}{35} & -\frac{2}{35} & \frac{2}{35} \\ -\frac{5}{14} & -\frac{3}{7} & -\frac{1}{14} \\ -\frac{1}{10} & \frac{2}{5} & \frac{1}{10} \end{bmatrix}$$

It follows that $P^{-1}AP = D$ or

$$\begin{bmatrix} \frac{3}{35} & -\frac{2}{35} & \frac{2}{35} \\ -\frac{5}{14} & -\frac{3}{7} & -\frac{1}{14} \\ -\frac{1}{10} & \frac{2}{5} & \frac{1}{10} \end{bmatrix} \begin{bmatrix} 2 & 2 & 0 \\ 2 & 1 & 1 \\ -7 & 2 & -3 \end{bmatrix} \begin{bmatrix} 1 & -2 & -2 \\ -3 & -1 & 1 \\ 13 & 2 & 4 \end{bmatrix}$$

$$= \begin{bmatrix} \frac{3}{35} & -\frac{2}{35} & \frac{2}{35} \\ -\frac{5}{14} & -\frac{3}{7} & -\frac{1}{14} \\ -\frac{1}{10} & \frac{2}{5} & \frac{1}{10} \end{bmatrix} \begin{bmatrix} -4 & -6 & -2 \\ 12 & -3 & 1 \\ -52 & 6 & 4 \end{bmatrix} = \begin{bmatrix} -4 & 0 & 0 \\ 0 & 3 & 0 \\ 0 & 0 & 1 \end{bmatrix}$$

This illustrates another important relationship between certain matrices that is embodied in the next definition.

Definition 5.6. Two matrices A and B are said to be similar if there exists a nonsingular matrix P such that $P^{-1}AP = B$.

Notice that while in the example B was a diagonal matrix, the general definition does not require this of B. A very important result of this relationship between matrices is given by the next property.

Property 5.1. If the matrix B is similar to the matrix A, then A and B have the same characteristic equation.

To see this, note that if B is similar to A, then by Definition 5.5, there exists a nonsingular matrix P such that $P^{-1}AP = B$. With this result the following is true.

$$
\begin{aligned}
|rI - B| &= |rIP^{-1}P - P^{-1}AP| = |P^{-1}rIP - P^{-1}AP| \\
&= |P^{-1}(rI - A)P| = |P^{-1}||rI - A||P| \\
&= |rI - A||P^{-1}||P| = |rI - A||P^{-1}P| \\
&= |rI - A||I| = |rI - A|
\end{aligned}
$$

Since the characteristic equation of the matrix A is $|rI - A| = 0$ and that of B is $|rI - B| = 0$, the above shows these are the same. This also shows that similar matrices have the same characteristic roots since these are the roots of the characteristic equation.

5.7 Similarity to a Diagonal Matrix

For an $n \times n$ matrix the characteristic roots are n in number, some or all of which may be real. In case they are all real and distinct, a set of characteristic vectors with real elements can be chosen, one for each root. This set of vectors can be used to form a matrix P. If the notation is chosen so that the ith characteristic vector P_i corresponds to the root r_i, then

$$
\begin{aligned}
AP &= A[P_1 \quad P_2 \quad \cdots \quad P_n] = [AP_1 \quad AP_2 \quad \cdots \quad AP_n] \\
&= [P_1 r_1 \quad P_2 r_2 \quad \cdots \quad P_n r_n]
\end{aligned}
$$

$$
= [P_1 \quad P_2 \quad \cdots \quad P_n]
\begin{bmatrix}
r_1 & 0 & \cdots & 0 \\
0 & r_2 & \cdots & 0 \\
\cdot & \cdot & \cdots & \cdot \\
\cdot & \cdot & \cdots & \cdot \\
\cdot & \cdot & \cdots & \cdot \\
0 & 0 & \cdots & r_n
\end{bmatrix}
= PD
$$

In this situation where the roots are real and distinct, the matrix P will be nonsingular so the relationship above can be written

$$P^{-1}AP = D$$

This means that the matrix A is similar to the diagonal matrix D by Definition 5.6. Note that in the general situation here, the characteristic roots of the diagonal matrix are the same as those of A as indicated by Property 5.1.

In the discussion above, it was specified that the characteristic roots were distinct and real so that the matrix is similar to a diagonal matrix. This is actually more restrictive than necessary. If there exists a set of n characteristic vectors that are linearly independent, one can form a nonsingular matrix P using these vectors so that A will be similar to a diagonal matrix. Not all matrices have this property for their characteristic vectors. A simple example of a matrix for which one cannot find three linearly independent characteristic vectors is the following:

$$C = \begin{bmatrix} 2 & 1 & 0 \\ 0 & 2 & 1 \\ 0 & 0 & 2 \end{bmatrix}$$

The characteristic equation for this matrix is

$$|rI - C| = \begin{vmatrix} r-2 & -1 & 0 \\ 0 & r-2 & -1 \\ 0 & 0 & r-2 \end{vmatrix} = (r-2)^3 = 0$$

One can find a characteristic vector corresponding to one root of 2 but all the other characteristic vectors are multiples of this one. To see this, form the homogeneous system corresponding to the root 2,

$$\begin{bmatrix} 0 & -1 & 0 \\ 0 & 0 & -1 \\ 0 & 0 & 0 \end{bmatrix} \begin{bmatrix} x_1 \\ x_2 \\ x_3 \end{bmatrix} = \begin{bmatrix} 0 \\ 0 \\ 0 \end{bmatrix}$$

This says $x_2 = x_3 = 0$ whereas x_1 can be arbitrary so all characteristic vectors must have the last two components zero. All such vectors are multiples of each other so that one cannot find three that are linearly independent.

There are other circumstances in which a matrix is similar to a diagonal matrix. One of these is when the minimum equation has distinct roots. The matrix B of Section 5.4 is in this category. Also if a matrix is symmetric it will be similar to a diagonal matrix. In the work to follow, the assumption will be made that the matrices considered are similar to diagonal matrices.

5.8 Numerical Technique for Finding the Dominant Root

Before giving a numerical method for finding approximations for characteristic roots and vectors, another result is needed. Suppose that a matrix A is similar to a matrix B. By Definition 5.6 there will exist a nonsingular matrix P such that $P^{-1}AP = B$. Consider the square of both sides of this expression

$$(P^{-1}AP)^2 = (P^{-1}AP)(P^{-1}AP) = P^{-1}APP^{-1}AP = P^{-1}A^2P$$
$$= B^2$$

In other words, the squares of A and B are also similar when A and B are similar. Next, consider the cubes

$$(P^{-1}AP)^3 = (P^{-1}AP)^2(P^{-1}AP) = (P^{-1}A^2P)(P^{-1}AP)$$
$$= P^{-1}A^2PP^{-1}AP = P^{-1}A^3P$$
$$= B^3$$

It is true in general that for any positive integer m

$$P^{-1}A^mP = B^m$$

This result says that if A and B are similar so are their mth powers. Furthermore, the same matrix P will relate their mth powers.

If the matrix B is diagonal, B^m is also diagonal and has for its elements the mth powers of the corresponding elements of B. Because the characteristic roots of a diagonal matrix are the elements on the diagonal, the characteristic roots of B^m are the mth powers of those of B. In other words, for a matrix similar to a diagonal matrix, raising it to the power m gives a matrix whose characteristic roots are mth powers of the characteristic roots of the original matrix.

Each characteristic root of a matrix A can be placed in one of three categories according to whether its absolute value is greater than 1, equal to 1, or less than 1. The absolute value of the corresponding root of A^m will also fall into the same category. However, the roots with absolute value greater than 1 will be larger in absolute value for A^m than the corresponding roots for A. In contrast, those with absolute value less than

1 will be smaller in absolute value than the corresponding roots in A. The mth powers of the characteristic roots whose absolute value is greater than 1 will increase in absolute value as m is increased, whereas the mth powers of those whose absolute value is less than 1 will decrease in absolute value. The absolute value of the mth powers of the roots with absolute value 1 will remain 1.

Any root with largest absolute value is called a *dominant root* and is denoted as r_1. If its absolute value is at least 1, its dominance, so to speak, will increase with higher powers. It will be assumed that there is only one dominant root and that it appears only once as a characteristic root. The situation where a root and its negative are both dominant will not be considered. Neither will the case for a complex dominant root since these both require special treatment.

The discussion above serves to introduce the key to the numerical procedure to be outlined now. For the diagonal matrix

$$D = \begin{bmatrix} r_1 & 0 & \cdots & 0 \\ 0 & r_2 & \cdots & 0 \\ \cdot & \cdot & \cdots & \cdot \\ \cdot & \cdot & \cdots & \cdot \\ \cdot & \cdot & \cdots & \cdot \\ 0 & 0 & \cdots & r_n \end{bmatrix}$$

one can define

$$D_1 = \frac{D}{r_1} = \begin{bmatrix} 1 & 0 & \cdots & 0 \\ 0 & r_2/r_1 & \cdots & 0 \\ \cdot & \cdot & \cdots & \cdot \\ \cdot & \cdot & \cdots & \cdot \\ \cdot & \cdot & \cdots & \cdot \\ 0 & 0 & \cdots & r_n/r_1 \end{bmatrix} = \begin{bmatrix} 1 & 0 & \cdots & 0 \\ 0 & t_2 & \cdots & 0 \\ \cdot & \cdot & \cdots & \cdot \\ \cdot & \cdot & \cdots & \cdot \\ \cdot & \cdot & \cdots & \cdot \\ 0 & 0 & \cdots & t_n \end{bmatrix}$$

where $t_i = r_i/r_1$. It will be true that for a specified degree of accuracy there is some value of m such that $(r_i/r_1)^m$ is approximately equal to zero for $i = 2, 3, \cdots, n$. For this accuracy and this value of m,

$$D_1^m = \begin{bmatrix} 1 & 0 & \cdots & 0 \\ 0 & t_2^m & \cdots & 0 \\ \cdot & \cdot & \cdots & \cdot \\ \cdot & \cdot & \cdots & \cdot \\ \cdot & \cdot & \cdots & \cdot \\ 0 & 0 & \cdots & t_n^m \end{bmatrix} \approx \begin{bmatrix} 1 & 0 & \cdots & 0 \\ 0 & 0 & \cdots & 0 \\ \cdot & \cdot & \cdots & \cdot \\ \cdot & \cdot & \cdots & \cdot \\ \cdot & \cdot & \cdots & \cdot \\ 0 & 0 & \cdots & 0 \end{bmatrix} \approx \begin{bmatrix} 1 & 0 & \cdots & 0 \\ 0 & t_2^{m+1} & \cdots & 0 \\ \cdot & \cdot & \cdots & \cdot \\ \cdot & \cdot & \cdots & \cdot \\ \cdot & \cdot & \cdots & \cdot \\ 0 & 0 & \cdots & t_n^{m+1} \end{bmatrix}$$

$$= D_1^{m+1}$$

where $\approx$ means "is approximately equal to." From this result and the fact that $r_1 D_1 = D$, it follows that

$$
\begin{aligned}
A^{m+1} = PD^{m+1}P^{-1} &= Pr_1^{m+1}D_1^{m+1}P^{-1} \\
&\approx r_1 Pr_1^m D_1^m P^{-1} = r_1 PD^m P^{-1} \\
&= r_1 A^m
\end{aligned}
$$

For any nonzero column vector Y this last statement implies

$$
A(A^m Y) = A^{m+1} Y
$$
$$
\approx r_1 A^m Y
$$

This result states that by taking a sufficiently large power of A and any nonzero vector Y, $A^m Y$ is an approximation for the characteristic vector of A corresponding to the approximation for the dominant characteristic root r_1. The accuracy desired will dictate the size of the integer m.

5.9 Application of the Technique

Now how does one go about using this technique? From the discussion above it would appear that a choice for Y is made, then it is multiplied repeatedly by A until a vector is obtained that is a multiple of the preceding one. This technique can be carried out rapidly if the absolute value of the dominant root is quite a bit larger than the absolute values of the other roots. If it is not, then several multiplications will have to be performed. The choice for Y will also have an effect on the number of steps required.

There is a modification of this basic process that enables one to determine quickly when a vector $A^{k+1} Y$ is a multiple of the vector $A^k Y$. This change also gives approximations for the characteristic root r_1. After the vector is multiplied by the matrix A, each element of the product vector is divided by a certain component of the vector to make this specified component 1. The vector is then said to be *normalized*. In the process one continues to multiply by the matrix A, normalize the resulting vector, and compare it with the vector found in the previous step. This is continued until one obtains the same vector, to the desired accuracy, for two successive steps. The quantity used as a divisor in the normalizing process is the dominant root r_1 and the vector is a characteristic vector corresponding to this root.

To illustrate this procedure with a numerical example, let

$$
A = \begin{bmatrix} 0 & 1 & 8 \\ 1 & -3 & 6 \\ 1 & -1 & 23 \end{bmatrix}
$$

The following table shows the results of the computations involved:

Y_0	$A Y_0$	Y_1	$A Y_1$	Y_2	$A Y_2$	Y_3	$A Y_3$	Y_4	$A Y_4$
0	9	1	19.85	1	23.70	1	23.08	1	23.114
1	3	0.33	14.65	0.74	16.00	0.68	15.76	0.682	15.778
1	22	2.44	56.79	2.87	66.27	2.80	64.72	2.804	64.810

Y_5	$A Y_5$	Y_6	$A Y_6$	Y_7	$A Y_7$	Y_8
1	23.1138	1	23.11313	1	23.113233	1
0.6826	15.7756	0.68252	15.77542	0.682529	15.775441	0.682529
2.8039	64.8071	2.80383	64.80557	2.803838	64.805745	2.803838

The table is formed by making a choice for Y_0 that is perfectly arbitrary. Then the product $A Y_0$ is formed and normalized on the first component to obtain Y_1; in other words, all components are divided by 9. The process is then repeated to find the successive Y_i. Notice that when the variation in the components of the vector get smaller, an increase in the number of decimal places is used. One thing about this process, if an error is made at any step, the only harm done would be a possible increase in the number of steps of the reduction. It is a self-correcting process. In this example, to four decimal place accuracy, the largest characteristic root is 23.1132 and a corresponding characteristic vector is

$$P_1 = \begin{bmatrix} 1.0000 \\ 0.6825 \\ 2.8038 \end{bmatrix}$$

Notice that the Y_7 and Y_8 are the same if rounded off to four decimal places. This means that the process is terminated with Y_8 since this is the accuracy desired.

In this example, the other two characteristic roots are much smaller than this largest one. For this reason only nine multiplications by A were necessary.

5.10 A Modification of the Technique

When the dominant characteristic root is only slightly larger than another root in absolute value, the method of the last section can take a number of steps. The process can be shortened by computing some power of A and using it as a multiplier instead of just A. If the resulting vector is normalized as before, the process can be carried out until the same vector is obtained in two successive steps.

Then a similar procedure is used with a lower power of A. If the power of A used the first time is not too large, one may go directly to using A as a multiplier. If not, one may want to decrease the power of A used as a multiplier in a number of steps. In either case, the final multiplication should be made using the matrix A. The advantage of use of powers of A in place of A lies in shortening the number of steps to build up $A^m Y$ to where m is sufficiently large. The drawbacks come in the computing of the powers of A and then working with the matrix so determined.

As an example, suppose that one is seeking the dominant characteristic root and a corresponding vector for the matrix of Section 5.2 where

$$A = \begin{bmatrix} 2 & 2 & 0 \\ 2 & 1 & 1 \\ -7 & 2 & -3 \end{bmatrix}$$

It can be verified that

$$A^2 = \begin{bmatrix} 8 & 6 & 2 \\ -1 & 7 & -2 \\ 11 & -18 & 11 \end{bmatrix} \qquad A^4 = \begin{bmatrix} 80 & 54 & 26 \\ -37 & 79 & -38 \\ 227 & -258 & 179 \end{bmatrix}$$

$$A^6 = \begin{bmatrix} 872 & 390 & 338 \\ -793 & 1015 & -650 \\ 4043 & -3666 & 2939 \end{bmatrix} \qquad A^8 = \begin{bmatrix} 10304 & 1878 & 4682 \\ -14509 & 14047 & -10766 \\ 68339 & -54306 & 47747 \end{bmatrix}$$

The following table shows the steps in the computation of an approximation to r_1 and P_1.

Y_0	$A^8 Y_0$	Y_1	$A^8 Y_1$	Y_2	$A^8 Y_2$	Y_3	$A^8 Y_3$	Y_4
1	16864	1	26313	1	56362	1	64319	1
1	−11228	−0.7	−64076	−2.4	−164495	−2.9	−191974	−3.0
1	61780	3.7	283017	10.8	714341	12.7	832213	12.9

$A^6 Y_4$	Y_5	$A^4 Y_5$	Y_6	$A^2 Y_6$	Y_7	$A Y_7$	Y_8
4062.2	1	256.50	1	16.008	1	−4.003	1
−12223.0	−3.01	−770.31	−3.003	−48.047	−3.001	12.004	−2.999
52954.1	13.04	3337.74	13.013	208.197	13.006	−52.019	12.997

It was shown before that the exact value for r_1 for this matrix is -4 and the corresponding normalized characteristic vector is

$$P_1 = \begin{bmatrix} 1 \\ -3 \\ 13 \end{bmatrix}$$

If the result in the table were rounded off to two decimal places, this exact answer would be obtained. If more computations were made, the result could be made to approximate the exact answer to more decimal places. In the table, notice that when the values seemed to be close, a lower power of A was used and the number of decimal places was increased. Finally, at the last step, A itself is the multiplier. The reason for doing this is to find r_1, for when one uses A^2, one obtains r_1^2 and not r_1.

With the illustrations of these two sections in mind, an outline of the method can now be given. First of all some vector Y_0 is chosen. It could be any column vector of A, it could be the choice used above which gives a vector that is the sum of the column vectors of A^k for $A^k Y_1$. If a rough approximation of the vector is known, that can be used. In applied engineering problems, it is sometimes possible to make a good guess for Y_0. One then computes a few $A Y_i$ to see if higher powers of A are needed. How high to go depends on how rapidly the numbers involved get large. With this highest power of A as a multiplier, the "correction" of Y_0 is speeded up. After the product $A^k Y_0$ is determined, a normalization on a fixed component is carried out to obtain Y_1. Then $A^k Y_1$ is formed and normalized to obtain Y_2. The product $A^k Y_2$ is found and normalized to get Y_3. The process is repeated over and over until two successive Y_i are nearly equal. Then lower powers of A are used in the process until finally the successive Y_i are again approximately equal, to the desired accuracy. The final multiplications are performed using the matrix A until the characteristic root is determined with the accuracy desired. This will give the value for the dominant root and a corresponding characteristic vector.

A word of warning is needed on the normalization process. If one finds the other components are increasing at each step, this probably means the component made 1 should be 0. In such a situation one simply chooses another component to normalize. Quite often the normalization is made on the numerically largest component to avoid this difficulty.

5.11 Finding the Other Characteristic Roots

The technique of the previous section gives only the dominant characteristic root. If other roots are needed they can be found, but the matrix A has to be replaced by another matrix B. This matrix B has the same characteristic roots as A except that it has a zero root in place of the dominant root r_1 of A.

Recall that A and A' have the same characteristic equation and so have the same characteristic roots. This means A' has the same dominant root as A. The process above, applied to A', will thus yield the same r_1. However, unless A is symmetric, the corresponding normalized characteristic vector will be different from the one found for the matrix A. Denote this dominant characteristic vector of A' as Q_1. If the matrix happened to be symmetric, $Q_1 = P_1$ so no new computation would be required to find Q_1. In the computation, one generally normalizes on the same component for the Q_1 as for the P_1. This is usually the first component, so assume that is done in what follows. A matrix is now formed by taking the product of the first column vector A_1 of A with Q_1'. This is a product of a column vector by a row vector so a square matrix is obtained of the same dimension as A. This matrix is then subtracted from A to obtain a new matrix B. This is the matrix that has r_1 replaced by 0, and all the other roots are the same as for the matrix A. After the process is illustrated, this assertion will be shown to be true.

For the example of Section 5.9 the calculation for Q_1 gives the following table.

Y_0	$A'Y_0$	Y_1	$A'Y_1$	Y_2	$A'Y_2$	Y_3	$A'Y_3$	Y_4
1	23	1	18.2	1	23.96	1	23.002	1
5	-32	-1.4	-14.4	-0.79	-21.38	-0.892	-20.218	-0.879
18	452	19.6	450.4	24.75	572.51	23.894	552.210	24.009

$A'Y_4$	Y_5	$A'Y_5$	Y_6	$A'Y_6$	Y_7	$A'Y_7$
23.130	1	23.1111	1	23.1135	1	23.1132
-20.372	-0.8808	-20.3495	-0.8805	-20.3525	-0.8805	-20.3522
554.933	23.9919	554.5289	23.9940	554.5790	23.9937	554.5721

Y_8	$A'Y_8$	Y_9	$A'Y_9$	Y_{10}
1	23.11320	1	23.113228	1
-0.88054	-20.35212	-0.880541	-20.352146	-0.880541
23.99374	554.57278	23.993769	554.573441	23.993768

An approximation for Q_1 would be

$$\begin{bmatrix} 1.0000 \\ -0.8805 \\ 23.9938 \end{bmatrix}$$

Using this value for Q_1, a matrix is formed by taking the product of the first column vector of A and the transpose of Q_1. This is the matrix

$$A_1 Q_1' = \begin{bmatrix} 0 \\ 1 \\ 1 \end{bmatrix} \begin{bmatrix} 1 & -0.8805 & 23.9938 \end{bmatrix} = \begin{bmatrix} 0 & 0 & 0 \\ 1 & -0.8805 & 23.9938 \\ 1 & -0.8805 & 23.9938 \end{bmatrix}$$

This matrix is then subtracted from A to obtain a new matrix B so

$$B = A - A_1 Q_1' = \begin{bmatrix} 0 & 1 & 8 \\ 1 & -3 & 6 \\ 1 & -1 & 23 \end{bmatrix} - \begin{bmatrix} 0 & 0 & 0 \\ 1 & -0.8805 & 23.9938 \\ 1 & -0.8805 & 23.9938 \end{bmatrix}$$

$$= \begin{bmatrix} 0 & 1 & 8 \\ 0 & -2.1195 & -17.9938 \\ 0 & -0.1195 & -0.9938 \end{bmatrix}$$

Notice the first column vector of B is the zero vector. This was accomplished deliberately by the choice of A_1 to form the matrix product. Since the first component of Q_1 was normalized to 1, the first column vector of A is used. If the second component had been normalized to 1, then the second column vector of A would have been used and the second column vector of B would have been zero. This can be seen by noting that the column vectors of the matrix product are multiples of the column vector A_1, the multiples being the components of Q_1'. Since the first component of this vector is 1, the first column vector of the matrix product is the same as A_1. Hence on subtraction, one obtains the zero column vector as the first column vector of B.

There is another way to modify the matrix A in case it is symmetric and $Q_1 = P_1$. This choice does not use the vector A_1. Suppose that one forms the product $P_1' P_1$ and calls it the scalar k_1. In Section 4.4 it was noted that this is the trace of the matrix $P_1 P_1'$. Now form a new matrix B using $(r_1/k_1) P_1$ in place of the A_1,

$$B = A - \frac{r_1}{k_1} P_1 P_1'$$

The matrix B is symmetric if A is symmetric as can be verified. This method is valid only if A is symmetric.

After the matrix B is determined, one repeats the method of the last section to find the dominant root and vector of B. A different component should be normalized; usually the second one is chosen. The following table shows the process applied to the example used in this section.

Y_0	BY_0	Y_1	BY_1	Y_2
1	1.40	-0.463	1.424	-0.4634
1	-3.02	1	-3.073	1
0.05	-0.17	0.053	-0.172	0.0560

BY_2	Y_3	BY_3	Y_4
1.4480	-0.4630	1.44800	-0.46304
-3.1272	1	-3.12715	1
-0.1752	0.0560	-0.17515	0.05601

Hence, the dominant characteristic root of B is -3.127 and a corresponding normalized characteristic vector is

$$P_2 = \begin{bmatrix} -0.463 \\ 1.000 \\ 0.056 \end{bmatrix}$$

To see how close this is to being a characteristic vector of A, consider

$$AP_2 = \begin{bmatrix} 0 & 1 & 8 \\ 1 & -3 & 6 \\ 1 & -1 & 23 \end{bmatrix} \begin{bmatrix} -0.463 \\ 1 \\ 0.056 \end{bmatrix} = \begin{bmatrix} 1.448 \\ -3.127 \\ -0.175 \end{bmatrix}$$

Notice the result is the same as BY_3 to three decimal places.

In order to show that the matrix B will have all roots the same as A except for the r_1, some computations are necessary. First consider the two ways of expressing

$$Q_1'AP_i = (Q_1'A)P_i = (A'Q_1)'P_i$$
$$= (r_1Q_1)'P_i = r_1Q_1'P_1$$

and

$$Q_1'AP_i = Q_1'(AP_i) = Q_1'(r_iP_i)$$
$$= r_iQ_1'P_i$$

Since these are the same product, the results on the right must be equal. Therefore,

$$r_1 Q_1' P_i = r_i Q_1' P_i \quad \text{or} \quad (r_1 - r_i) Q_1' P_i = 0$$

If $r_1 \neq r_i$, then $r_1 - r_i \neq 0$, so it must be true that $Q_1' P_i = 0$ for $i \neq 1$. On multiplying $B = A - A_1 Q_1'$ by P_i one obtains

$$BP_i = (A - A_1 Q_1') P_i = A P_i - A_1 Q_1' P_i$$
$$= r_i P_i - A_1 \cdot 0 = r_i P_i$$

This says that B has the same characteristic roots and vectors as A except for the dominant root r_1 of A. This much would be true if any $n \times 1$ vector is used in place of A_1. However, in order for the other root of B to be zero, one of the two choices given must be used. Both techniques subtract from A a matrix whose trace is r_1. This means the trace of B is that much less than the trace of A. Since all characteristic roots of A except the dominant one are characteristic roots of B, one root of B must be zero.

To see that the matrix subtracted in each method has trace r_1, consider the first case. Here $T(A_1 Q_1') = Q_1' A_1$ by the result noted in Section 5.4. Now, by definition,

$$Q_1' A = Q_1' [A_1 \quad A_2 \quad \cdots \quad A_n]$$
$$= [Q_1' A_1 \quad Q_1' A_2 \quad \cdots \quad Q_1' A_n]$$
$$= r_1 Q_1'$$

Since the first component of Q_1' is 1, the first component of $r_1 Q_1'$ is r_1. This must be equal to the first component $Q_1' A_1$ of $Q_1' A$. Thus,

$$Q_1' A_1 = r_1 \quad \text{and} \quad T(A_1 Q_1') = r_1$$

For the method used with symmetric matrices, the result of Section 5.4 is needed since $P_1 P_1'$ is the product of a column and a row vector. In this case,

$$T\left(\frac{r_1}{k_1} P_1 P_1'\right) = \frac{r_1}{k_1} T(P_1 P_1') = \frac{r_1}{k_1} P_1' P_1$$
$$= \frac{r_1}{k_1} k_1 = r_1$$

For the numerical example of this section, the process will be applied again to find the last root. This would not be done in general for a 3×3 matrix. One can find an approximation to the third root knowing the trace and two of the roots. However, for purposes of illustration and finding a characteristic vector, this has value.

First of all, the computations for a characteristic vector of B' give rise to the following table.

Y_0	$B'Y_0$	Y_1	$B'Y_1$	Y_2	$B'Y_2$	Y_3
0	0	0	0	0	0	0
1	-3.0755	1	-3.1233	1	-3.1269	1
8	-25.9442	8.4	-26.3417	8.43	-26.3715	8.433

$B'Y_3$	Y_4	$B'Y_4$	Y_5	$B'Y_5$	Y_6
0	0	0	0	0	0
-3.1272	1	-3.12734	1	-3.127340	1
-26.3743	8.4339	-26.37540	8.43381	-26.375320	8.433787

Notice that the first component must be zero because the first row of B' is zero.

Since normalization is on the second component, B_2 will be used in forming C. Thus,

$$B_2 Q_2' = \begin{bmatrix} 1 \\ -2.1195 \\ -0.1195 \end{bmatrix} \begin{bmatrix} 0 & 1 & 8.4338 \end{bmatrix} = \begin{bmatrix} 0 & 1 & 8.4338 \\ 0 & -2.1195 & -17.8754 \\ 0 & -0.1195 & -1.0078 \end{bmatrix}$$

so

$$C = B - B_2 Q_2' = \begin{bmatrix} 0 & 0 & -0.4338 \\ 0 & 0 & -0.1180 \\ 0 & 0 & -0.0140 \end{bmatrix}$$

Notice that the first two columns of C are now zero. The last column vector is a characteristic vector of the third characteristic root of A. The last component of this vector is the third characteristic root. To see this, form the product

$$CP_3 = \begin{bmatrix} 0 & 0 & -0.4338 \\ 0 & 0 & -0.1180 \\ 0 & 0 & -0.0140 \end{bmatrix} \begin{bmatrix} -0.4338 \\ -0.1180 \\ -0.0140 \end{bmatrix} = (-0.0140) \begin{bmatrix} -0.4338 \\ -0.1180 \\ -0.0140 \end{bmatrix}$$

In the general situation, after r_2 is found, a characteristic vector corresponding to r_2 of B' is found; call it Q_2. This vector is then used to modify

B to form the new matrix

$$C = B - B_2 Q_2' \quad \text{or} \quad C = B - \frac{r_2}{k_2} P_2 P_2'$$

where B_2 is the column vector whose index is the same as the component of Q_2 that is made 1. This will not be the same as the one used for Q_1 since this component of Q_2 will be zero. This matrix C will have two column vectors that are zero. If B is symmetric, the second method could be used to retain the symmetry. The process can theoretically be used to find all the characteristic roots. However, the accuracy decreases as more "round-off" errors are brought into the calculations.

Programs for digital computers have been worked out to utilize this method of finding the dominant characteristic roots of matrices. Besides the saving in work and time, greater accuracy can be obtained with the digital computers.

On rare occasions, one might not obtain the dominant characteristic root for A or A' by this method. This could happen if the choice for Y_0 or Z_0 is a linear combination of characteristic vectors corresponding to roots other than the dominant one. This becomes apparent when the dominant root of A' is found in the nonsymmetric case. If the calculated root for A' is larger than the one for A, then a new choice has to be made for Y_0 and the calculations carried out again. If the calculated root for A is larger, it means that one has to make a new choice for Z_0. In case the matrix A is symmetric so that one is using $Q_1 = P_1$, then it would not be detected that the root found is not dominant. However, it will make no real difference since the elimination of a root does not require that it be dominant.

5.12 Companion Matrix

Associated with every polynomial of degree n with coefficient of x^n equal to 1, is an $n \times n$ matrix known as the *companion matrix* of the polynomial. This matrix will have the given polynomial as its characteristic polynomial. For example, if the polynomial were of degree four,

$$f(x) = x^4 - a_1 x^3 - a_2 x^2 - a_3 x - a_4$$

then its companion matrix would be

$$C(f) = \begin{bmatrix} 0 & 1 & 0 & 0 \\ 0 & 0 & 1 & 0 \\ 0 & 0 & 0 & 1 \\ a_4 & a_3 & a_2 & a_1 \end{bmatrix}$$

Notice that above the main diagonal are a series of ones, whereas along the bottom row are coefficients of the polynomial.

For the general situation let the polynomial be

$$f(x) = x^n - a_1 x^{n-1} - a_2 x^{n-2} - \cdots - a_{n-1} x - a_n$$

Then the companion matrix is given by

$$C(f) = \begin{bmatrix} 0 & 1 & \cdots & 0 & 0 \\ 0 & 0 & \cdots & 0 & 0 \\ \cdot & \cdot & \cdots & \cdot & \cdot \\ \cdot & \cdot & \cdots & \cdot & \cdot \\ \cdot & \cdot & \cdots & \cdot & \cdot \\ a_n & a_{n-1} & \cdots & a_2 & a_1 \end{bmatrix}$$

For an example consider the companion matrix of the characteristic polynomial of the example matrix A of Section 5.2. Recall that the polynomial in r was $r^3 - 13r + 12$. Putting this into the form above in the variable x gives

$$x^3 - 0x^2 - 13x - (-12)$$

so its companion matrix is

$$C(f) = \begin{bmatrix} 0 & 1 & 0 \\ 0 & 0 & 1 \\ -12 & 13 & 0 \end{bmatrix}$$

The characteristic matrix for $C(f)$ can be simplified as follows:

$$\begin{bmatrix} r & -1 & 0 \\ 0 & r & -1 \\ 12 & -13 & r \end{bmatrix} \xleftrightarrow[C2 + rC3]{} \begin{bmatrix} r & -1 & 0 \\ 0 & 0 & -1 \\ 12 & -13 + r^2 & r \end{bmatrix}$$

$$\xleftrightarrow[C1 + rC2]{} \begin{bmatrix} 0 & -1 & 0 \\ 0 & 0 & -1 \\ 12 - 13r + r^3 & -13 + r^2 & r \end{bmatrix}$$

Expansion along the first column vector shows that the determinant of this matrix is $(r^3 - 13r + 12)(1)$. This of course is the polynomial from which the companion matrix was formed. It is true of all companion matrices that their characteristic polynomials are the polynomials used to form them. This is usually proved by simplifying the characteristic matrix as above. Notice that all the r's on the diagonal except the one in the last column, are eliminated in order from right to left. The characteristic polynomial is then the only nonzero element in the first column.

5.13 Finding the Roots of a Polynomial Equation

The numerical procedure for finding dominant characteristic roots of matrices can be used to find roots of some polynomial equations with real coefficients. One could form the companion matrix of the polynomial and then apply the process of finding the characteristic roots of this matrix. If the polynomial equation has no pairs of complex roots or pairs of roots that are negatives of each other, then all of its roots could be found. Instead of utilizing the companion matrix directly, one can use the following formulae.

$$d_1 = 1$$

$$d_2 = a_1 d_1$$

$$d_3 = a_2 d_1 + a_1 d_2$$

$$d_4 = a_3 d_1 + a_2 d_2 + a_1 d_3$$

$$\cdot \quad \cdot \quad \cdot \quad \cdot \quad \cdot \quad \cdot \quad \cdot \quad \cdot \quad \cdot \quad \cdot \quad \cdot \quad \cdot$$

$$d_{i+1} = a_i d_1 + a_{i-1} d_2 + \cdots + a_1 d_i \qquad\qquad i \leq n$$

$$d_{n+1} = a_n d_1 + a_{n-1} d_2 + \cdots + a_1 d_n$$

$$d_{n+2} = a_n d_2 + a_{n-1} d_3 + \cdots + a_1 d_{n+1}$$

$$\cdot \quad \cdot \quad \cdot \quad \cdot \quad \cdot \quad \cdot \quad \cdot \quad \cdot \quad \cdot \quad \cdot \quad \cdot \quad \cdot$$

$$d_{n+j} = a_n d_j + a_{n-1} d_{j+1} + \cdots + a_1 d_{n+j-1}$$

$$t_i = \frac{d_i}{d_{i-1}}$$

These formulae are derived from the process for finding the dominant characteristic root of a matrix. What is involved in this method is the computation of successive d_i until the ratio t_i remains constant to the desired degree of accuracy. Then this t_i will be the dominant root r_1 of the polynomial equation.

To see how this follows from the numerical procedure introduced in this chapter, consider the polynomial equation of degree four whose companion matrix was given in Section 5.12. The following table could be constructed using the definitions above with normalization on the last component.

Y_1	CY_1	CY_1	Y_2	CY_2	CY_2	CY_2	Y_3
0	0	0	0	0	0	0	0
0	0	0	0	$\dfrac{d_1}{d_2}$	$\dfrac{d_1}{d_2}$	$\dfrac{d_1}{d_2}$	$\dfrac{d_1}{d_3}$
0	1	$\dfrac{d_1}{d_1}$	$\dfrac{d_1}{d_2}$	1	$\dfrac{d_2}{d_2}$	$\dfrac{d_2}{d_2}$	$\dfrac{d_2}{d_3}$
1	a_1	$\dfrac{d_2}{d_1}$	1	$\dfrac{a_2 d_1}{d_2}+a_1$	$\dfrac{a_2 d_1 + a_1 d_2}{d_2}$	$\dfrac{d_3}{d_2}$	1

CY_3	CY_3	Y_4	CY_4	Y_5	$\cdots$	CY_{m-1}	Y_m
$\dfrac{d_1}{d_3}$	$\dfrac{d_1}{d_3}$	$\dfrac{d_1}{d_4}$	$\dfrac{d_2}{d_4}$	$\dfrac{d_2}{d_5}$		$\dfrac{d_{m-3}}{d_{m-1}}$	$\dfrac{d_{m-3}}{d_m}$
$\dfrac{d_2}{d_3}$	$\dfrac{d_2}{d_3}$	$\dfrac{d_2}{d_4}$	$\dfrac{d_3}{d_4}$	$\dfrac{d_3}{d_5}$		$\dfrac{d_{m-2}}{d_{m-1}}$	$\dfrac{d_{m-2}}{d_m}$
1	$\dfrac{d_3}{d_3}$	$\dfrac{d_3}{d_4}$	$\dfrac{d_4}{d_4}$	$\dfrac{d_4}{d_5}$		$\dfrac{d_{m-1}}{d_{m-1}}$	$\dfrac{d_{m-1}}{d_m}$
$\dfrac{a_3 d_1 + a_2 d_2 + a_1 d_3}{d_3}$	$\dfrac{d_4}{d_3}$	1	$\dfrac{d_5}{d_4}$	1		$\dfrac{d_m}{d_{m-1}}$	1

Note that the normalizing factor at each step that determines r_1 is just the t_i that was defined.

As an example of the computation of the dominant root, consider the polynomial

$$f(x) = x^3 - 3x^2 - 16x - 12$$

whose companion matrix is

$$C = \begin{bmatrix} 0 & 1 & 0 \\ 0 & 0 & 1 \\ 12 & 16 & 3 \end{bmatrix}$$

The calculations for the dominant root yield the following table.

$d_1 = 1$

$d_2 = 3(1) = 3$ $t_2 = d_2/d_1 = 3$

$d_3 = 16(1) + 3(3) = 25$ $t_3 = d_3/d_2 = 8.3$

$d_4 = 12(1) + 16(3) + 3(25) = 135$ $t_4 = d_4/d_3 = 5.4$

$d_5 = 12(3) + 16(25) + 3(135) = 841$ $t_5 = d_5/d_4 = 6.2$

$d_6 = 12(25) + 16(135) + 3(841) = 4983$ $t_6 = d_6/d_5 = 5.925$

$d_7 = 12(135) + 16(841) + 3(4983) = 30025$ $t_7 = d_7/d_6 = 6.025$

$d_8 = 12(841) + 16(4983) + 3(30025) = 179895$ $t_8 = d_8/d_7 = 5.9915$

$d_9 = 12(4983) + 16(30025) + 3(179895) = 1079881$ $t_9 = 6.0028$

$d_{10} = 12(30025) + 16(179895) + 3(1079881) = 6478263$ $t_{10} = 5.9991$

$d_{11} = 12(179895) + 16(1079881) + 3(6478263) = 38871625$ $t_{11} = 6.0003$

If the t_{10} and t_{11} are rounded off to two decimal places, this would give the value of $r_1 = 6.00$. This of course is the exact value as can be shown.

It is not necessary to compute all the t_i for one can form ratios of the d_i where the subscripts differ by more than one. It is true that such a ratio will approximate the power of r_1 that is equal to the difference of these subscripts. For instance, one might compute eight of the d_i and evaluate the ratios d_7/d_3, d_8/d_4 which are approximations for r_1^4. Unless these ratios are nearly equal in value there is no need to compute the $t_1, t_2, \cdots, t_7$. Instead one should compute more of the d_i and compare d_9/d_5, d_{10}/d_6, etc., until two successive ones are close in value. Then one compares ratios where the subscripts differ by only two. These are approximations for r_1^2 that can be used until two successive ones are nearly the same. Finally, one can compute the t_i and, hence, r_1.

To find the other roots, one first forms the polynomial equation of lower degree that has roots the same as those of the original polynomial equation except for r_1. The coefficients for this equation are given as follows:

$$b_1 = a_1 - r_1$$

$$b_2 = a_2 + b_1 r_1$$

$$b_3 = a_3 + b_2 r_1$$

$$\cdot \quad \cdot \quad \cdot \quad \cdot \quad \cdot \quad \cdot$$

$$b_{n-1} = a_{n-1} + b_{n-2} r_1$$

To see that this is true for the reduction of the general fourth degree polynomial equation, one needs to show that

$$x^4 - a_1x^3 - a_2x^2 - a_3x - a_4 = (x^3 - b_1x^2 - b_2x - b_3)(x - r_1)$$

Multiplying the right side, one obtains

$$x^4 - (b_1 + r_1)x^3 - (b_2 - b_1r_1)x^2 - (b_3 - b_2r_1)x + b_3r_1$$

From the definitions above,

$$b_1 + r_1 = a_1 \qquad b_2 - b_1r_1 = a_2 \quad \text{and} \quad b_3 - b_2r_1 = a_3$$

It remains only to show that $-b_3r_1 = a_4$. Since r_1 satisfies the equation

$$r_1^4 - a_1r_1^3 - a_2r_1^2 - a_3r_1 - a_4 = 0$$

solving this for a_4, one obtains

$$
\begin{aligned}
a_4 &= (r_1 - a_1)r_1^3 - a_2r_1^2 - a_3r_1 \\
&= -b_1r_1^3 - a_2r_1^2 - a_3r_1 \\
&= -(b_1r_1 + a_2)r^2 - a_3r_1 \\
&= -b_2r_1^2 - a_3r_1 \\
&= -b_3r_1
\end{aligned}
$$

For the general polynomial equation of degree n, it can be shown in a similar manner that the b_i are the coefficients of the polynomial equation of degree $n - 1$ that has the same roots as the original polynomial equation of degree n except for the dominant root r_1.

Using these b_i, one can carry through the process of finding a new set of d_i. These will give the dominant root of the reduced equation. Just to illustrate the process, since $r_1 = 6$ for the given example, the b_i are

$$b_1 = 3 - 6 = -3$$

$$b_2 = 16 + (-3)(6) = -2$$

This means the reduced equation is the quadratic equation

$$x^2 + 3x + 2 = 0$$

The computation for the d_i for this equation gives the next table.

$d_1 = 1$

$d_2 = -3 \cdot 1 = -3$	$t_2 = -3$
$d_3 = -2 \cdot 1 + -3 \cdot -3 = 7$	$t_3 = -2.3$
$d_4 = -2 \cdot -3 + -3 \cdot 7 = -15$	$t_4 = -2.1$
$d_5 = -2 \cdot 7 + -3 \cdot -15 = 31$	$t_5 = -2.07$
$d_6 = -2 \cdot -15 + -3 \cdot 31 = -63$	$t_6 = -2.03$
$d_7 = -2 \cdot 31 + -3 \cdot -63 = 127$	$t_7 = -2.016$
$d_8 = -2 \cdot -63 + -3 \cdot 127 = -255$	$t_8 = -2.001$
$d_9 = -2 \cdot 127 + -3 \cdot -255 = 511$	$t_9 = -2.0004$

Solving the quadratic equation would show that its dominant root is -2.

One could repeat this cycle over and over, reducing the degree of the polynomial by one at each step. The process could be terminated with the polynomial of degree two and the quadratic formula used to find the remaining roots.

One can use this process when the polynomial equation has a pair of conjugate roots or a pair with the same absolute value. However, only those roots that have larger absolute value than these could be found.

PROBLEMS

1. Determine a 4×4 matrix (not I_4) that will transform:

(a) All 4×1 vectors with 0 third component into themselves.

(b) All 4×1 vectors with 0 second and fourth components, into themselves.

(c) All 4×1 vectors into vectors whose components are double the corresponding components of the original vectors.

(d) All 4×1 vectors into vectors whose components are $-\frac{1}{3}$ of the corresponding components of the original vectors.

2. Given the matrix

$$A = \begin{bmatrix} -1 & -2 & -1 \\ -2 & 1 & 1 \\ -3 & 8 & 3 \end{bmatrix}$$

carry through the analysis of finding a scalar r and a vector X such that $AX = rX$. Find all such r's and the corresponding vectors. Verify that you have correct solutions. What is the trace of this matrix? What is the determinant of this matrix? Show that the trace is equal to the sum of the characteristic roots and the determinant is their product.

3. Go thróugh part of the analysis of Section 5.2 of $BX = rX$ with B as the general 2×2 matrix. Go as far as setting up the characteristic equation.

4. Show that A and B of Problem 2 and 3 satisfy their characteristic equations. Using the minimum equation for A, find A^{-1}.

5. For the matrix A of Problem 2, find a matrix P so that $P^{-1}AP = B$ where B is the diagonal matrix with the characteristic roots of A as diagonal elements. Verify that

$$P^{-1}A^2P = B^2 \quad \text{and} \quad P^{-1}A^3P = B^3$$

6. Extend the accuracy of the computation of the characteristic roots and vectors for the matrix A of Section 5.9 to one more decimal place accuracy in all the roots.

7. For the matrix

$$A = \begin{bmatrix} 5 & 1 & 0 \\ 1 & 3 & 1 \\ 0 & 1 & 4 \end{bmatrix}$$

find

(a) A^2, A^4, A^6, and A^8.

(b) If the elements of a matrix B are 0.1 times those of the corresponding elements of A, then what is the relative size of the elements of B^8 as compared to the corresponding elements of A^8?

(c) Find all the characteristic roots and vectors of A.

8. By the method in Section 5.13 find the dominant root of the polynomial equation

$$f(x) = x^3 - 7x^2 - 40x + 100 = 0$$

Determine a reduced polynomial equation that has for roots the other two roots of $f(x)$. Find the dominant root of this polynomial equation using a new set of d_i.

6

Inversion of Matrices

6.1 Introduction

In Chapter 2 a general system of n equations in m unknowns was written in the matrix form $AX = G$. If $m = n$, the matrix A is square and might be nonsingular. In this case, one can multiply the matrix equation on the left by A^{-1} and obtain the explicit form

$$X = A^{-1}G$$

for the solution vector. If the matrix A has an inverse that is not known, there are situations where it would be advantageous to compute it. Such would be the case if one had several systems of equations all with the same coefficient matrix A. Knowing the inverse matrix would reduce the problem of determining the solutions for these systems to one of matrix multiplication. There is another advantage to discussing techniques for inverting matrices in that some of these methods are readily adapted to finding a solution X for a system of equations.

In previous chapters, there were methods given for finding the inverse of a matrix. If the matrix is of small size, one of these will give the inverse without too much trouble. However, for larger matrices and for matrices whose elements are numbers that are approximations, these techniques are not too satisfactory. As a result, a large number of numerical approximation methods for determining the inverse of a matrix have been developed. These methods are sometimes set up so that desk calculators may be used to best advantage.

There are two essentially different types of approximating techniques to be considered. In this chapter the direct solution type will be discussed whereas the iterative technique will be considered in the next chapter. The direct solution techniques are characterized by being methods where one carries out a specified process only once, whereas in the iterative techniques the process is carried out repeatedly. In the direct solution, the accuracy of the final result is determined by the accuracy of the computations. In the iterative technique, the desired accuracy in the final result is obtained by the repetition of the process. The method of approximating the characteristic root and vector of the last chapter was an example of an iterative procedure.

The technique of Sections 2.6 and 2.8 of using elementary row or column operations to obtain a canonical form B for the matrix A, forms the basis for the first numerical direct process for finding the inverse of a matrix. It was pointed out in Section 2.7 that by performing the same operations in the same order on the identity matrix, a new matrix P was obtained. Then either $PA = B$ or $AP = B$ depending upon whether row or column operations are used. In case the canonical matrix B is the identity matrix then $P = A^{-1}$.

This technique will now be modified. Instead of having to perform the same elementary operations a second time with the identity matrix in place of A, suppose that they are performed on both A and I simultaneously. One way to do this is to augment the matrix A with the identity matrix and simplify the resulting matrix using elementary row operations. One could also place the identity matrix below the matrix to be inverted and use elementary column operations. The first method can be illustrated using the matrix

$$A = \begin{bmatrix} 1 & -2 & -1 \\ 4 & -3 & 1 \\ 3 & -1 & -2 \end{bmatrix}$$

If this matrix is augmented on the right by the identity matrix, this new matrix can be simplified as follows

$$\begin{bmatrix} 1 & -2 & -1 & 1 & 0 & 0 \\ 4 & -3 & 1 & 0 & 1 & 0 \\ 3 & -1 & -2 & 0 & 0 & 1 \end{bmatrix} \xrightarrow[\substack{R2-4R1 \\ R3-3R1}]{} \begin{bmatrix} 1 & -2 & -1 & 1 & 0 & 0 \\ 0 & 5 & 5 & -4 & 1 & 0 \\ 0 & 5 & 1 & -3 & 0 & 1 \end{bmatrix}$$

$$\xleftrightarrow[0.2R2]{} \begin{bmatrix} 1 & -2 & -1 & 1 & 0 & 0 \\ 0 & 1 & 1 & -0.8 & 0.2 & 0 \\ 0 & 5 & 1 & -3 & 0 & 1 \end{bmatrix}$$

$$\xleftrightarrow[\substack{R1+2R2 \\ R3-5R2}]{} \begin{bmatrix} 1 & 0 & 1 & -0.6 & 0.4 & 0 \\ 0 & 1 & 1 & -0.8 & 0.2 & 0 \\ 0 & 0 & -4 & 1 & -1 & 1 \end{bmatrix}$$

$$\xleftrightarrow[-0.25R3]{} \begin{bmatrix} 1 & 0 & 1 & -0.6 & 0.4 & 0 \\ 0 & 1 & 1 & -0.8 & 0.2 & 0 \\ 0 & 0 & 1 & -0.25 & 0.25 & -0.25 \end{bmatrix}$$

$$\xleftrightarrow[\substack{R1-1R3 \\ R2-1R3}]{} \begin{bmatrix} 1 & 0 & 0 & -0.35 & 0.15 & 0.25 \\ 0 & 1 & 0 & -0.55 & -0.05 & 0.25 \\ 0 & 0 & 1 & -0.25 & 0.25 & -0.25 \end{bmatrix}$$

Since the last three columns are the result of the row operations on I,

$$A^{-1} = \begin{bmatrix} -0.35 & 0.15 & 0.25 \\ -0.55 & -0.05 & 0.25 \\ -0.25 & 0.25 & -0.25 \end{bmatrix}$$

In this process notice that one starts with the matrix augmented by I and ends with I augmented by A^{-1}. How does this procedure differ from what was done in Chapter 2? There the operations were performed on A augmented by G instead of A augmented by the matrix I as is done here. This means the elementary row operations are performed on G as well as on A. This will be typical of the procedures to be given; one simply replaces I by G to find the solution X for a given system.

One can also use both elementary row and column operations to find the inverse of the matrix A. Suppose A is reduced to I using elementray operations. In Section 2.9, it was found that there would exist matrices P and Q such that $PAQ = I$. If one multiplies this equation on the left by Q and on the right by Q^{-1},

$$Q(PAQ)Q^{-1} = QIQ^{-1} \quad \text{or} \quad (QP)A = I$$

This result shows that the inverse of the matrix A is the matrix QP.

    To find the P and Q that will reduce a given nonsingular matrix A to I, one can place the identity matrix of A below A and also to the right of A. Then a zero matrix can be placed in the lower right corner to form an enlarged matrix. This corner submatrix should always remain a zero matrix. Any column operation performed on A will also be performed on the identity matrix placed below it so this will become the matrix Q. Similarly the row operations will also be applied to the identity placed to the right of A and will determine the matrix P. None of these operations will affect the zero matrix in the lower right-hand corner. One can thus easily determine the Q and P that are needed.

    As an example, consider the following reduction of the matrix used as an illustration in this section.

$$
\begin{bmatrix}
1 & -2 & -1 & 1 & 0 & 0 \\
4 & -3 & 1 & 0 & 1 & 0 \\
3 & -1 & -2 & 0 & 0 & 1 \\
1 & 0 & 0 & 0 & 0 & 0 \\
0 & 1 & 0 & 0 & 0 & 0 \\
0 & 0 & 1 & 0 & 0 & 0
\end{bmatrix}
\xrightarrow[R3-3R1]{\overset{\longleftarrow}{R2-4R1}}
\begin{bmatrix}
1 & -2 & -1 & 1 & 0 & 0 \\
0 & 5 & 5 & -4 & 1 & 0 \\
0 & 5 & 1 & -3 & 0 & 1 \\
1 & 0 & 0 & 0 & 0 & 0 \\
0 & 1 & 0 & 0 & 0 & 0 \\
0 & 0 & 1 & 0 & 0 & 0
\end{bmatrix}
$$

$$
\xrightarrow[C3+1C1]{\overset{\longleftarrow}{C2+2C1}}
\begin{bmatrix}
1 & 0 & 0 & 1 & 0 & 0 \\
0 & 5 & 5 & -4 & 1 & 0 \\
0 & 5 & 1 & -3 & 0 & 1 \\
1 & 2 & 1 & 0 & 0 & 0 \\
0 & 1 & 0 & 0 & 0 & 0 \\
0 & 0 & 1 & 0 & 0 & 0
\end{bmatrix}
\xrightarrow{\overset{\longleftarrow}{R3-1R2}}
\begin{bmatrix}
1 & 0 & 0 & 1 & 0 & 0 \\
0 & 5 & 5 & -4 & 1 & 0 \\
0 & 0 & -4 & 1 & -1 & 1 \\
1 & 2 & 1 & 0 & 0 & 0 \\
0 & 1 & 0 & 0 & 0 & 0 \\
0 & 0 & 1 & 0 & 0 & 0
\end{bmatrix}
$$

$$\overset{\longleftrightarrow}{C3 - 1C2}\begin{bmatrix} 1 & 0 & 0 & 1 & 0 & 0 \\ 0 & 5 & 0 & -4 & 1 & 0 \\ 0 & 0 & -4 & 1 & -1 & 1 \\ 1 & 2 & -1 & 0 & 0 & 0 \\ 0 & 1 & -1 & 0 & 0 & 0 \\ 0 & 0 & 1 & 0 & 0 & 0 \end{bmatrix}$$

$$\begin{matrix} \overset{\longleftrightarrow}{0.2R2} \\ -0.25C3 \end{matrix}\begin{bmatrix} 1 & 0 & 0 & 1 & 0 & 0 \\ 0 & 1 & 0 & -0.8 & 0.2 & 0 \\ 0 & 0 & 1 & 1 & -1 & 1 \\ 1 & 2 & 0.25 & 0 & 0 & 0 \\ 0 & 1 & 0.25 & 0 & 0 & 0 \\ 0 & 0 & -0.25 & 0 & 0 & 0 \end{bmatrix}$$

The inverse matrix is given by

$$QP = \begin{bmatrix} 1 & 2 & 0.25 \\ 0 & 1 & 0.25 \\ 0 & 0 & -0.25 \end{bmatrix}\begin{bmatrix} 1 & 0 & 0 \\ -0.8 & 0.2 & 0 \\ 1 & -1 & 1 \end{bmatrix} = \begin{bmatrix} -0.35 & 0.15 & 0.25 \\ -0.55 & -0.05 & 0.25 \\ -0.25 & 0.25 & -0.25 \end{bmatrix}$$

which is the result obtained previously.

6.2 The Crout Process; the Forward Solution

One of the better known of the numerical direct techniques of inverting a matrix is the Crout method. There are two parts to this process, the first part is called the *forward solution* and the second part the *backward solution*. It is not until both parts are completed that one has the inverse of the given matrix. The forward solution will be discussed in this section while the backward solution will be discussed in the next section.

In the Crout process, the matrix to be inverted is first augmented with the identity matrix. The elements in each row of this new matrix are then added together and these sums used to form a column to the right of the columns of the identity matrix. The elements of this latter column are used as a check on the computations. To make the notation uniform, the elements of the identity matrix and the row sums are written using the regular a_{rs} symbols. This gives the augmented matrix the form

$$\begin{bmatrix} a_{11} & a_{12} & \cdots & a_{1t} \\ a_{21} & a_{22} & \cdots & a_{2t} \\ \cdot & \cdot & \cdots & \cdot \\ \cdot & \cdot & \cdots & \cdot \\ \cdot & \cdot & \cdots & \cdot \\ a_{n1} & a_{n2} & \cdots & a_{nt} \end{bmatrix}$$

where $t = 2n + 1$. Those a_{rs} whose s varies from 1 to n constitute the matrix to be inverted. Those where s varies from $n + 1$ to $2n$ form the identity matrix. The elements in the last column are simply the sum of the other elements in each row. From this matrix, a table of values for the forward solution is computed. The elements of the table are determined in a series of steps. In the following display, those elements computed at a given step are blocked off and the number of the step at which they are computed is indicated. At each step, one computes all elements of a certain row or column that were not determined at a previous step.

c_{11}	c_{12}	c_{13}	c_{14} $\cdots$	c_{1n}	$c_{1, n+1}$ $\cdots$ c_{1t}	[2]
c_{21}	c_{22}	c_{23}	c_{24} $\cdots$	c_{2n}	$c_{2, n+1}$ $\cdots$ c_{2t}	[4]
c_{31}	c_{32}	c_{33}	c_{34} $\cdots$	c_{3n}	$c_{3, n+1}$ $\cdots$ c_{3t}	[6]
$\cdot$	$\cdot$	$\cdot$	$\cdot$			
$\cdot$	$\cdot$	$\cdot$	$\cdot$			
$\cdot$	$\cdot$	$\cdot$	$\cdot$			
c_{n1}	c_{n2}	c_{n3}	$\cdots$	c_{nn}	$c_{n, n+1}$ $\cdots$ c_{nt}	[2n]
[1]	[3]	[5]		[2n − 1]		

Note that the first set of c_{r1} to be computed are in the first column while the next set of c_{s1} are in the first row. One then calculates the remaining elements in the second column and then the second row. This is followed by determining the rest of the third column and row and so on down to the nth column and row.

The columns and rows are computed using the formulae,

1. $c_{r1} = a_{r1}$ $\qquad\qquad\qquad r = 1, \cdots, n$

2. $c_{1s} = \dfrac{a_{1s}}{c_{11}}$ $\qquad\qquad\qquad s = 2, \cdots, t$

3. $c_{r2} = a_{r2} - c_{12}c_{r1}$ $\qquad\qquad\qquad r = 2, \cdots, n$

4. $c_{2s} = \dfrac{a_{2s} - c_{21}c_{1s}}{c_{22}}$ $\qquad\qquad\qquad s = 3, \cdots, t$

$$\bullet \quad \bullet \quad \bullet$$

$2j - 1.$ $c_{rj} = a_{rj} - \displaystyle\sum_{k=1}^{j-1} c_{kj}c_{rk}$ $\qquad\qquad r = j, \cdots, n$

$2j.$ $c_{js} = \dfrac{a_{js} - \displaystyle\sum_{k=1}^{j-1} c_{jk}c_{ks}}{c_{jj}}$ $\qquad\qquad s = j+1, \cdots, t$

if all $c_{jj} \neq 0$. The case where some $c_{jj} = 0$ is considered at the end of Section 6.3. These formulae are numbered to correspond to the number of the step indicated in the table for the forward solution. Formula 1 indicates that the first column of the c_{r1} is to be the same as the first column of the matrix A. The restrictions placed on the values for r and s are to emphasize that previously computed c_{rs} are not to be evaluated again.

As a simple example of this technique, consider the matrix

$$A = \begin{bmatrix} 1 & -2 & -1 & 2 \\ -2 & 6 & 3 & 0 \\ -1 & 3 & -2 & 2 \\ 2 & 0 & 2 & 4 \end{bmatrix}$$

The augmented matrix would have the form

$$\begin{bmatrix} 1 & -2 & -1 & 2 & 1 & 0 & 0 & 0 & 1 \\ -2 & 6 & 3 & 0 & 0 & 1 & 0 & 0 & 8 \\ -1 & 3 & -2 & 2 & 0 & 0 & 1 & 0 & 3 \\ 2 & 0 & 2 & 4 & 0 & 0 & 0 & 1 & 9 \end{bmatrix}$$

The table for the forward solution is

1	-2	-1	2	1	0	0	0	1	[2]
-2	2	$\frac{1}{2}$	2	1	$1\frac{1}{2}$	0	0	5	[4]
-1	1	$-\frac{7}{2}$	$-\frac{4}{7}$	0	$\frac{1}{7}$	$-\frac{2}{7}$	0	$\frac{2}{7}$	[6]
2	4	2	$-\frac{8}{7}$	$\frac{7}{8}$	$\frac{1}{3}$	$-\frac{1}{12}$	$-\frac{7}{48}$	$\frac{95}{48}$	[8]
[1]	[3]	[5]	[7]						

In this example $c_{11} = 1$ so the c_{1s} can be written down at once. To find the other elements, the following computations are made.

$$[3]. \quad c_{22} = a_{22} - c_{12}c_{21} = 6 - (-2)(-2) = 2$$

$$c_{32} = a_{32} - c_{12}c_{31} = 3 - (-2)(-1) = 1$$

$$c_{42} = a_{42} - c_{12}c_{41} = 0 - (-2)(2) = 4$$

$$[4]. \quad c_{23} = \frac{a_{23} - c_{21}c_{13}}{c_{22}} = \frac{3 - (-2)(-1)}{2} = \frac{1}{2}$$

$$c_{24} = \frac{a_{24} - c_{21}c_{14}}{c_{22}} = \frac{0 - (-2)(2)}{2} = 2$$

$$c_{25} = \frac{a_{25} - c_{21}c_{15}}{c_{22}} = \frac{0 - (-2)(0)}{2} = 1$$

$$c_{26} = \frac{a_{26} - c_{21}c_{16}}{c_{22}} = \frac{1 - (-2)(0)}{2} = \frac{1}{2}$$

$$c_{27} = \frac{a_{27} - c_{21}c_{17}}{c_{22}} = \frac{0 - (-2)(0)}{2} = 0$$

$$c_{28} = \frac{a_{28} - c_{21}c_{18}}{c_{22}} = \frac{0 - (-2)(0)}{2} = 0$$

$$c_{29} = \frac{a_{29} - c_{21}c_{19}}{c_{22}} = \frac{8 - (-2)(1)}{2} = 5$$

$$[5]. \quad c_{33} = a_{33} - c_{13}c_{31} - c_{23}c_{32} = -\frac{7}{2}$$

$$c_{43} = a_{43} - c_{13}c_{41} - c_{23}c_{42} = 2$$

$$[6]. \quad c_{34} = \frac{a_{34} - c_{31}c_{14} - c_{32}c_{24}}{c_{33}} = -\frac{4}{7}$$

$$c_{35} = \frac{a_{35} - c_{31}c_{15} - c_{32}c_{25}}{c_{33}} = 0$$

$$c_{36} = \frac{a_{36} - c_{31}c_{16} - c_{32}c_{26}}{c_{33}} = \frac{1}{7}$$

$$c_{37} = \frac{a_{37} - c_{31}c_{17} - c_{32}c_{27}}{c_{33}} = -\frac{2}{7}$$

$$c_{38} = \frac{a_{38} - c_{31}c_{18} - c_{32}c_{28}}{c_{33}} = 0$$

$$c_{39} = \frac{a_{39} - c_{31}c_{19} - c_{32}c_{29}}{c_{33}} = \frac{2}{7}$$

$$[7]. \quad c_{44} = a_{44} - c_{14}c_{41} - c_{24}c_{42} - c_{34}c_{43} = -\frac{48}{7}$$

$$[8]. \quad c_{45} = \frac{a_{45} - c_{41}c_{15} - c_{42}c_{25} - c_{43}c_{35}}{c_{44}} = \frac{7}{8}$$

$$c_{46} = \frac{a_{46} - c_{41}c_{16} - c_{42}c_{26} - c_{43}c_{36}}{c_{44}} = \frac{1}{3}$$

$$c_{47} = \frac{a_{47} - c_{41}c_{17} - c_{42}c_{27} - c_{43}c_{37}}{c_{44}} = -\frac{1}{12}$$

$$c_{48} = \frac{a_{48} - c_{41}c_{18} - c_{42}c_{28} - c_{43}c_{38}}{c_{44}} = -\frac{7}{48}$$

$$c_{49} = \frac{a_{49} - c_{41}c_{19} - c_{42}c_{29} - c_{43}c_{39}}{c_{44}} = \frac{95}{48}$$

To check the calculations, those elements blocked off to the right in each row of the table are considered, that is, those computed at the even numbered steps. The last element should exceed the sum of the others by 1. This is called the "row-sum check." For this example, the row-sum check indicates that there are probably no errors made in the computations.

There is a close relationship between the computations involved in the Crout process and those that are required in simplifying the augmented matrix using elementary row operations. The relationship can be seen in the following reduction. Certain parts of the matrices at each step are blocked off to emphasize the connection. Consider the reduction,

$$\begin{bmatrix} 1 & -2 & -1 & 2 & 1 & 0 & 0 & 0 & 1 \\ -2 & 6 & 3 & 0 & 0 & 1 & 0 & 0 & 8 \\ -1 & 3 & -2 & 2 & 0 & 0 & 1 & 0 & 3 \\ 2 & 0 & 2 & 4 & 0 & 0 & 0 & 1 & 9 \end{bmatrix}$$

$$\xrightarrow{1R1} \begin{bmatrix} 1 & -2 & -1 & 2 & 1 & 0 & 0 & 0 & 1 \\ -2 & 6 & 3 & 0 & 0 & 1 & 0 & 0 & 8 \\ -1 & 3 & -2 & 2 & 0 & 0 & 1 & 0 & 3 \\ 2 & 0 & 2 & 4 & 0 & 0 & 0 & 1 & 9 \end{bmatrix}$$

$$\xrightarrow[\substack{R2-(-2)R1 \\ R3-(-1)R1 \\ R4-2R1}]{} \begin{bmatrix} 1 & -2 & -1 & 2 & 1 & 0 & 0 & 0 & 1 \\ 0 & 2 & 1 & 4 & 2 & 1 & 0 & 0 & 10 \\ 0 & 1 & -3 & 4 & 1 & 0 & 1 & 0 & 4 \\ 0 & 4 & 4 & 0 & -2 & 0 & 0 & 1 & 7 \end{bmatrix}$$

$$\xrightarrow{\frac{1}{2}R2} \begin{bmatrix} 1 & -2 & -1 & 2 & 1 & 0 & 0 & 0 & 1 \\ 0 & 1 & \frac{1}{2} & 2 & 1 & \frac{1}{2} & 0 & 0 & 5 \\ 0 & 1 & -3 & 4 & 1 & 0 & 1 & 0 & 4 \\ 0 & 4 & 4 & 0 & -2 & 0 & 0 & 1 & 7 \end{bmatrix}$$

$$\xrightarrow[\substack{R3-1R2 \\ R4-4R2}]{} \begin{bmatrix} 1 & -2 & -1 & 2 & 1 & 0 & 0 & 0 & 1 \\ 0 & 1 & \frac{1}{2} & 2 & 1 & \frac{1}{2} & 0 & 0 & 5 \\ 0 & 0 & -\frac{7}{2} & 2 & 0 & -\frac{1}{2} & 1 & 0 & -1 \\ 0 & 0 & 2 & -8 & -6 & -2 & 0 & 1 & -13 \end{bmatrix}$$

$$-\tfrac{2}{7}R3 \quad \begin{bmatrix} 1 & -2 & -1 & 2 & 1 & 0 & 0 & 0 & 1 \\ 0 & 1 & \tfrac{1}{2} & 2 & 1 & \tfrac{1}{2} & 0 & 0 & 5 \\ 0 & 0 & 1 & \boxed{-\tfrac{4}{7} \quad 0 \quad \tfrac{1}{7} \quad -\tfrac{2}{7} \quad 0 \quad \tfrac{2}{7}} \\ 0 & 0 & 2 & -8 & -6 & -2 & 0 & 1 & -13 \end{bmatrix}$$

$$R4 - 2R3 \quad \begin{bmatrix} 1 & -2 & -1 & 2 & 1 & 0 & 0 & 0 & 1 \\ 0 & 1 & \tfrac{1}{2} & 2 & 1 & \tfrac{1}{2} & 0 & 0 & 5 \\ 0 & 0 & 1 & -\tfrac{4}{7} & 0 & \tfrac{1}{7} & -\tfrac{2}{7} & 0 & \tfrac{2}{7} \\ 0 & 0 & 0 & \boxed{-\tfrac{48}{7}} & -6 & -\tfrac{16}{7} & \tfrac{4}{7} & 1 & -\tfrac{95}{7} \end{bmatrix}$$

$$-\tfrac{7}{48}R4 \quad \begin{bmatrix} 1 & -2 & -1 & 2 & 1 & 0 & 0 & 0 & 1 \\ 0 & 1 & \tfrac{1}{2} & 2 & 1 & \tfrac{1}{2} & 0 & 0 & 5 \\ 0 & 0 & 1 & -\tfrac{4}{7} & 0 & \tfrac{1}{7} & -\tfrac{2}{7} & 0 & \tfrac{2}{7} \\ 0 & 0 & 0 & 1 & \boxed{\tfrac{7}{8} \quad \tfrac{1}{3} \quad -\tfrac{1}{12} \quad -\tfrac{7}{48} \quad \tfrac{95}{48}} \end{bmatrix}$$

At each step notice that the numbers blocked off are the same as the set of c_{rs} computed at the corresponding step. Furthermore, the numbers in the rows that are blocked off on the even numbered steps are left unchanged thereafter. The numbers in the columns that are blocked off at the odd numbered steps are changed in the next two steps. The first element is 1 at the next step and the others are 0 at the following step. To see why this is, notice that for the first operation the reciprocal of c_{11} is used as a multiplier of the first row. Then at the next step the multiples of the first row that are needed to modify the other three rows are the c_{r1}. This makes these elements in the first column 0 after the second step. The numbers blocked off in the second column are then used in a similar manner to determine the next two steps. The reciprocal of the element c_{22} is used as a multiplier for the second row. The other c_{r2} that are blocked off determine the multiples of the second row that are used at the fourth step. This cycle is repeated until all calculations have been made. In other words, the numbers in the columns blocked off at the odd steps in the Crout calculations serve only to give the necessary numbers needed in the altering of the rows in the next two steps. Notice that what has been done is that the matrix A was reduced to triangular form by elementary row operations.

In the Crout process these elementary operations are used in an order that differs from the order used in Chapter 2. These changes are made so that it is easy to perform the computations on a desk calculator.

6.3 The Backward Solution

To complete the task of determining the inverse of the matrix, one more step is needed. This is known as finding the backward solution. For this, a matrix $D = (d_{rs})$ is computed using the c_{rs} determined on the forward solution. The rows of D are calculated in order, starting with its last row and ending with its first row. The elements of D are determined from the formulae,

$$d_{ns} = c_{n,\ n+s}$$

$$d_{rs} = c_{r,\ n+s} - \sum_{k=r+1}^{n} c_{rk}d_{ks} \qquad r = n-1, n-2, \cdots, 1$$

where $s = 1, 2, \cdots, t - n$.

In the formulae, the d_{rs} are obtained by altering the c_{rs} with second index greater than n. The multiples used in the process are the c_{rk}, where $k = r + 1, \cdots, n$, that is, those whose second index exceeds the first but is still less than or equal to n. The last row of D requires no new calculations.

Note the similarity of these formulae to the even numbered ones used in determining the forward solution. The formulae for the d_{rs} are simpler because there is no division by an element c_{rr} since these elements were made 1 in the forward solution.

For the numerical example of the previous section, the formulae will give

$s =:$	1	2	3	4	5
$d_{1s}:$	$-\frac{9}{4}$	-1	$\frac{1}{2}$	$\frac{7}{8}$	$-\frac{7}{8}$
$d_{2s}:$	-1	$-\frac{1}{3}$	$\frac{1}{3}$	$\frac{1}{3}$	$\frac{1}{3}$
$d_{3s}:$	$\frac{1}{2}$	$\frac{1}{3}$	$-\frac{1}{3}$	$-\frac{1}{12}$	$\frac{17}{12}$
$d_{4s}:$	$\frac{7}{8}$	$\frac{1}{3}$	$-\frac{1}{12}$	$-\frac{7}{48}$	$\frac{95}{48}$

The calculations are made starting with the d_{4s} and concluding with the d_{1s}. They are written in the above order for convenience. Fractions are retained in the result to obtain an exact answer. In practice, the matrices to be inverted usually have elements that are decimal approximations. The elements of D are then also written as decimal approximations.

The matrix formed from the first four columns of this table is A^{-1}. The last column is again the check column. Its elements should exceed the sum of the other elements in the corresponding rows by 1. This is true for this example so the calculations are probably correct.

The backward solution can also be interpreted in terms of elementary row operations. For this, one starts with the final form of the matrix that illustrated the forward solution and reduces it to obtain the identity matrix in the first n columns. The multiples that are used at each step are the elements c_{rk}, where $k = r + 1, \cdots, n$, that is, the same elements used in the determination of the d_{rs}. These operations give

$$
\begin{bmatrix}
1 & -2 & -1 & 2 & 1 & 0 & 0 & 0 & 1 \\
0 & 1 & \frac{1}{2} & 2 & 1 & \frac{1}{2} & 0 & 0 & 5 \\
0 & 0 & 1 & -\frac{4}{7} & 0 & \frac{1}{7} & -\frac{2}{7} & 0 & \frac{2}{7} \\
0 & 0 & 0 & 1 & \frac{7}{8} & \frac{1}{3} & -\frac{1}{12} & -\frac{7}{48} & \frac{95}{48}
\end{bmatrix}
$$

$$
\begin{array}{l}
\\
\\
\xleftarrow{\hspace{1cm}}\rightarrow \\
R3 - (-\frac{4}{7})R4 \\
R2 - 2R4 \\
R1 - 2R4
\end{array}
\begin{bmatrix}
1 & -2 & -1 & 0 & -\frac{3}{4} & -\frac{2}{3} & \frac{1}{6} & \frac{7}{24} & -\frac{71}{24} \\
0 & 1 & \frac{1}{2} & 0 & -\frac{3}{4} & -\frac{1}{6} & \frac{1}{6} & \frac{7}{24} & \frac{22}{24} \\
0 & 0 & 1 & 0 & \frac{1}{2} & \frac{1}{3} & -\frac{1}{3} & -\frac{1}{12} & \frac{17}{12} \\
0 & 0 & 0 & 1 & \frac{7}{8} & \frac{1}{3} & -\frac{1}{12} & -\frac{7}{48} & \frac{95}{48}
\end{bmatrix}
$$

$$
\begin{array}{l}
\\
\\
\xleftarrow{\hspace{1cm}}\rightarrow \\
R2 - \frac{1}{2}R3 \\
R1 - (-1)R3
\end{array}
\begin{bmatrix}
1 & -2 & 0 & 0 & -\frac{1}{4} & -\frac{1}{3} & -\frac{1}{6} & \frac{5}{24} & -\frac{37}{24} \\
0 & 1 & 0 & 0 & -1 & -\frac{1}{3} & \frac{1}{3} & \frac{1}{3} & \frac{1}{3} \\
0 & 0 & 1 & 0 & \frac{1}{2} & \frac{1}{3} & -\frac{1}{3} & -\frac{1}{12} & \frac{17}{12} \\
0 & 0 & 0 & 1 & \frac{7}{8} & \frac{1}{3} & -\frac{1}{12} & -\frac{7}{48} & \frac{95}{48}
\end{bmatrix}
$$

$$
\begin{array}{l}
\\
\\
\xleftarrow{\hspace{1cm}}\rightarrow \\
R1 - (-2)R2
\end{array}
\begin{bmatrix}
1 & 0 & 0 & 0 & -\frac{9}{4} & -1 & \frac{1}{2} & \frac{7}{8} & -\frac{7}{8} \\
0 & 1 & 0 & 0 & -1 & -\frac{1}{3} & \frac{1}{3} & \frac{1}{3} & \frac{1}{3} \\
0 & 0 & 1 & 0 & \frac{1}{2} & \frac{1}{3} & -\frac{1}{3} & -\frac{1}{12} & \frac{17}{12} \\
0 & 0 & 0 & 1 & \frac{7}{8} & \frac{1}{3} & -\frac{1}{12} & -\frac{7}{48} & \frac{95}{48}
\end{bmatrix}
$$

The last five columns are the values obtained for the d_{rs} using the formulae. The computations required to find them are the same as those involved in the elementary row operations that are needed to complete the determination of the inverse matrix.

There is another check that can be used on the backward solution in place of the row sum check. This check utilizes the fact that if one has the inverse, the product of its row vectors with the column vectors of A must give either 0 or 1, since the product of the matrices is the identity matrix. One starts with the set of d_{ns} computed at the first step. Those with the second index ranging from 1 to n form the nth row of the inverse matrix. The product of this row vector with the last column vector of A must give an approximation to 1. As a further check, one can use some other column vectors of A to see if the product with this row vector is nearly 0. After the check is made, the next to last row of the inverse is computed. It will consist of the $d_{n-1, s}$, where s ranges from 1 to n. This row vector is multiplied by the next to last column vector of A to see if the result is reasonably close to 1. Again as a further check on this row, one can consider its product with another column vector of A to see if the result is almost 0. One can continue in this fashion, checking each row of the inverse for errors. This checking should be made for each row since all later computations use rows that have already been determined.

A word of warning is needed about the use of the above method and the method to be discussed in the next section. There is always a possibility of a diagonal element becoming 0 in the simplification. In such an event, division by this element is not possible. Also, if the diagonal element is nearly 0 in comparison with the other elements in its row, the division may introduce large errors. These two situations can be taken care of by interchanging this row with some row that has not been altered at this point. Then to find the inverse of the original matrix, one must interchange the corresponding columns of the inverse of this new matrix. (In Section 7.3 there will be a discussion of why this must be done). As an alternative to this interchange of columns, the corresponding rows of the original matrix could be interchanged and this new matrix used in place of the starting matrix.

6.4 The Doolittle Process

In case the matrix A that is to be inverted is symmetric, there is a simplification of the Crout method that can be used. This modified process is known as the Doolittle method. The starting point is the same augmented matrix formed in the Crout technique. A table this time is built up row by row instead of alternating between columns and rows. It is given in the following form.

$$
\begin{array}{cccccccc}
b_{11} & b_{12} & b_{13} & \cdots & b_{1n} & \cdots & b_{1t} \\
1 & c_{12} & c_{13} & \cdots & c_{1n} & \cdots & c_{1t} \\
 & b_{22} & b_{23} & \cdots & b_{2n} & \cdots & b_{2t} \\
 & 1 & c_{23} & \cdots & c_{2n} & \cdots & c_{2t} \\
 & & b_{33} & \cdots & b_{3n} & \cdots & b_{3t} \\
 & & 1 & \cdots & c_{3n} & \cdots & c_{3t} \\
 & & & \cdot & \cdot & \cdot & \\
 & & & & b_{nn} & \cdots & b_{nt} \\
 & & & & 1 & \cdots & c_{nt}
\end{array}
$$

These entries are computed using the formulae

$$b_{1s} = a_{1s}$$

$$b_{rs} = a_{rs} - \sum_{k=1}^{r-1} c_{kr}b_{ks} = a_{rs} - \sum_{k=1}^{r-1} b_{kr}c_{ks} \qquad s = r, \cdots, t$$

$$c_{rs} = \frac{b_{rs}}{b_{rr}} \quad (b_{rr} \neq 0) \qquad s = r, \cdots, t$$

Either formula can be used to find b_{rs} since by the formula for c_{rs}

$$c_{kr}b_{ks} = \frac{b_{kr}}{b_{kk}}(b_{ks}) = (b_{kr})\frac{b_{ks}}{b_{kk}} = b_{kr}c_{ks}$$

This time, in the row sum check, the elements of the last column must be exactly equal to the sum of the other elements in the corresponding row. There are no computations required to find the b_{1s} since these are the same as the elements in the first row of the augmented matrix.

Before showing how this process is related to the Crout process, consider its application to the matrix used in Section 6.2. That matrix is symmetric so that the Doolittle method is applicable. The augmented matrix is

$$
\begin{bmatrix}
1 & -2 & -1 & 2 & 1 & 0 & 0 & 0 & 1 \\
-2 & 6 & 3 & 0 & 0 & 1 & 0 & 0 & 8 \\
-1 & 3 & -2 & 2 & 0 & 0 & 1 & 0 & 3 \\
2 & 0 & 2 & 4 & 0 & 0 & 0 & 1 & 9
\end{bmatrix}
$$

As can be verified, the table for the forward solution would be

$s =$:	1	2	3	4	5	6	7	8	9
b_{1s}:	1	-2	-1	2	1	0	0	0	1
c_{1s}:	1	-2	-1	2	1	0	0	0	1
b_{2s}:		2	1	4	2	1	0	0	10
c_{2s}:		1	$\frac{1}{2}$	2	1	$\frac{1}{2}$	0	0	5
b_{3s}:			$-\frac{7}{2}$	2	0	$-\frac{1}{2}$	1	0	-1
c_{3s}:			1	$-\frac{4}{7}$	0	$\frac{1}{7}$	$-\frac{2}{7}$	0	$\frac{2}{7}$
b_{4s}:				$-\frac{48}{7}$	-6	$-\frac{16}{7}$	$\frac{4}{7}$	1	$-\frac{95}{7}$
c_{4s}:				1	$\frac{7}{8}$	$\frac{1}{3}$	$-\frac{1}{12}$	$-\frac{7}{48}$	$\frac{95}{48}$

To see that this is a modification of the Crout process, some observations need to be made. Basically the b_{rs}, with index ranging up to n, are the same as the c_{rs} computed at the odd steps in the Crout method when the matrix is symmetric. The c_{rs} are exactly the same as the c_{rs} of the Crout process except for the c_{rr} which is 1 in the Doolittle method. To see this, compare the formulae, remembering for the odd numbered formulae that $a_{sr} = a_{rs}$,

[1] $$b_{1s} = a_{1s} = a_{s1} = c_{s1} \qquad s = 1, \cdots, n$$

[2] $$c_{1s} = \frac{b_{1s}}{b_{11}} = \frac{a_{1s}}{c_{11}} = c_{1s} \qquad s = 2, \cdots, t$$

[3] $$b_{2s} = a_{2s} - c_{12}b_{1s}$$
$$= a_{s2} - c_{12}c_{s1} = c_{s2} \qquad s = 2, \cdots, n$$

[4] $$c_{2s} = \frac{b_{2s}}{b_{22}} = \frac{a_{2s} - b_{12}c_{1s}}{b_{22}}$$
$$= \frac{a_{2s} - c_{21}c_{1s}}{c_{22}} = c_{2s} \qquad s = 3, \cdots, t$$

$$\cdot \quad \cdot \quad \cdot$$

[2j − 1] $$b_{js} = a_{js} - \sum_{k=1}^{j-1} c_{kj}b_{ks} = a_{sj} - \sum_{k=1}^{j-1} c_{kj}c_{sk} = c_{sj} \qquad s = j, \cdots, n$$

[2j] $$c_{js} = \frac{b_{js}}{b_{jj}} = \frac{a_{js} - \sum_{k=1}^{j-1} b_{kj}c_{ks}}{b_{jj}} = \frac{a_{js} - \sum_{k=1}^{j-1} c_{jk}c_{ks}}{c_{jj}} = c_{js}$$
$$s = j + 1, \cdots, t$$

This relationship can be illustrated by comparing the tables for the forward solution of the Crout and Doolittle techniques for the numerical examples. It is even more apparent in the justification for the Doolittle formulae in terms of elementary row operations. Consider the reduction of the augmented matrix where certain elements of the matrices are again blocked off.

$$
\begin{bmatrix}
1 & -2 & -1 & 2 & 1 & 0 & 0 & 0 & 1 \\
-2 & 6 & 3 & 0 & 0 & 1 & 0 & 0 & 8 \\
-1 & 3 & -2 & 2 & 0 & 0 & 1 & 0 & 3 \\
2 & 0 & 2 & 4 & 0 & 0 & 0 & 1 & 9
\end{bmatrix}
$$

$$
\xleftrightarrow{1R1}
\begin{bmatrix}
1 & -2 & -1 & 2 & 1 & 0 & 0 & 0 & 1 \\
-2 & 6 & 3 & 0 & 0 & 1 & 0 & 0 & 8 \\
-1 & 3 & -2 & 2 & 0 & 0 & 1 & 0 & 3 \\
2 & 0 & 2 & 4 & 0 & 0 & 0 & 1 & 9
\end{bmatrix}
$$

$$
\begin{matrix}
\xleftrightarrow{} \\
R2-(-2)R1 \\
R3-(-1)R1 \\
R4-2R1
\end{matrix}
\begin{bmatrix}
1 & -2 & -1 & 2 & 1 & 0 & 0 & 0 & 1 \\
0 & 2 & 1 & 4 & 2 & 1 & 0 & 0 & 10 \\
0 & 1 & -3 & 4 & 1 & 0 & 1 & 0 & 4 \\
0 & 4 & 4 & 0 & -2 & 0 & 0 & 1 & 7
\end{bmatrix}
$$

$$
\xleftrightarrow{\frac{1}{2}R2}
\begin{bmatrix}
1 & -2 & -1 & 2 & 1 & 0 & 0 & 0 & 1 \\
0 & 1 & \frac{1}{2} & 2 & 1 & \frac{1}{2} & 0 & 0 & 5 \\
0 & 1 & -3 & 4 & 1 & 0 & 1 & 0 & 4 \\
0 & 4 & 4 & 0 & -2 & 0 & 0 & 1 & 7
\end{bmatrix}
$$

$$
\begin{matrix}
\xleftrightarrow{} \\
R3-1R2 \\
R4-4R2
\end{matrix}
\begin{bmatrix}
1 & -2 & -1 & 2 & 1 & 0 & 0 & 0 & 1 \\
0 & 1 & \frac{1}{2} & 2 & 1 & \frac{1}{2} & 0 & 0 & 5 \\
0 & 0 & -\frac{7}{2} & 2 & 0 & -\frac{1}{2} & 1 & 0 & -1 \\
0 & 0 & 2 & -8 & -6 & -2 & 0 & 1 & -13
\end{bmatrix}
$$

$$-\tfrac{2}{7}R3 \qquad \begin{bmatrix} 1 & -2 & -1 & 2 & 1 & 0 & 0 & 0 & 1 \\ 0 & 1 & \tfrac{1}{2} & 2 & 1 & \tfrac{1}{2} & 0 & 0 & 5 \\ 0 & 0 & 1 & \boxed{-\tfrac{4}{7} \quad 0 \quad \tfrac{1}{7} \quad -\tfrac{2}{7} \quad 0 \quad \tfrac{2}{7}} \\ 0 & 0 & 2 & -8 & -6 & -2 & 0 & 1 & -13 \end{bmatrix}$$

$$R4 - 2R3 \qquad \begin{bmatrix} 1 & -2 & -1 & 2 & 1 & 0 & 0 & 0 & 1 \\ 0 & 1 & \tfrac{1}{2} & 2 & 1 & \tfrac{1}{2} & 0 & 0 & 5 \\ 0 & 0 & 1 & -\tfrac{4}{7} & 0 & \tfrac{1}{7} & -\tfrac{2}{7} & 0 & \tfrac{2}{7} \\ 0 & 0 & 0 & \boxed{-\tfrac{48}{7}} & -6 & -\tfrac{16}{7} & \tfrac{4}{7} & 1 & -\tfrac{95}{7} \end{bmatrix}$$

$$-\tfrac{7}{48}R4 \qquad \begin{bmatrix} 1 & -2 & -1 & 2 & 1 & 0 & 0 & 0 & 1 \\ 0 & 1 & \tfrac{1}{2} & 2 & 1 & \tfrac{1}{2} & 0 & 0 & 5 \\ 0 & 0 & 1 & -\tfrac{4}{7} & 0 & \tfrac{1}{7} & -\tfrac{2}{7} & 0 & \tfrac{2}{7} \\ 0 & 0 & 0 & 1 & \boxed{\tfrac{7}{8} \quad \tfrac{1}{3} \quad -\tfrac{1}{12} \quad -\tfrac{7}{48} \quad \tfrac{95}{48}} \end{bmatrix}$$

Notice that at all steps the same numbers are blocked off in this reduction and in the one for the forward solution of the Crout process. The only difference is that at the odd steps the numbers are now in a row vector instead of a column vector. It should be emphasized that this is true only because the original matrix A is symmetric.

The process as outlined gives only the forward solution for this method. In terms of elementary row operations, both the Crout and Doolittle methods reduce the agumented matrix to the same form. Both are techniques that reduce the elements below the diagonal of the starting matrix to 0 and also make the diagonal elements 1. This means that the task of finally finding the inverse is the same for both. For this reason there is no need to discuss the backward solution for the Doolittle method. One uses the technique outlined in Section 6.3 for the Crout method.

Both the Crout and Doolittle techniques are readily adaptable to finding the solution X for a system of linear equations. In place of the identity matrix, one uses the constant vector G to augment the coefficient matrix. If solutions for more than one system with the same coefficient matrix are desired, the coefficient matrix can be augmented with the constant vectors for each system. A check column can be formed by adding the elements in each row as before. The notation is readily adaptable to any number of systems of equations with the same coefficient matrix, by varying the value of t in the table. On the backward solution, there would be a column of D associated with each system of equations. These columns would be the solutions X for the corresponding system of equations. If a check column is used, it would be the last column vector of D.

6.5 Inversion by Partitioning

Another direct method for inverting a matrix is one that depends upon partitioning of the matrix into four submatrices. This is advantageous if the partitioned matrix has for its diagonal elements two square matrices whose inverses are easy to find. If the matrix is 6×6 or smaller, one could partition the matrix so that the diagonal matrices are no larger than 3×3. It is not too difficult to find the inverses of matrices of this size. As a matter of fact, one can write down at once the inverse of a 2×2 matrix. For the general 2×2 matrix A,

$$A = \begin{bmatrix} a_{11} & a_{12} \\ a_{21} & a_{22} \end{bmatrix} \qquad \text{adj } A = \begin{bmatrix} a_{22} & -a_{12} \\ -a_{21} & a_{11} \end{bmatrix} \qquad |A| = a_{11}a_{22} - a_{12}a_{21} = d$$

so that

$$A^{-1} = \frac{\text{adj } A}{|A|} = \begin{bmatrix} \dfrac{a_{22}}{d} & -\dfrac{a_{12}}{d} \\ -\dfrac{a_{21}}{d} & \dfrac{a_{11}}{d} \end{bmatrix}$$

This says the inverse of a 2×2 matrix A is formed by interchanging the diagonal elements of A, changing the signs of the other two elements, and dividing by the determinant of A.

Suppose the matrix A is partitioned into four submatrices so that the matrices on the diagonal are square. If A^{-1} is denoted as D, the product AD can be written as

$$\begin{bmatrix} A_{11} & A_{12} \\ A_{21} & A_{22} \end{bmatrix} \begin{bmatrix} D_{11} & D_{12} \\ D_{21} & D_{22} \end{bmatrix} = \begin{bmatrix} I & 0 \\ 0 & I \end{bmatrix}$$

where all the matrices are partitioned in the same manner. Performing the multiplication on the left gives the equality

$$\begin{bmatrix} A_{11}D_{11} + A_{12}D_{21} & A_{11}D_{12} + A_{12}D_{22} \\ A_{21}D_{11} + A_{22}D_{21} & A_{21}D_{12} + A_{22}D_{22} \end{bmatrix} = \begin{bmatrix} I & 0 \\ 0 & I \end{bmatrix}$$

Since the two sides are assumed to have the same partitioning, the four corresponding submatrices must be equal, that is

$$A_{11}D_{11} + A_{12}D_{21} = I \qquad A_{11}D_{12} + A_{12}D_{22} = 0$$

$$A_{21}D_{11} + A_{22}D_{21} = 0 \qquad A_{21}D_{12} + A_{22}D_{22} = I$$

One can use these four equations to find the four submatrices of D in terms of submatrices of A. To do this one solves for D_{21} and D_{12} in the equations with constant term of 0. This would give:

$$D_{21} = -A_{22}^{-1}A_{21}D_{11} \qquad D_{12} = -A_{11}^{-1}A_{12}D_{22}$$

These expressions can now be substituted into the other two equations to obtain equations in D_{11} and D_{22} alone. Substituting, one obtains

$$A_{11}D_{11} + A_{12}(-A_{22}^{-1}A_{21}D_{11}) = I \qquad A_{21}(-A_{11}^{-1}A_{12}D_{22}) + A_{22}D_{22} = I$$

Collecting the coefficients of D_{11} and D_{22},

$$(A_{11} - A_{12}A_{22}^{-1}A_{21})D_{11} = I \qquad (A_{22} - A_{21}A_{11}^{-1}A_{12})D_{22} = I$$

These two equations imply

$$D_{11}^{-1} = (A_{11} - A_{12}A_{22}^{-1}A_{21}) \qquad D_{22}^{-1} = (A_{22} - A_{21}A_{11}^{-1}A_{12})$$

or

$$D_{11} = (A_{11} - A_{12}A_{22}^{-1}A_{21})^{-1} \qquad D_{22} = (A_{22} - A_{21}A_{11}^{-1}A_{12})^{-1}$$

This means that in order to find the inverse by this technique, the expressions inside the parentheses must also have inverses. If so, D_{12} and D_{21} can be computed from

$$D_{21} = -A_{22}^{-1}A_{21}D_{11} \qquad D_{12} = -A_{11}^{-1}A_{12}D_{22}$$

This procedure can be illustrated with the example of Section 6.2. Suppose that matrix is partitioned into four 2×2 submatrices as follows:

$$A = \begin{bmatrix} 1 & -2 & -1 & 2 \\ -2 & 6 & 3 & 0 \\ -1 & 3 & -2 & 2 \\ 2 & 0 & 2 & 4 \end{bmatrix} = \begin{bmatrix} A_{11} & A_{12} \\ A_{21} & A_{22} \end{bmatrix}$$

The following computations are performed to obtain the inverse of A.

$$A_{22}^{-1}A_{21} = \begin{bmatrix} -\frac{1}{3} & \frac{1}{6} \\ \frac{1}{6} & \frac{1}{6} \end{bmatrix} \begin{bmatrix} -1 & 3 \\ 2 & 0 \end{bmatrix} = \begin{bmatrix} \frac{2}{3} & -1 \\ \frac{1}{6} & \frac{1}{2} \end{bmatrix}$$

$$A_{11}^{-1}A_{12} = \begin{bmatrix} 3 & 1 \\ 1 & \frac{1}{2} \end{bmatrix} \begin{bmatrix} -1 & 2 \\ 3 & 0 \end{bmatrix} = \begin{bmatrix} 0 & 6 \\ \frac{1}{2} & 2 \end{bmatrix}$$

$$D_{11}^{-1} = A_{11} - A_{12}A_{22}^{-1}A_{21} = \begin{bmatrix} 1 & -2 \\ -2 & 6 \end{bmatrix} - \begin{bmatrix} -\frac{1}{3} & 2 \\ 2 & -3 \end{bmatrix} = \begin{bmatrix} \frac{4}{3} & -4 \\ -4 & 9 \end{bmatrix}$$

$$D_{22}^{-1} = A_{22} - A_{21}A_{11}^{-1}A_{12} = \begin{bmatrix} -2 & 2 \\ 2 & 4 \end{bmatrix} - \begin{bmatrix} \frac{3}{2} & 0 \\ 0 & 12 \end{bmatrix} = \begin{bmatrix} -\frac{7}{2} & 2 \\ 2 & -8 \end{bmatrix}$$

so

$$D_{11} = \begin{bmatrix} -\frac{9}{4} & -1 \\ -1 & -\frac{1}{3} \end{bmatrix} \qquad\qquad D_{22} = \begin{bmatrix} -\frac{1}{3} & -\frac{1}{12} \\ -\frac{1}{12} & -\frac{7}{48} \end{bmatrix}$$

$$D_{21} = -A_{22}^{-1}A_{21}D_{11} = \begin{bmatrix} \frac{1}{2} & \frac{1}{3} \\ \frac{7}{8} & \frac{1}{3} \end{bmatrix} \qquad D_{12} = -A_{11}^{-1}A_{12}D_{22} = \begin{bmatrix} \frac{1}{2} & \frac{7}{8} \\ \frac{1}{3} & \frac{1}{3} \end{bmatrix}$$

$$A^{-1} = \begin{bmatrix} D_{11} & D_{12} \\ D_{21} & D_{22} \end{bmatrix} = \begin{bmatrix} -\frac{9}{4} & -1 & \frac{1}{2} & \frac{7}{8} \\ -1 & -\frac{1}{3} & \frac{1}{3} & \frac{1}{3} \\ \frac{1}{2} & \frac{1}{3} & -\frac{1}{3} & -\frac{1}{12} \\ \frac{7}{8} & \frac{1}{3} & -\frac{1}{12} & -\frac{7}{48} \end{bmatrix}$$

This result checks with the value computed previously for A^{-1} by the other methods of this chapter.

In case the partitioning can be made so that either A_{12} or A_{21} is a zero matrix, the inverse of A is much easier to find. For, if $A_{12} = 0$, the formulae for the D's would give

$$D_{11} = (A_{11} - 0 \cdot A_{22}^{-1}A_{21})^{-1} = A_{11}^{-1}$$

$$D_{22} = (A_{22} - A_{21}A_{11}^{-1} \cdot 0)^{-1} = A_{22}^{-1}$$

$$D_{21} = -A_{22}^{-1}A_{21}D_{11} = -A_{22}^{-1}A_{21}A_{11}^{-1}$$

$$D_{12} = -A_{11}^{-1} \cdot 0 \cdot D_{22} = 0$$

Similarly, if $A_{21} = 0$, then

$$D_{11} = A_{11}^{-1} \qquad D_{22} = A_{22}^{-1} \qquad D_{21} = 0 \quad \text{and} \quad D_{12} = -A_{11}^{-1}A_{12}A_{22}^{-1}$$

6.6 Extension of the Partitioning Method

The inverse of a matrix can be computed in a series of steps using the process of the last section. That technique reduced the inversion problem to finding the inverses of smaller matrices. The inverses of these smaller matrices could be found using the same method. In other words, one could apply the partitioning process repeatedly until one has to invert only small size matrices. The price paid, of course, is an increase in the number of matrices to be inverted. This can be illustrated using the partitioned matrix

$$A = \left[\begin{array}{cccc:cc}
1 & -2 & -1 & 2 & 1 & -2 \\
-2 & 6 & 3 & 0 & -3 & 4 \\
-1 & 3 & -2 & 2 & -1 & 2 \\
2 & 0 & 2 & 4 & 2 & -4 \\
\hdashline
-1 & -2 & 1 & -3 & 1 & -2 \\
3 & 4 & -2 & 2 & -1 & 3
\end{array}\right] = \begin{bmatrix} A_{11} & A_{12} \\ A_{21} & A_{22} \end{bmatrix}$$

The inverse of the submatrix A_{11} was found in the last section by partitioning. The matrix A_{22} is only a 2×2 so its inverse is easily evaluated. The computations required for A^{-1} are

$$A_{22}^{-1}A_{21} = \begin{bmatrix} 3 & 2 \\ 1 & 1 \end{bmatrix}\begin{bmatrix} -1 & -2 & 1 & -3 \\ 3 & 4 & -2 & 2 \end{bmatrix} = \begin{bmatrix} 3 & 2 & -1 & -5 \\ 2 & 2 & -1 & -1 \end{bmatrix}$$

$$A_{11}^{-1}A_{12} = \begin{bmatrix} -\frac{9}{4} & -1 & \frac{1}{2} & \frac{7}{8} \\ -1 & -\frac{1}{3} & \frac{1}{3} & \frac{1}{3} \\ \frac{1}{2} & \frac{1}{3} & -\frac{1}{3} & -\frac{1}{12} \\ \frac{7}{8} & \frac{1}{3} & -\frac{1}{12} & -\frac{7}{48} \end{bmatrix}\begin{bmatrix} 1 & -2 \\ -3 & 4 \\ -1 & 2 \\ 2 & -4 \end{bmatrix} = \begin{bmatrix} 2 & -2 \\ \frac{1}{3} & 0 \\ -\frac{1}{3} & 0 \\ -\frac{1}{3} & 0 \end{bmatrix}$$

$$D_{11}^{-1} = \begin{bmatrix} 1 & -2 & -1 & 2 \\ -2 & 6 & 3 & 0 \\ -1 & 3 & -2 & 2 \\ 2 & 0 & 2 & 4 \end{bmatrix} - \begin{bmatrix} -1 & -2 & 1 & -3 \\ -1 & 2 & -1 & 11 \\ 1 & 2 & -1 & 3 \\ -2 & -4 & 2 & -6 \end{bmatrix}$$

$$= \begin{bmatrix} 2 & 0 & -2 & 5 \\ -1 & 4 & 4 & -11 \\ -2 & 1 & -1 & -1 \\ 4 & 4 & 0 & 10 \end{bmatrix}$$

$$D_{22}^{-1} = \begin{bmatrix} 1 & -2 \\ -1 & 3 \end{bmatrix} - \begin{bmatrix} -2 & 2 \\ \frac{22}{3} & -6 \end{bmatrix} = \begin{bmatrix} 3 & -4 \\ -\frac{25}{3} & 9 \end{bmatrix}$$

The matrix D_{22} is easy to compute since it is 2×2. However, to find D_{11} the process of the last section will be used. For notation, let

$$E = D_{11}^{-1} \quad \text{and} \quad F = E^{-1} = D_{11}$$

Let the matrix E be partitioned into four 2×2 submatrices. The results of the computations to find $F = D_{11}$ are as follows:

$$E_{22}^{-1}E_{21} = \begin{bmatrix} -1 & -\frac{1}{10} \\ 0 & \frac{1}{10} \end{bmatrix}\begin{bmatrix} -2 & 1 \\ 4 & 4 \end{bmatrix} = \begin{bmatrix} \frac{8}{5} & -\frac{7}{5} \\ \frac{2}{5} & \frac{2}{5} \end{bmatrix}$$

$$E_{11}^{-1}E_{12} = \begin{bmatrix} \frac{1}{2} & 0 \\ \frac{1}{8} & \frac{1}{4} \end{bmatrix}\begin{bmatrix} -2 & 5 \\ 4 & -11 \end{bmatrix} = \begin{bmatrix} -1 & \frac{5}{2} \\ \frac{3}{4} & -\frac{17}{8} \end{bmatrix}$$

$$F_{11}^{-1} = E_{11} - E_{12}E_{11}^{-1}E_{21} = \begin{bmatrix} 2 & 0 \\ -1 & 4 \end{bmatrix} - \begin{bmatrix} -\frac{6}{5} & \frac{24}{5} \\ 2 & -10 \end{bmatrix} = \begin{bmatrix} \frac{16}{5} & -\frac{24}{5} \\ -3 & 14 \end{bmatrix}$$

$$F_{22}^{-1} = E_{22} - E_{21}E_{11}^{-1}E_{12} = \begin{bmatrix} -1 & -1 \\ 0 & 10 \end{bmatrix} - \begin{bmatrix} \frac{11}{4} & -\frac{57}{8} \\ -1 & \frac{3}{2} \end{bmatrix} = \begin{bmatrix} -\frac{15}{4} & \frac{49}{8} \\ 1 & \frac{17}{2} \end{bmatrix}$$

$$F_{11} = \begin{bmatrix} \frac{35}{76} & \frac{3}{19} \\ \frac{15}{152} & \frac{2}{19} \end{bmatrix} \qquad\qquad F_{22} = \begin{bmatrix} -\frac{17}{76} & \frac{49}{304} \\ \frac{1}{38} & \frac{15}{152} \end{bmatrix}$$

$$F_{21} = -E_{22}^{-1}E_{21}F_{11} = \begin{bmatrix} -\frac{91}{152} & -\frac{2}{19} \\ \\ -\frac{17}{76} & -\frac{2}{19} \end{bmatrix}$$

$$F_{12} = -E_{11}^{-1}E_{12}F_{22} = \begin{bmatrix} -\frac{11}{38} & -\frac{13}{152} \\ \\ \frac{17}{76} & \frac{27}{304} \end{bmatrix}$$

Therefore,

$$D_{11} = \begin{bmatrix} \frac{35}{76} & \frac{3}{19} & -\frac{11}{38} & -\frac{13}{152} \\ \\ \frac{15}{152} & \frac{2}{19} & \frac{17}{76} & \frac{27}{304} \\ \\ -\frac{91}{152} & -\frac{2}{19} & -\frac{17}{76} & \frac{49}{304} \\ \\ -\frac{17}{76} & -\frac{2}{19} & \frac{1}{38} & \frac{15}{152} \end{bmatrix} \qquad D_{22} = \begin{bmatrix} -\frac{27}{19} & -\frac{12}{19} \\ \\ -\frac{25}{19} & -\frac{9}{19} \end{bmatrix}$$

From these results, the remaining submatrices of D are found to be

$$D_{21} = -A_{22}^{-1}A_{21}D_{11} = \begin{bmatrix} -\frac{501}{152} & -\frac{25}{19} & \frac{25}{76} & \frac{223}{304} \\ \\ -\frac{295}{152} & -\frac{14}{19} & -\frac{5}{76} & \frac{77}{304} \end{bmatrix}$$

$$D_{12} = -A_{11}^{-1}A_{12}D_{22} = \begin{bmatrix} \frac{4}{19} & \frac{6}{19} \\ \\ \frac{9}{19} & \frac{4}{19} \\ \\ -\frac{9}{19} & -\frac{4}{19} \\ \\ -\frac{9}{19} & -\frac{4}{19} \end{bmatrix}$$

The inverse can now be written as

$$A^{-1} = D = \begin{bmatrix} \frac{35}{76} & \frac{3}{19} & -\frac{11}{38} & -\frac{13}{152} & \frac{4}{19} & \frac{6}{19} \\ \\ \frac{15}{152} & \frac{2}{19} & \frac{17}{76} & \frac{27}{304} & \frac{9}{19} & \frac{4}{19} \\ \\ -\frac{91}{152} & -\frac{2}{19} & -\frac{17}{76} & \frac{49}{304} & -\frac{9}{19} & -\frac{4}{19} \\ \\ -\frac{17}{76} & -\frac{2}{19} & \frac{1}{38} & \frac{15}{152} & -\frac{9}{19} & -\frac{4}{19} \\ \\ -\frac{501}{152} & -\frac{25}{19} & \frac{25}{76} & \frac{223}{304} & -\frac{27}{19} & -\frac{12}{19} \\ \\ -\frac{295}{152} & -\frac{14}{19} & -\frac{5}{76} & \frac{77}{304} & -\frac{25}{19} & -\frac{9}{19} \end{bmatrix}$$

That this matrix is the inverse can be verified. The result is left in exact fractional form to aid in this check.

The technique outlined in this section is a modification of one known as Gutemans Enlargement. In this process one builds up step by step the inverse of a matrix from the inverses of matrices of smaller dimension.

PROBLEMS

1. By the Crout method, find an approximation for the inverses of the following matrices correct to two decimal places.

(a)
$$\begin{bmatrix} 4 & 4 & -1 & -1 \\ 4 & -4 & 4 & 5 \\ -1 & 4 & -4 & 6 \\ -1 & 5 & 6 & -2 \end{bmatrix}$$

(b)
$$\begin{bmatrix} 2 & 1 & 4 & 3 \\ 6 & -1 & 2 & -4 \\ 3 & -2 & 5 & 1 \\ -5 & 6 & 4 & -1 \end{bmatrix}$$

(c)
$$\begin{bmatrix} 2 & 1 & 1 & 1 \\ -1 & 2 & 1 & 2 \\ 1 & 1 & 1 & 2 \\ 2 & 2 & 1 & 1 \end{bmatrix}$$

2. By the Doolittle method, find an approximation for the inverses of the following matrices correct to two decimal places.

(a) The matrix of Problem 1(a)

(b)
$$\begin{bmatrix} 4 & 7 & 7 & -2 \\ 7 & -2 & 0 & 2 \\ 7 & 0 & 10 & 5 \\ -2 & 2 & 5 & -2 \end{bmatrix}$$

3. Find an inverse for the matrices of Problems 1(a) and 2(b) by the technique of Chapter 2 and verify the results above.

4. By the method of partitioning find an approximation for the inverses of the following matrices correct to two decimal places.

(a) The matrix of Problem 1(c)

(b)
$$
\begin{bmatrix}
1 & 3 & -2 & 4 \\
-1 & -4 & 3 & 7 \\
2 & 1 & 7 & 0 \\
1 & -3 & -1 & 1
\end{bmatrix}
$$

(c)
$$
\begin{bmatrix}
1.31 & 6.15 & 3.14 \\
7.40 & -2.10 & 6.30 \\
5.10 & 6.42 & 1.00
\end{bmatrix}
$$

7

Inversion of Matrices by Iteration

7.1 Matrices Whose Powers Approach the Zero Matrix

In the last chapter, direct techniques for finding the inverse of a matrix were discussed. In this chapter, iterative techniques for finding the inverse of a matrix and for finding the solution for systems of linear equations will be considered. As noted at the beginning of Chapter 6, the iterative techniques are methods that employ a cycle of computations. The cycle is repeated until an answer with a prescribed accuracy is obtained.

In the iterative technique for finding the inverse of a matrix, the raising of an error matrix to higher and higher powers is basically involved. In order for the approximations for the inverse to approach the desired accuracy, the elements of these higher powers of the error matrix must become numerically smaller and approach 0. Fortunately, there is a simple test that can be used to determine when a matrix has this property. For this test, the sums of the absolute values of the elements in each row of the matrix are determined. If these sums are all less than 1, the matrix has the desired property. One can use the same test on the columns as well. It is possible for the set of row sums to have the property and the set of column sums not to have it or vice versa. The validity of this row sum test will be discussed later in this section.

177

To illustrate the assertions just made about the row sum test, consider the powers of the matrix E where

$$E = \begin{bmatrix} 0.7 & -0.1 & 0.1 \\ -0.3 & 0.4 & 0.1 \\ 0.2 & 0.4 & -0.3 \end{bmatrix} \qquad E^2 = \begin{bmatrix} 0.54 & -0.07 & 0.03 \\ -0.31 & 0.23 & -0.02 \\ -0.04 & 0.02 & 0.15 \end{bmatrix}$$

$$E^3 = \begin{bmatrix} 0.405 & -0.070 & 0.038 \\ -0.290 & 0.115 & -0.002 \\ -0.004 & 0.072 & -0.047 \end{bmatrix}$$

$$E^4 = \begin{bmatrix} 0.3121 & -0.0533 & 0.0221 \\ -0.2379 & 0.0742 & -0.0169 \\ -0.0338 & 0.0104 & 0.0209 \end{bmatrix}$$

The row sums for these matrices are

	E	E^2	E^3	E^4
$R1$	0.9	0.64	0.513	0.3875
$R2$	0.8	0.56	0.407	0.3290
$R3$	0.9	0.21	0.123	0.0651

It is apparent from this table that there is a decrease in corresponding row sums as the power of E is increased. This is not true for the absolute values of the corresponding elements of the matrices except for the elements of E^4.

In the matrices E^2, E^3, and E^4, some of the elements are numerically smaller than they would have been if all the elements of E were positive numbers. To see this, consider the powers of the matrix F where

$$F = \begin{bmatrix} 0.7 & 0.1 & 0.1 \\ 0.3 & 0.4 & 0.1 \\ 0.2 & 0.4 & 0.3 \end{bmatrix} \qquad F^2 = \begin{bmatrix} 0.54 & 0.15 & 0.11 \\ 0.35 & 0.23 & 0.10 \\ 0.32 & 0.30 & 0.15 \end{bmatrix}$$

$$F^3 = \begin{bmatrix} 0.445 & 0.158 & 0.102 \\ 0.334 & 0.167 & 0.088 \\ 0.344 & 0.212 & 0.107 \end{bmatrix} \qquad F^4 = \begin{bmatrix} 0.3793 & 0.1485 & 0.0909 \\ 0.3015 & 0.1354 & 0.0765 \\ 0.3258 & 0.1620 & 0.0877 \end{bmatrix}$$

The elements of F are chosen as the absolute values of the corresponding elements of E. Notice that every element of F^2, F^3, and F^4, is larger than the corresponding element of E^2, E^3, and E^4 except for the diagonal elements of F^2. This is a consequence of the fact that there were terms of different signs added to form the elements of E^2, E^3, and E^4. Still the row sums of powers of F decrease with an increase in the exponent m, for these sums are

	F	F^2	F^3	F^4
$R1$	0.9	0.80	0.705	0.6187
$R2$	0.8	0.68	0.589	0.5134
$R3$	0.9	0.77	0.663	0.5755.

This is true in general for any matrix F formed from a matrix E by taking the absolute values of its elements. This enables one to consider only matrices whose elements are positive in showing that the test is valid. When it is known that F^m is approximately equal to the zero matrix for some m, then E^m is approximately equal to the zero matrix.

The matrix F is also an example of a matrix whose column sums are not all less than 1. These sums are

	F	F^2	F^3	F^4
$C1$	1.2	1.21	1.123	1.0066
$C2$	0.9	0.68	0.537	0.4459
$C3$	0 5	0.36	0.297	0.2551.

Notice that the first column sum is greater than 1 in all four matrices but does decrease from a largest value in F^2 to a smallest value in F^4. It can be verified that the first column sum of F^5 is less than 1.

It remains to show that powers of a matrix whose row sums are all less than 1 will approach the zero matrix. This will follow from a consideration of the row sums of a given matrix B. There is at least one row sum of B of largest value p where $p < 1$. All other row sums of B are no larger than p. It will be shown that the row sums of B^m are no larger than p^m. This is done by noting that all row sums of a product of two matrices AB are no larger than p times the corresponding row sums of A. It will follow that all the row sums of B^m approach 0 as m is increased because p^m will approach 0. For the example matrices E and F, notice that $p = 0.9$. In the tables of row sums for F^k none exceeds $(0.9)^k$ as can be verified. As a matter of fact, the row sums in all cases are actually less than $(0.9)^k$.

Before taking up the general case, the row sums of the product of two 3×3 general matrices A and B will be considered. It will be assumed that all elements of the matrices are positive and that p is the value of the largest row sum of B. To simplify the proof, the notation $kRSC$ will be used to indicate the sum of the elements in the kth row of any matrix C. With these assumptions, consider the product of the two matrices,

$$AB = \begin{bmatrix} a_{11} & a_{12} & a_{13} \\ a_{21} & a_{22} & a_{23} \\ a_{31} & a_{32} & a_{33} \end{bmatrix} \begin{bmatrix} b_{11} & b_{12} & b_{13} \\ b_{21} & b_{22} & b_{23} \\ b_{31} & b_{32} & b_{33} \end{bmatrix}$$

$$= \begin{bmatrix} a_{11}b_{11} + a_{12}b_{21} + a_{13}b_{31} & a_{11}b_{12} + a_{12}b_{22} + a_{13}b_{32} & a_{11}b_{13} + a_{12}b_{23} + a_{13}b_{33} \\ a_{21}b_{11} + a_{22}b_{21} + a_{23}b_{31} & a_{21}b_{12} + a_{22}b_{22} + a_{23}b_{32} & a_{21}b_{13} + a_{22}b_{23} + a_{23}b_{33} \\ a_{31}b_{11} + a_{32}b_{21} + a_{33}b_{31} & a_{31}b_{12} + a_{32}b_{22} + a_{33}b_{32} & a_{31}b_{13} + a_{32}b_{23} + a_{33}b_{33} \end{bmatrix}$$

$$= \begin{bmatrix} \sum_{k=1}^{3} a_{1k}b_{k1} & \sum_{k=1}^{3} a_{1k}b_{k2} & \sum_{k=1}^{3} a_{1k}b_{k3} \\ \sum_{k=1}^{3} a_{2k}b_{k1} & \sum_{k=1}^{3} a_{2k}b_{k2} & \sum_{k=1}^{3} a_{2k}b_{k3} \\ \sum_{k=1}^{3} a_{3k}b_{k1} & \sum_{k=1}^{3} a_{3k}b_{k2} & \sum_{k=1}^{3} a_{3k}b_{k3} \end{bmatrix}$$

In this product matrix the sum of the elements in the first row is

$$(a_{11}b_{11} + a_{12}b_{21} + a_{13}b_{31}) + (a_{11}b_{12} + a_{12}b_{22} + a_{13}b_{32})$$

$$+ (a_{11}b_{13} + a_{12}b_{23} + a_{13}b_{33}) = a_{11}(b_{11} + b_{12} + b_{13}) + a_{12}(b_{21} + b_{22} + b_{23})$$

$$+ a_{13}(b_{31} + b_{32} + b_{33}) = a_{11}(1RSB) + a_{12}(2RSB) + a_{13}(3RSB)$$

$$\leq a_{11}p + a_{12}p + a_{13}p = p(1RSA)$$

In the derivation above notice that the terms are rearranged to include one set with a factor of a_{11}, one with a factor of a_{12}, and finally, the rest have a factor of a_{13}. These elements are factored out and what is inside the parentheses is then a row sum of B. Since p is the value of the largest row sum of B, $rRSB$ is less than or equal to p for $r = 1, 2, 3$.

For the second row sum the elements a_{21}, a_{22}, and a_{23} will appear in place of the a_{11}, a_{12}, and a_{13} so one has the inequality

$$2RSAB \leq p(2RSA)$$

Similarly, for the third row sum of AB the elements factored out are those of the third row vector of A. Hence, the third row has the same property as the other two.

The expressions above for $1RSAB$ could be shortened using the summation notation. These relationships for the $rRSAB$ could be written in the form

$$rRSAB = \sum_{k=1}^{3} a_{rk}b_{k1} + \sum_{k=1}^{3} a_{rk}b_{k2} + \sum_{k=1}^{3} a_{rk}b_{k3}$$

$$= a_{r1} \sum_{s=1}^{3} b_{1s} + a_{r2} \sum_{s=1}^{3} b_{2s} + a_{r3} \sum_{s=1}^{3} b_{3s}$$

$$= a_{r1}(1RSB) + a_{r2}(2RSB) + a_{r3}(3RSB)$$

$$\leq a_{r1}p + a_{r2}p + a_{r3}p = p(rRSA)$$

This result shows that the row sums of AB are no greater than the product of the maximum row sum of B and the corresponding row sum of A.

This result can be extended to the product of two general $n \times n$ matrices A and B. Let p be the value of the largest row sum of B so that $kRSB$ is no larger than p for $k = 1, 2, \cdots, n$. The product

$$AB = (a_{rs})(b_{rs}) = \left(\sum_{k=1}^{n} a_{rk}b_{ks} \right)$$

Considering only the elements in the rth row, that is, the elements obtained for a fixed r and for s varying from 1 to n,

$$rRSAB = \sum_{k=1}^{n} a_{rk}b_{k1} + \sum_{k=1}^{n} a_{rk}b_{k2} + \cdots + \sum_{k=1}^{n} a_{rk}b_{kn}$$

$$= \sum_{s=1}^{n} \sum_{k=1}^{n} a_{rk}b_{ks}$$

$$= \sum_{k=1}^{n} a_{rk} \sum_{s=1}^{n} b_{ks} = \sum_{k=1}^{n} a_{rk}kRSB$$

$$\leq \sum_{k=1}^{n} pa_{rk} = p(rRSA)$$

If the matrix $A = B$, the discussion above shows that the row sums of B^2 are less than or equal to the product of p and the corresponding row sum of B. This means for this case that the row sums of B^2 are no larger than p^2. Letting $A = B^2$, one can conclude that the row sums of B^3 are no larger than the product of p and the corresponding row sum of B^2. Since the largest row sum of B^2 is no greater than p^2, the row sums of B^3 are all less than or equal to p^3. In a similar manner, one can conclude by letting $A = B^k$ that the row sums of B^{k+1} are no larger than the product of p and the corresponding row sums of B^k. Since the row sums of B^k are no larger than p^k, the row sums of B^{k+1} are no larger than p^{k+1}. By assumption, p is less than 1 so that p^k will approach 0 as k increases. This means that for some integer m, p^m is approximately equal to 0. Because the row sums of B^m are no larger than p^m, they must all be approximately equal to 0. Since the elements in each of the rows of the powers of the matrix B are all assumed to be positive numbers, their sum approaching 0 as the power is increased implies that each element must approach 0. In other words, for some positive integer m, B^m is approximately equal to the zero matrix.

One can make a similar argument using column sums in place of row sums. The column sums of the product BA are less than or equal to the product of the maximum column sum of B by the corresponding column sums of A if both A and B have all column sums less than 1. By letting $A = B^k$, one can conclude that the column sums of B^{k+1} will approach 0 as k is increased. Hence, for some m, B^m is approximately equal to the zero matrix.

7.2 An Iterative Method

With the background of the last section, the basic iterative procedure for finding the inverse of a matrix can be discussed. For this, assume an approximation D_0 for A^{-1} which is to be improved. For this process, the following sequence is defined.

$$D_1 = (2I - D_0 A)D_0$$

$$D_2 = (2I - D_1 A)D_1$$

$$\cdot \quad \cdot \quad \cdot$$

$$D_m = (2I - D_{m-1} A)D_{m-1}$$

Also let

$$C = I - D_0 A$$

This last statement says the error in using D_0 as the inverse of A is given by the matrix C. It will be shown that the error made in using the successive approximations $D_1, D_2, \cdots, D_m$ will be higher and higher powers of C.

This means that if the D_0 is close enough to A^{-1} so that C has either its row or column sums all less than 1, then an approximation for A^{-1} can be obtained to any accuracy required. To see that powers of the matrix C are the errors in the use of the D_1 D_2, $\cdots$, D_m, consider the following derivations of the $I - D_k A$.

The definition of C implies that

$$(1) \qquad\qquad D_0 A = I - C$$

$$(2) \qquad\qquad I + C = 2I - D_0 A$$

The first expression is obtained by solving for $D_0 A$ in the definition of C. The second expression is derived by adding I to both sides of the definition. If Equation (1) is multiplied by A^{-1} on the right, it becomes

$$D_0 = (I - C) A^{-1}$$

This result and Equation (2) give the factors for

$$D_1 = (2I - D_0 A) D_0 = (I + C)(I - C) A^{-1} = (I - C^2) A^{-1}$$

Multiplying on the right by A,

$$D_1 A = I - C^2$$

and hence,

$$C^2 = I - D_1 A \qquad I + C^2 = 2I - D_1 A$$

The expression for C^2 says that this is the error in using D_1 as the inverse of A. The last relation and the original one for D_1 enables one to write

$$D_2 = (2I - D_1 A) D_1 = (I + C^2)(I - C^2) A^{-1}$$
$$= (I - C^4) A^{-1}$$

so that

$$D_2 A = I - C^4 \qquad C^4 = I - D_2 A \qquad I + C^4 = 2I - D_2 A$$

Again notice that this shows that C^4 is the error in using D_2 as the inverse.

Going through the cycle again gives

$$D_3 = (2I - D_2 A) D_2 = (I + C^4)(I - C^4) A^{-1} = (I - C^8) A^{-1}$$
$$C^8 = I - D_3 A \qquad I + C^8 = 2I - D_3 A$$

In general then,

$$D_m = (2I - D_{m-1} A) D_{m-1} = (I + C^{2^{m-1}})(I - C^{2^{m-1}}) A^{-1} = (I - C^{2^m}) A^{-1}$$
$$C^{2^m} = I - D_m A \qquad I + C^{2^m} = 2I - D_m A$$

What has been shown is that the error made decreases geometrically with the successive D_k. This means the accuracy should improve fairly rapidly. When one finds that C^{2^m} is approximately equal to the zero matrix, then $D_m A$ is approximately equal to the identity matrix so D_m is approximately equal to A^{-1}. To illustrate this, consider the matrix

$$A = \begin{bmatrix} 1 & -2 & -1 \\ 4 & -3 & 1 \\ 3 & -1 & -2 \end{bmatrix}$$

As an approximation to the inverse of A, let

$$D_0 = \begin{bmatrix} -0.4 & 0.1 & 0.3 \\ -0.6 & -0.1 & 0.2 \\ -0.3 & 0.2 & -0.2 \end{bmatrix}$$

Forming the product

$$D_0 A = \begin{bmatrix} -0.4 & 0.1 & 0.3 \\ -0.6 & -0.1 & 0.2 \\ -0.3 & 0.2 & -0.2 \end{bmatrix} \begin{bmatrix} 1 & -2 & -1 \\ 4 & -3 & 1 \\ 3 & -1 & -2 \end{bmatrix} = \begin{bmatrix} 0.9 & 0.2 & -0.1 \\ -0.4 & 1.3 & 0.1 \\ -0.1 & 0.2 & 0.9 \end{bmatrix}$$

Subtracting this product from the identity matrix gives the error matrix

$$C = I - D_0 A = \begin{bmatrix} 1 & 0 & 0 \\ 0 & 1 & 0 \\ 0 & 0 & 1 \end{bmatrix} - \begin{bmatrix} 0.9 & 0.2 & -0.1 \\ -0.4 & 1.3 & 0.1 \\ -0.1 & 0.2 & 0.9 \end{bmatrix}$$

$$= \begin{bmatrix} 0.1 & -0.2 & 0.1 \\ 0.4 & -0.3 & -0.1 \\ 0.1 & -0.2 & 0.1 \end{bmatrix}$$

A quick check shows that this error matrix has its row sums all less than 1. As a check on the computations for the D_i, certain powers of C

need to be found. This will also be an aid in deciding how far it is necessary to go in the process to obtain the desired accuracy. These powers are

$$C^2 = \begin{bmatrix} -0.06 & 0.02 & 0.04 \\ -0.09 & 0.03 & 0.06 \\ -0.06 & 0.02 & 0.04 \end{bmatrix} \quad C^4 = \begin{bmatrix} -0.0006 & 0.0002 & 0.0004 \\ -0.0009 & 0.0003 & 0.0006 \\ -0.0006 & 0.0002 & 0.0004 \end{bmatrix}$$

$$C^8 = \begin{bmatrix} -0.00000006 & 0.00000002 & 0.00000004 \\ -0.00000009 & 0.00000003 & 0.00000006 \\ -0.00000006 & 0.00000002 & 0.00000004 \end{bmatrix}$$

From this it follows that D_3 would give an approximation for the inverse of A good to six decimal places. To find D_3, first of all compute

$$D_1 = (2I - D_0 A)D_0 = \begin{bmatrix} 1.1 & -0.2 & 0.1 \\ 0.4 & 0.7 & -0.1 \\ 0.1 & -0.2 & 1.1 \end{bmatrix} \begin{bmatrix} -0.4 & 0.1 & 0.3 \\ -0.6 & -0.1 & 0.2 \\ -0.3 & 0.2 & -0.2 \end{bmatrix}$$

and

$$D_1 A = \begin{bmatrix} -0.35 & 0.15 & 0.27 \\ -0.55 & -0.05 & 0.28 \\ -0.25 & 0.25 & -0.23 \end{bmatrix} \begin{bmatrix} 1 & -2 & -1 \\ 4 & -3 & 1 \\ 3 & -1 & -2 \end{bmatrix}$$

$$= \begin{bmatrix} 1.06 & -0.02 & -0.04 \\ 0.09 & 0.97 & -0.06 \\ 0.06 & -0.02 & 0.96 \end{bmatrix}$$

As a check, this matrix should differ from the identity matrix by the matrix C^2. It can easily be seen that this is true.

With this result it follows that

$$D_2 = (2I - D_1 A)D_1 = \begin{bmatrix} 0.94 & 0.02 & 0.04 \\ -0.09 & 1.03 & 0.06 \\ -0.06 & 0.02 & 1.04 \end{bmatrix} \begin{bmatrix} -0.35 & 0.15 & 0.27 \\ -0.55 & -0.05 & 0.28 \\ -0.25 & 0.25 & -0.23 \end{bmatrix}$$

and

$$D_2A = \begin{bmatrix} -0.3500 & 0.1500 & 0.2502 \\ -0.5500 & -0.0500 & 0.2503 \\ -0.2500 & 0.2500 & -0.2498 \end{bmatrix} \begin{bmatrix} 1 & -2 & -1 \\ 4 & -3 & 1 \\ 3 & -1 & -2 \end{bmatrix}$$

$$= \begin{bmatrix} 1.0006 & -0.0002 & -0.0004 \\ 0.0009 & 0.9997 & -0.0006 \\ 0.0006 & -0.0002 & 0.9996 \end{bmatrix}$$

Again comparing this with the identity matrix it is seen that their difference is equal to the matrix C^4. Finally then,

$$D_3 = (2I - D_2A)D_2$$

$$= \begin{bmatrix} 0.9994 & 0.0002 & 0.0004 \\ -0.0009 & 1.0003 & 0.0006 \\ -0.0006 & 0.0002 & 1.0004 \end{bmatrix} \begin{bmatrix} -0.3500 & 0.1500 & 0.2502 \\ -0.5500 & -0.0500 & 0.2503 \\ -0.2500 & 0.2500 & -0.2498 \end{bmatrix}$$

$$= \begin{bmatrix} -0.35000000 & 0.15000000 & 0.25000002 \\ -0.55000000 & -0.05000000 & 0.25000003 \\ -0.25000000 & 0.25000000 & -0.24999998 \end{bmatrix}$$

If the product D_3A is formed, it will be found that when it is subtracted from I that the difference is C^8. This means that apparently no errors have been made in the computations.

Rounding off D_3 to 6 decimal places,

$$D_3 = \begin{bmatrix} -0.350000 & 0.150000 & 0.250000 \\ -0.550000 & -0.050000 & 0.250000 \\ -0.250000 & 0.250000 & -0.250000 \end{bmatrix}$$

For this problem one might suspect this is the exact answer. That assumption is correct as can be easily verified by comparison with the inverse found for this matrix in Section 6.1.

It should be noted that in case one obtains a D_i which is exact so that $D_iA = I$, then

$$D_{i+1} = (2I - D_iA)D_i = (2I - I)D_i = ID_i = D_i$$

Thus the process would terminate when two successive D_i were the same and each would be the desired inverse.

7.3 Strongly Diagonal Matrices

There is a type of matrix with real elements whose inverse is easily approximated so that the above procedure could be applied. This type of matrix is known as a *strongly diagonal matrix*. It is also called "essentially diagonal." This refers to a matrix whose diagonal elements each have absolute value in excess of the sum of the absolute values of the other elements in its row. If each of the rows of a strongly diagonal matrix is divided by its diagonal element, the resulting matrix will be one whose row sums are all less than 2. This means that the matrix that is equal to the difference between the identity matrix and this new matrix has row sums less than 1 so this new matrix has the property described in Section 7.1.

Using this as a clue, a process for finding the inverse of a strongly diagonal matrix can be outlined. The first step is to choose D_0 as the diagonal matrix,

$$D_0 = \begin{bmatrix} a_{11}^{-1} & 0 & \cdots & 0 \\ 0 & a_{22}^{-1} & \cdots & 0 \\ \cdot & \cdot & \cdots & \cdot \\ \cdot & \cdot & \cdots & \cdot \\ \cdot & \cdot & \cdots & \cdot \\ 0 & 0 & \cdots & a_{nn}^{-1} \end{bmatrix}$$

Then $C = I - D_0A$ is a matrix whose row sums are less than 1 for it is the matrix mentioned in the last paragraph. As a simple numerical example, let

$$A = \begin{bmatrix} 4 & -2.8 & 1 \\ 1 & -2 & -0.8 \\ 0.3 & -1 & -2 \end{bmatrix}$$

A check of the rows of this matrix shows that for

$$\text{row 1: } 2.8 + 1 = 3.8 < 4$$

$$\text{row 2: } 1 + 0.8 = 1.8 < 2$$

$$\text{row 3: } 0.3 + 1 = 1.3 < 2$$

so the matrix is strongly diagonal. Let

$$D_0 = \begin{bmatrix} 0.25 & 0 & 0 \\ 0 & -0.5 & 0 \\ 0 & 0 & -0.5 \end{bmatrix}$$

Then,

$$C = I - D_0 A = \begin{bmatrix} 1 & 0 & 0 \\ 0 & 1 & 0 \\ 0 & 0 & 1 \end{bmatrix} - \begin{bmatrix} 1 & -0.7 & 0.25 \\ -0.5 & 1 & 0.4 \\ -0.15 & 0.5 & 1 \end{bmatrix}$$

$$= \begin{bmatrix} 0 & 0.7 & -0.25 \\ 0.5 & 0 & -0.4 \\ 0.15 & -0.5 & 0 \end{bmatrix}$$

Notice that

$$1 RSC = 0.70 + 0.25 = 0.95 < 1$$
$$2 RSC = 0.50 + 0.40 = 0.90 < 1$$
$$3 RSC = 0.15 + 0.50 = 0.65 < 1$$

This means the matrix C has the desired property of Section 7.1. Thus this D_0 can be used to find A^{-1} by the method of that section.

It is possible to put some matrices into strongly diagonal form. This can be done by first locating the element of A of maximum numerical value. By interchanging row vectors, this maximal element is placed on the diagonal. Then one deletes from A the row and column vector to which this dominant element belongs in its new position. In the submatrix formed, the process is repeated. The dominant element is determined and then placed on the diagonal. The associated vectors are deleted and the cycle repeated until all diagonal elements are determined. The final result of this procedure can be checked to see if the matrix formed is strongly diagonal. If so, one can find the inverse of the original matrix using the method of this section. This is done by first finding the inverse of the strongly diagonal matrix to the desired accuracy. Then one performs on the columns of this matrix the same interchanges, but in reverse order, as were made on the rows of A to make it strongly diagonal. The result will be A^{-1}. To show that this is true, suppose that one determines a strongly diagonal matrix B by performing on A the elementary row operations of type one whose matrices are E_1, E_2, $\cdots$, E_t, so that

$$B = E_t \cdots E_2 E_1 A$$

Multiplying on the right by A^{-1} and on the left by B^{-1}, one has

$$B^{-1} B A^{-1} = B^{-1} E_t \cdots E_2 E_1 A A^{-1}$$

Simplyifying this equation, one obtains the new matrix equation,

$$A^{-1} = B^{-1} E_t \cdots E_2 E_1$$

This says the columns of B^{-1} are interchanged in the reverse order to that of the interchanges of the rows of A to obtain B. This means that one has to keep track of the row interchanges made on A.

It is possible to alter A by using column operations. The B^{-1} this time would have to have the corresponding row operations performed on it in reverse order to obtain A^{-1}. Finally one can use a combination of both row and column operations. One might want to order the dominant elements on the diagonal. If so, then a combination of the row and column operations could be used. In determining A^{-1}, one would have to take great care that the elementary operations of type one that are used to alter A are changed from row operations to column operations and vice versa, and that their order is reversed.

7.4 Solutions of Systems of Linear Equations

The technique of the last section has its counterpart for solving systems of equations. This method is known as the Gauss-Seidel process. It is assumed that the system has a coefficient matrix that is strongly diagonal. If not, it might be possible that by reordering the equations, one could make the coefficient matrix strongly diagonal. Of course, not all systems have this property so this method will not always be applicable.

The first step in the process involves a simplification of the coefficient matrix A for the system of equations. The matrix D_0 of Section 7.3 is used to multiply on the left, the matrix equation $AX = G$ of the system. This would give $D_0 A$ as the coefficient matrix of the new system of equations and $D_0 G$ as the constant vector. Defining $D_0 A = I - C$ and $D_0 G = H$, the new system can be written in the form

$$(I - C)X = H$$

where the matrix C would have row sums less than 1. Adding CX to both sides of the matrix equation, one has

$$X = CX + H$$

as a new way of writing the system of equations.

Next assume an approximation for the solution X to the system and let it be denoted as $X^{[0]}$. Define the following series of successive approximations

$$X^{[1]} = CX^{[0]} + H$$

$$X^{[2]} = CX^{[1]} + H$$

$$X^{[3]} = CX^{[2]} + H$$

$$\cdot \quad \cdot \quad \cdot$$

$$X^{[i+1]} = CX^{[i]} + H$$

In order to show that this method will give better approximations for the solution X, consider the following expressions for them in terms of the initial approximation.

$$X^{[2]} = CX^{[1]} + H = C(CX^{[0]} + H) + H = C^2X^{[0]} + CH + H$$

$$X^{[3]} = CX^{[2]} + H = C(C^2X^{[0]} + CH + H) + H$$
$$= C^3X^{[0]} + C^2H + CH + H$$

$$X^{[4]} = CX^{[3]} + H = C(C^3X^{[0]} + C^2H + CH + H) + H$$
$$= C^4X^{[0]} + C^3H + C^2H + CH + H$$

$$\cdot \quad \cdot \quad \cdot$$

$$X^{[i]} = CX^{[i-1]} + H = C(C^{i-1}X^{[0]} + C^{i-2}H + \cdots + CH + H) + H$$
$$= C^iX^{[0]} + C^{i-1}H + \cdots + C^2H + CH + H$$

$$X^{[i+1]} = CX^{[i]} + H = C(C^iX^{[0]} + C^{i-1}H + \cdots + CH + H) + H$$
$$= C^{i+1}X^{[0]} + C^iH + \cdots + C^2H + CH + H$$

The differences between successive pairs of approximations are

$$X^{[2]} - X^{[1]} = (C^2 - C)X^{[0]} + CH$$

$$X^{[3]} - X^{[2]} = (C^3 - C^2)X^{[0]} + C^2H$$

$$X^{[4]} - X^{[3]} = (C^4 - C^3)X^{[0]} + C^3H$$

$$\cdot \quad \cdot \quad \cdot$$

$$X^{[i+1]} - X^{[i]} = (C^{i+1} - C^i)X^{[0]} + C^iH$$

Since the matrix C has row sums less than 1, for some positive integer m, C^m is approximately equal to the zero matrix. This means that the difference between two successive approximations for X must approach 0, or in other words, they must be nearly equal. This would mean that if $X^{[m+1]}$ is nearly equal to $X^{[m]}$, then in the equation

$$X^{[m+1]} = CX^{[m]} + H$$

one can replace $X^{[m+1]}$ by $X^{[m]}$. The resulting equation

$$X^{[m]} = CX^{[m]} + H$$

is of the form used in writing the problem down. In other words, $X^{[m]}$ is a solution to the system with the desired degree of accuracy.

To illustrate this process, consider the system of equations

$$-4x_1 - 5x_2 + 20x_3 = 4$$
$$8x_1 - 2x_2 + 3x_3 = 1$$
$$-1x_1 + 10x_2 + 2x_3 = 3$$

The coefficient matrix here is not strongly diagonal in its present form. If the equations are rewritten as

$$8x_1 - 2x_2 + 3x_3 = 1$$
$$-1x_1 + 10x_2 + 2x_3 = 3$$
$$-4x_1 - 5x_2 + 20x_3 = 4$$

then the coefficient matrix of this system is strongly diagonal. For this system, the matrix D_0 is

$$D_0 = \begin{bmatrix} 0.125 & 0 & 0 \\ 0 & 0.1 & 0 \\ 0 & 0 & 0.05 \end{bmatrix}$$

$$D_0 A = \begin{bmatrix} 1.000 & -0.250 & 0.375 \\ -0.100 & 1.000 & 0.200 \\ -0.200 & -0.250 & 1.000 \end{bmatrix}$$

$$= \begin{bmatrix} 1 & 0 & 0 \\ 0 & 1 & 0 \\ 0 & 0 & 1 \end{bmatrix} - \begin{bmatrix} 0.000 & 0.250 & -0.375 \\ 0.100 & 0.000 & -0.200 \\ 0.200 & 0.250 & 0.000 \end{bmatrix} = I - C$$

and

$$H = D_0G = \begin{bmatrix} 0.125 \\ 0.300 \\ 0.200 \end{bmatrix}$$

This system can be written in the form

$$\begin{bmatrix} x_1 \\ x_2 \\ x_3 \end{bmatrix} = \begin{bmatrix} 0.000 & 0.250 & -0.375 \\ 0.100 & 0.000 & -0.200 \\ 0.200 & 0.250 & 0.000 \end{bmatrix} \begin{bmatrix} x_1 \\ x_2 \\ x_3 \end{bmatrix} + \begin{bmatrix} 0.125 \\ 0.300 \\ 0.200 \end{bmatrix}$$

As a first approximation, let

$$X^{[0]} = H = \begin{bmatrix} 0.125 \\ 0.300 \\ 0.200 \end{bmatrix}$$

The following table gives the results of the calculations for

$$X^{[i]} = CX^{[i-1]} + H.$$

$X^{[0]}$	$CX^{[0]}$	$X^{[1]}$	$CX^{[1]}$	$X^{[2]}$	$CX^{[2]}$	$X^{[3]}$	$CX^{[3]}$
0.125	0.0000	0.1250	−0.0444	0.0806	−0.0494	0.0756	−0.0427
0.300	−0.0275	0.2725	−0.0475	0.2525	−0.0519	0.2481	−0.0483
0.200	0.1000	0.3000	0.1000	0.3000	0.0792	0.2792	0.0771

$X^{[4]}$	$CX^{[4]}$	$X^{[5]}$	$CX^{[5]}$	$X^{[6]}$	$CX^{[6]}$	$X^{[7]}$
0.0823	−0.0410	0.0840	−0.04158	0.08342	−0.041870	0.083130
0.2517	−0.0472	0.2528	−0.04748	0.25252	−0.047658	0.252342
0.2771	0.0794	0.2794	0.08000	0.28000	0.079814	0.279814

$CX^{[7]}$	$X^{[8]}$	$CX^{[8]}$	$X^{[9]}$	$CX^{[9]}$	$X^{[10]}$
−0.041845	0.083155	−0.041800	0.083200	−0.041801	0.083199
−0.047650	0.252350	−0.047624	0.252376	−0.047624	0.252376
0.079712	0.279700	0.079718	0.279719	0.079734	0.279734

The answer to four decimal places would be

$$X = \begin{bmatrix} 0.0832 \\ 0.2524 \\ 0.2797 \end{bmatrix}$$

7.5 *Extension of the Gauss-Seidel Method*

In the last section, each new approximation for the vector X was deter-mined from the previous one by matrix multiplication. Each equation in the system $X = CX + H$ was used to determine a new approximation for one unknown as a linear combination of a constant from H and the old approximations for the other unknowns. If one were to take, in order, only one equation at a time and use the last approximation for each variable, the number of approximations for each variable should be less. To illustrate this for the 3×3 case, let the first approximation $X^{[1]}$ be given by

$$x_1^{[1]} = (0)x_1^{[0]} + c_{12}x_2^{[0]} + c_{13}x_3^{[0]} + h_1$$

$$x_2^{[1]} = c_{21}x_1^{[1]} + (0)x_2^{[0]} + c_{23}x_3^{[0]} + h_2$$

$$x_3^{[1]} = c_{31}x_1^{[1]} + c_{32}x_2^{[1]} + (0)x_3^{[0]} + h_3$$

Notice that in the second and third equations, the new approximation is used for x_1 and in the third there is also the new approximation for x_2.

The problem now is to express this technique in terms of matrix multi-plication. This requires rewriting the equation $X = CX + H$ for the 3×3 case in the slightly different form

$$x_1 = (0)x_1 + c_{12}x_2 + c_{13}x_3 + h_1 \cdot 1$$

$$x_2 = c_{21}x_1 + (0)x_2 + c_{23}x_3 + h_2 \cdot 1$$

$$x_3 = c_{31}x_1 + c_{32}x_2 + (0)x_3 + h_3 \cdot 1$$

$$1 = (0)x_1 + (0)x_2 + (0)x_3 + 1 \cdot 1$$

or written in matrix notation this is

$$\begin{bmatrix} x_1 \\ x_2 \\ x_3 \\ 1 \end{bmatrix} = \begin{bmatrix} 0 & c_{12} & c_{13} & h_1 \\ c_{21} & 0 & c_{23} & h_2 \\ c_{31} & c_{32} & 0 & h_3 \\ 0 & 0 & 0 & 1 \end{bmatrix} \begin{bmatrix} x_1 \\ x_2 \\ x_3 \\ 1 \end{bmatrix}$$

Notice that in this form the last equation is simply $1 = 1$. This device is a useful way to incorporate the constants into a coefficient matrix,

The new approximation $x_1^{[1]}$ is determined by the first equation. The following matrix product will give this new approximation for x_1 while leaving the other unknowns unchanged.

$$
\begin{bmatrix} x_1^{[1]} \\ x_2^{[0]} \\ x_3^{[0]} \\ 1 \end{bmatrix}
=
\begin{bmatrix} 0 & c_{12} & c_{13} & h_1 \\ 0 & 1 & 0 & 0 \\ 0 & 0 & 1 & 0 \\ 0 & 0 & 0 & 1 \end{bmatrix}
\begin{bmatrix} x_1^{[0]} \\ x_2^{[0]} \\ x_3^{[0]} \\ 1 \end{bmatrix}
$$

In a similar manner, the change in the second variable can be expressed as the matrix product

$$
\begin{bmatrix} x_1^{[1]} \\ x_2^{[1]} \\ x_3^{[0]} \\ 1 \end{bmatrix}
=
\begin{bmatrix} 1 & 0 & 0 & 0 \\ c_{21} & 0 & c_{23} & h_2 \\ 0 & 0 & 1 & 0 \\ 0 & 0 & 0 & 1 \end{bmatrix}
\begin{bmatrix} x_1^{[1]} \\ x_2^{[0]} \\ x_3^{[0]} \\ 1 \end{bmatrix}
$$

Finally, the change in the last variable is determined by

$$
\begin{bmatrix} x_1^{[1]} \\ x_2^{[1]} \\ x_3^{[1]} \\ 1 \end{bmatrix}
=
\begin{bmatrix} 1 & 0 & 0 & 0 \\ 0 & 1 & 0 & 0 \\ c_{31} & c_{32} & 0 & h_3 \\ 0 & 0 & 0 & 1 \end{bmatrix}
\begin{bmatrix} x_1^{[1]} \\ x_2^{[1]} \\ x_3^{[0]} \\ 1 \end{bmatrix}
$$

If the 4×4 matrices in the products are designated by T_1, T_2, and T_3, respectively, then

$$
T_3 T_2 T_1 \begin{bmatrix} x_1^{[0]} \\ x_2^{[0]} \\ x_3^{[0]} \\ 1 \end{bmatrix}
= T_3 T_2 \begin{bmatrix} x_1^{[1]} \\ x_2^{[0]} \\ x_3^{[0]} \\ 1 \end{bmatrix}
= T_3 \begin{bmatrix} x_1^{[1]} \\ x_2^{[1]} \\ x_3^{[0]} \\ 1 \end{bmatrix}
= \begin{bmatrix} x_1^{[1]} \\ x_2^{[1]} \\ x_3^{[1]} \\ 1 \end{bmatrix}
$$

In other words, it takes the product of three matrices to obtain the new approximation for all three variables. The advantage here is that one obtains better approximations for the last variables to be considered than were found in the previous section. However, the price paid is the increased complexity of having to perform more matrix multiplications. If one defines $T = T_3 T_2 T_1$ and

$$X^{[i]} = \begin{bmatrix} x_1^{[i]} \\ x_2^{[i]} \\ x_3^{[i]} \\ 1 \end{bmatrix}$$

then the successive approximations can be written as

$$X^{[1]} = TX^{[0]}$$

$$X^{[2]} = TX^{[1]}$$

$$\cdot \quad \cdot \quad \cdot$$

$$X^{[i+1]} = TX^{[i]}$$

This procedure can be illustrated with the system used in Section 7.4. For that system, the matrix T is determined by the product

$$T_3 T_2 T_1 = T_3 \begin{bmatrix} 1 & 0 & 0 & 0 \\ 0.1 & 0 & -0.2 & 0.3 \\ 0 & 0 & 1 & 0 \\ 0 & 0 & 0 & 1 \end{bmatrix} \begin{bmatrix} 0 & 0.25 & -0.375 & 0.125 \\ 0 & 1 & 0 & 0 \\ 0 & 0 & 1 & 0 \\ 0 & 0 & 0 & 1 \end{bmatrix}$$

$$= \begin{bmatrix} 1 & 0 & 0 & 0 \\ 0 & 1 & 0 & 0 \\ 0.2 & 0.25 & 0 & 0.2 \\ 0 & 0 & 0 & 1 \end{bmatrix} \begin{bmatrix} 0 & 0.25 & -0.375 & 0.125 \\ 0 & 0.025 & -0.2375 & 0.3125 \\ 0 & 0 & 1 & 0 \\ 0 & 0 & 0 & 1 \end{bmatrix}$$

$$= \begin{bmatrix} 0 & 0.25 & -0.375 & 0.125 \\ 0 & 0.025 & -0.2375 & 0.3125 \\ 0 & 0.05625 & -0.134375 & 0.303125 \\ 0 & 0 & 0 & 1 \end{bmatrix}$$

The following table shows the results of the computations involved in finding $X^{[i+1]} = TX^{[i]}$.

$X^{[0]}$	$X^{[1]}$	$X^{[2]}$	$X^{[3]}$	$X^{[4]}$	$X^{[5]}$
0.125	0.1250	0.0832	0.08276	0.083239	0.083194
0.300	0.2725	0.2497	0.25246	0.252390	0.252363
0.200	0.2931	0.2791	0.27967	0.279745	0.279731
1	1	1	1	1	1

Therefore,

$$X = \begin{bmatrix} 0.0832 \\ 0.2524 \\ 0.2797 \end{bmatrix}$$

to four decimal places.

This result is the same X that was found in Section 7.4. Notice that fewer steps were required. However, one disadvantage to this process is the necessity for computing the matrix T. Any errors brought into its computation will cause errors in the result obtained.

The generalization of this process to the case of n equations in n unknowns can be made. One has to find n different matrices, each one of which will change only one variable using the last approximation for each of the others. The ordered product of these matrices can be formed to give the matrix T.

There are two other ways that one can compute the matrix T. The first one can be illustrated using the system of three equations used at the beginning of this section. This system can be written in the matrix form

$$\begin{bmatrix} 1 & 0 & 0 & 0 \\ 0 & 1 & 0 & 0 \\ 0 & 0 & 1 & 0 \\ 0 & 0 & 0 & 1 \end{bmatrix}\begin{bmatrix} x_1^{[1]} \\ x_2^{[1]} \\ x_3^{[1]} \\ 1 \end{bmatrix} = \begin{bmatrix} 0 & c_{12} & c_{13} & h_1 \\ 0 & 0 & c_{23} & h_2 \\ 0 & 0 & 0 & h_3 \\ 0 & 0 & 0 & 1 \end{bmatrix}\begin{bmatrix} x_1^{[0]} \\ x_2^{[0]} \\ x_3^{[0]} \\ 1 \end{bmatrix} + \begin{bmatrix} 0 & 0 & 0 & 0 \\ c_{21} & 0 & 0 & 0 \\ c_{31} & c_{32} & 0 & 0 \\ 0 & 0 & 0 & 0 \end{bmatrix}\begin{bmatrix} x_1^{[1]} \\ x_2^{[1]} \\ x_3^{[1]} \\ 1 \end{bmatrix}$$

Subtracting the second matrix product on the right from both sides of the equation, one finds that

$$\begin{bmatrix} 1 & 0 & 0 & 0 \\ -c_{21} & 1 & 0 & 0 \\ -c_{31} & -c_{32} & 1 & 0 \\ 0 & 0 & 0 & 1 \end{bmatrix}\begin{bmatrix} x_1^{[1]} \\ x_2^{[1]} \\ x_3^{[1]} \\ 1 \end{bmatrix} = \begin{bmatrix} 0 & c_{12} & c_{13} & h_1 \\ 0 & 0 & c_{23} & h_2 \\ 0 & 0 & 0 & h_3 \\ 0 & 0 & 0 & 1 \end{bmatrix}\begin{bmatrix} x_1^{[0]} \\ x_2^{[0]} \\ x_3^{[0]} \\ 1 \end{bmatrix}$$

Notice the coefficient matrix on the left is nonsingular since it is triangular with all nonzero elements on the diagonal. Multiplying both sides of the equation by the inverse of this matrix, one obtains

$$
\begin{bmatrix} x_1^{[1]} \\ x_2^{[1]} \\ x_3^{[1]} \\ 1 \end{bmatrix} = \begin{bmatrix} 1 & 0 & 0 & 0 \\ -c_{21} & 1 & 0 & 0 \\ -c_{31} & -c_{32} & 1 & 0 \\ 0 & 0 & 0 & 1 \end{bmatrix}^{-1} \begin{bmatrix} 0 & c_{12} & c_{13} & h_1 \\ 0 & 0 & c_{23} & h_2 \\ 0 & 0 & 0 & h_3 \\ 0 & 0 & 0 & 1 \end{bmatrix} \begin{bmatrix} x_1^{[0]} \\ x_2^{[0]} \\ x_3^{[0]} \\ 1 \end{bmatrix}
$$

Comparing this with the formulae for the successive approximations shows that the product of the two 4×4 matrices must be the matrix T.

For the numerical example of this section,

$$
T = \begin{bmatrix} 1 & 0 & 0 & 0 \\ -0.1 & 1 & 0 & 0 \\ -0.2 & -0.25 & 1 & 0 \\ 0 & 0 & 0 & 1 \end{bmatrix}^{-1} \begin{bmatrix} 0 & 0.25 & -0.375 & 0.125 \\ 0 & 0 & -0.2 & 0.3 \\ 0 & 0 & 0 & 0.2 \\ 0 & 0 & 0 & 1 \end{bmatrix}
$$

Computing the inverse of the first matrix, and forming the product for T, one finds that

$$
T = \begin{bmatrix} 1 & 0 & 0 & 0 \\ 0.1 & 1 & 0 & 0 \\ 0.225 & 0.25 & 1 & 0 \\ 0 & 0 & 0 & 1 \end{bmatrix} \begin{bmatrix} 0 & 0.25 & -0.375 & 0.125 \\ 0 & 0 & -0.2 & 0.3 \\ 0 & 0 & 0 & 0.2 \\ 0 & 0 & 0 & 1 \end{bmatrix}
$$

$$
= \begin{bmatrix} 0 & 0.25 & -0.375 & 0.125 \\ 0 & 0.025 & -0.2375 & 0.3125 \\ 0 & 0.05625 & 0.134375 & 0.303125 \\ 0 & 0 & 0 & 1 \end{bmatrix}
$$

This result is in agreement with the previous expression for T.

For the general system of n equations in n unknowns, the matrix T can be computed from the product of two matrices as for the example above. The disadvantage of this lies in the need to invert a matrix first.

One can compute the matrix T directly using formulae. To simplify the notation, let $h_r = c_{r,\,n+1}$. Also recall that the first column vector of T is always a zero vector since the first column vector of T_1 is the zero vector. The last row vector will have a 1 in the last position and zeros elsewhere since this is true for all T_i. The formulae for the remaining elements of T are

$$t_{1s} = c_{1s}$$

$$t_{2s} = c_{21}t_{1s} \qquad\qquad s < 2$$

$$t_{2s} = c_{21}t_{1s} + c_{2s} \qquad\quad s \geq 2$$

$$\cdot \quad \cdot \quad \cdot$$

$$t_{rs} = \sum_{k=1}^{r-1} c_{rk}t_{ks} \qquad\qquad s < r$$

$$t_{rs} = \sum_{k=1}^{r-1} c_{rk}t_{ks} + c_{rs} \qquad s \geq r$$

These formulae can be applied to determine T for the numerical example of this section. It can be verified that one does obtain the same matrix T that has been computed before.

As a final observation, notice that in this technique using the matrix T, one multiplies each approximation vector $X^{[i]}$ by a matrix T to obtain a new approximation. This is a familiar process for it is one used to find the dominant characteristic root and vector. However, no normalization is required since the last component of the vector is always 1.

7.6 The Relaxation Method

The basic procedure in the last section involved changing the unknowns one at a time in order starting with the first one. A matrix T was determined so that a complete cycle of changes could be accomplished by matrix multiplication. There is a modification of this process that drops the changing of the unknowns in order and the use of the matrix multiplication. Before describing how to determine which variable to change at each step, some results of Section 7.4 are needed. In that section the successive approximations were expressed in the form,

$$X^{[i+1]} = CX^{[i]} + H$$

The new approximation $X^{[i+1]}$ is a vector that will differ from the vector $X^{[i]}$ by another vector that can be designated as $R^{[i]}$. The process involves trying to make this vector approach zero. This column vector is called the *residual vector*. With this notation, the equation above can be expressed as

$$X^{[i]} + R^{[i]} = CX^{[i]} + H$$

Solving this matrix equation for $R^{[i]}$,

$$R^{[i]} = (CX^{[i]} + H) - X^{[i]} = (C - I)X^{[i]} + H$$

To illustrate the procedure in detail, consider the system of equations of Section 7.4, where

$$
\begin{bmatrix} x_1^{[i+1]} \\ x_2^{[i+1]} \\ x_3^{[i+1]} \end{bmatrix}
=
\begin{bmatrix} 0 & 0.250 & -0.375 \\ 0.100 & 0 & -0.200 \\ 0.200 & 0.250 & 0 \end{bmatrix}
\begin{bmatrix} x_1^{[i]} \\ x_2^{[i]} \\ x_3^{[i]} \end{bmatrix}
+
\begin{bmatrix} 0.125 \\ 0.300 \\ 0.200 \end{bmatrix}
$$

Making the suggested change using $R^{[i]}$,

$$
\begin{bmatrix} x_1^{[i]} \\ x_2^{[i]} \\ x_3^{[i]} \end{bmatrix}
+
\begin{bmatrix} r_1^{[i]} \\ r_2^{[i]} \\ r_3^{[i]} \end{bmatrix}
=
\begin{bmatrix} 0 & 0.250 & -0.375 \\ 0.100 & 0 & -0.200 \\ 0.200 & 0.250 & 0 \end{bmatrix}
\begin{bmatrix} x_1^{[i]} \\ x_2^{[i]} \\ x_3^{[i]} \end{bmatrix}
+
\begin{bmatrix} 0.125 \\ 0.300 \\ 0.200 \end{bmatrix}
$$

To simplify the computations, the system can be put in the form,

$$
\begin{bmatrix} r_1^{[i]} \\ r_2^{[i]} \\ r_3^{[i]} \end{bmatrix}
=
\begin{bmatrix} -1 & 0.250 & -0.375 \\ 0.100 & -1 & -0.200 \\ 0.200 & 0.250 & -1 \end{bmatrix}
\begin{bmatrix} x_1^{[i]} \\ x_2^{[i]} \\ x_3^{[i]} \end{bmatrix}
+
\begin{bmatrix} 0.125 \\ 0.300 \\ 0.200 \end{bmatrix}
$$

The new process involves computing the $R^{[i]}$ for a given approximation. Then the numerically largest of the $r^{[i]}$ is noted. The corresponding $x^{[i]}$ is the one that is changed at this step. It is usually altered by adding the residual to the previous approximation for this unknown. At the next step the residual for this unknown would be equal to 0. To illustrate this method with the numerical example, let the initial approximation $X^{[0]}$ be the constant vector H. The following table can then be constructed.

$X^{[0]}$	$R^{[0]}$	$X^{[1]}$	$R^{[1]}$	$X^{[2]}$	$R^{[2]}$	$X^{[3]}$	$R^{[3]}$
0.125	0.000	0.125	-0.0375	0.1250	-0.0494	0.0756	0
0.300	-0.028	0.300	-0.0475	0.2525	0	0.2525	-0.00494
0.200	0.100	0.300	0	0.3000	-0.0119	0.3000	-0.02175

$X^{[4]}$	$R^{[4]}$	$X^{[5]}$	$R^{[5]}$	$X^{[6]}$	$R^{[6]}$
0.07560	0.00818	0.08378	0	0.083780	-0.000612
0.25250	-0.00059	0.25250	0.000228	0.252500	-0.000099
0.27825	0	0.27825	0.001636	0.279886	0

$X^{[7]}$	$R^{[7]}$	$X^{[8]}$	$R^{[8]}$	$X^{[9]}$	$R^{[9]}$
0.083168	0	0.083168	-0.000040	0.083168	0.000023
0.252500	-0.000160	0.252340	-0.000001	0.252340	0.000033
0.279886	-0.000127	0.279886	-0.000167	0.279719	0

$X^{[10]}$	$R^{[10]}$	$X^{[11]}$	$R^{[11]}$	$X^{[12]}$	$R^{[12]}$
0.083168	0.000031	0.083199	0	0.083199	-0.000005
0.252373	0	0.252373	0.000003	0.252373	0.000000
0.279719	0.000008	0.279719	0.000014	0.279733	0

For the first approximation it just happened that the residual in the first equation was 0. The largest numerical residual was in the third equation, so 0.1 was added to $x_3^{[0]}$ to obtain the new approximation 0.3. Thus, $r_3^{[1]}$ is equal to 0 and $r_2^{[1]}$ is the largest residual at this step. This value is used to reduce the $x_2^{[1]}$ to 0.2525. At the next step the x_1 is changed so all three variables have been changed from their original values at this point. Notice how only one variable is changed at each step throughout the table and how the residual for that variable is 0 at the next step. The final approximation for X is the same one to four decimal places that was found for this system in Section 7.5.

Unfortunately, this process does not always work as well as it did with this example. There are some problems where, after a cycle of changes, the residuals may not have been reduced very much, or they may change a variable back to a value close to its first approximation. The usual techique in this case is to over or under compensate. In other words, the residual is not made exactly 0 but changes in the other variables are utilized to reduce its value at later stages. This takes skill and practice to do effectively so this technique will not be discussed.

7.7 *Conclusion*

The literature contains many methods for inverting matrices and for solving systems of equations by numerical devices. In the bibliography there are references where one may find other techniques discussed or variations of the methods considered in these two chapters. The purpose in this discussion has been to consider basic techniques and to note just why they are valid. Some of the better known methods have been included. There is a notable lack of uniformity in the notation that is used in discussing inversion of matrices or solving systems of equations. An attempt has been made in these two chapters to develop a standard notation that is easy to use and to understand. In reading the literature one has to "translate" the given notation into notation which one is accustomed to using.

Finally, it should be noted that the advent of the high speed computer has greatly facilitated the inversion of matrices. Their great speed and accuracy make them ideal for this sort of computation. However, unless one has several matrices to invert, or a large matrix to invert or several systems of equations to solve, it is usually not economical to use a high speed computer.

PROBLEMS

1. By the iteration method, improve the accuracy for the inverse of the matrix computed in Problem 4(c) of Chapter 6, to four decimal places.

2. Find the inverse of the following matrix by iteration, obtaining five decimal place accuracy.

$$\begin{bmatrix} 1 & -10 & -1 & -1 \\ 1 & 1 & -1 & 10 \\ 10 & 1 & 1 & 1 \\ -1 & 1 & 10 & 1 \end{bmatrix}$$

3. Solve the following systems of equations by the Gauss-Seidel method, obtaining 3 decimal place accuracy.

(a)
$$6x_1 - 2x_2 - x_3 = 9$$
$$x_1 + 7x_2 + x_3 = 10$$
$$x_1 - x_2 + 8x_3 = 9$$

(b)
$$12.4x_1 - x_2 - 2.0x_3 = 27.8$$
$$2.1x_1 + 17.5x_2 - 3.1x_3 = -10.2$$
$$1.2x_1 - 0.5x_2 + 11.1x_3 = -8.2$$

4. Solve the system of equations of 3(b) by the relaxation method.

8

Homogeneous Forms

8.1 The Linear Form

A very useful concept in mathematics is that of homogeneous forms. These involve linear combinations of variables where the coefficients and the variables are usually real numbers. There are several types of homogeneous forms, each characterized by the degree of the variables involved. When a specific type is referred to, the adjective "homogeneous" is usually omitted. This practice will be adopted in this chapter.

The simplest kind of homogeneous form is the linear form. It is a linear function of a set of independent variables x_i written as

$$f(X) = a_1x_1 + a_2x_2 + \cdots + a_mx_m$$

The right-hand side of this expression should look familiar. It could be thought of as the side of a linear equation that involves the unknowns x_i. Because each term contains only one x_i of the first degree, this is called a linear form. The expression could be written as the product of a constant row vector and a column vector in the x_i because

$$f(X) = \begin{bmatrix} a_1 & a_2 & \cdots & a_m \end{bmatrix} \begin{bmatrix} x_1 \\ x_2 \\ \cdot \\ \cdot \\ \cdot \\ x_m \end{bmatrix} = AX$$

The column vector in the x_i is denoted with the same symbol X used in the functional description. The vector X is referred to as the variable of the form. Since the linear form is determined as soon as the row vector A is known, it is said to "characterize" the form.

By assigning values to each x_i in the set, one determines a particular X for the linear form. When this vector X is multiplied by the row vector A of the form, a scalar is obtained. By assigning different values to X, a set of values for the linear form is found. This set of values is called the *range* of the form. More than one value for X may give the same constant in the range of a form.

If a set of linear forms is considered, each form would have some specified range of values. Suppose a particular value is chosen for each linear form from its range of values, is it possible to find a vector X that will determine each of these values for the corresponding linear form? In other words, if the linear forms and the row vectors of the set are numbered, is there an X such that

$$f_1(X) = A_1X = g_1$$

$$f_2(X) = A_2X = g_2$$

$$\cdot \quad \cdot \quad \cdot$$

$$f_n(X) = A_nX = g_n$$

where the g_i are values in the ranges of each of the linear forms. The set of equations on the right can be considered as equality of components between two vectors, so they can be written in the form

$$\begin{bmatrix} A_1X \\ A_2X \\ \cdot \\ \cdot \\ \cdot \\ A_nX \end{bmatrix} = \begin{bmatrix} A_1 \\ A_2 \\ \cdot \\ \cdot \\ \cdot \\ A_n \end{bmatrix} X = \begin{bmatrix} g_1 \\ g_2 \\ \cdot \\ \cdot \\ \cdot \\ g_n \end{bmatrix}$$

If one defined a matrix A as one whose row vectors are $A_1, A_2, \cdots, A_n$, then this equation is also expressible as

$$AX = G$$

This matrix equation is the familiar one that represents a system of linear equations. Thus, the finding a vector X which will give a set of specified values for a certain set of linear forms is equivalent to the determination of a solution to a system of linear equations.

8.2 Bilinear Forms

A slightly more complicated homogeneous form is the bilinear form. In this form two sets of variables are involved. Each term in the form has one and only one variable to the first power from each set. The "bi" of the term "bilinear" indicates two sets of variables are involved whereas the "linear" part refers to the degree of the variables in each term. As an example, let

(1) $f(Y, X) = 2y_1x_1 + 3y_2x_1 + 8y_1x_2 + 7y_2x_2 - 5y_1x_3 - 3y_2x_3$

Notice that in each term there is exactly one x_i of the first degree and exactly one y_j of the first degree.

The general bilinear form contains terms with every possible combination of a variable from each of the two sets. The form can be written as the double summation

$$f(Y, X) = \sum_{i=1}^{n} \sum_{j=1}^{m} a_{ij} y_i x_j$$

For the example above, the a_{ij} are

$$a_{11} = 2 \qquad a_{21} = 3 \qquad a_{12} = 8$$

$$a_{22} = 7 \qquad a_{13} = -5 \qquad a_{23} = -3$$

If the form (1) is factored by grouping, it can be written as

$$f(Y, X) = (2y_1 + 3y_2)x_1 + (8y_1 + 7y_2)x_2 + (-5y_1 - 3y_2)x_3$$

This looks like a linear form in X but one with coefficients that are linear forms in Y. Suppose that this is first written as a linear form in X with the variable coefficients, then

$$f(Y, X) = \begin{bmatrix} 2y_1 + 3y_2 & 8y_1 + 7y_2 & -5y_1 - 3y_2 \end{bmatrix} \begin{bmatrix} x_1 \\ x_2 \\ x_3 \end{bmatrix}$$

The transpose of the row vector in this product is the column vector

$$\begin{bmatrix} 2y_1 + 3y_2 \\ 8y_1 + 7y_2 \\ -5y_1 - 3y_2 \end{bmatrix}$$

Each component of this column vector is a linear form in the same variables so this vector can be written as the product

$$
\begin{bmatrix} 2 & 3 \\ 8 & 7 \\ -5 & -3 \end{bmatrix} \begin{bmatrix} y_1 \\ y_2 \end{bmatrix} = A'Y
$$

Since this vector is the transpose of the row vector in $f(Y, X)$, that row vector could be expressed as

$$
(A'Y)' = Y'A = \begin{bmatrix} y_1 & y_2 \end{bmatrix} \begin{bmatrix} 2 & 8 & -5 \\ 3 & 7 & -3 \end{bmatrix}
$$

Using this result, the expression for the bilinear form can be written

$$
f(Y, X) = \begin{bmatrix} y_1 & y_2 \end{bmatrix} \begin{bmatrix} 2 & 8 & -5 \\ 3 & 7 & -3 \end{bmatrix} \begin{bmatrix} x_1 \\ x_2 \\ x_3 \end{bmatrix} = Y'AX
$$

This illustrates how the general bilinear form $f(Y, X)$ can be expressed as a matrix product. It can be verified that

$$
f(Y, X) = \sum_{i=1}^{n} \sum_{j=1}^{m} a_{ij} y_i x_j = Y'AX
$$

where the matrix $A = (a_{rs})$ is formed from the coefficients a_{ij}. The index of the variable y_i is associated with the row index of the elements of the matrix A. The column index of the elements of the matrix is associated with the x_j. The matrix A is called the *matrix of the bilinear form* since it determines the form completely. The vectors X and Y are referred to as the variables of the form. By assigning values to the vectors Y and X, one obtains a set of values for the bilinear form. The set of all possible values is called the *range* of the bilinear form.

Since a bilinear form is a scalar, it can be considered as a 1×1 matrix and so is equal to its transpose. In terms of the matrix representation, this means

$$
f(Y, X) = (f(Y, X))' = (Y'AX)' = X'A'Y = g(X, Y)
$$

where $g(X, Y)$ is a bilinear form in X and Y with matrix A'. Note in the equivalent bilinear forms $f(Y, X)$ and $g(X, Y)$, that the roles of the two variables X and Y are interchanged and the matrices are transposes of each other. In other words, if one reverses the roles of the variables, the matrix of the new bilinear form is the transpose of the original matrix.

In Section 2.8 it was shown that a change of variable in a system of linear equations could be expressed as a product of a matrix and a vector involving a new set of variables. Suppose that in the bilinear form $f(Y, X)$ that both the variables Y and X are replaced by new variables V and U. This change could be expressed by writing

$$Y = P'V \qquad X = QU$$

If these values are substituted for Y and X in the bilinear form, it becomes

$$f(Y, X) = Y'AX = (P'V)'A(QU) = V'(PAQ)U = V'BU = g(V, U)$$

The form is now one in the variables V and U, as indicated by calling it $g(V, U)$. The matrix B of this new form is PAQ. This suggests the reduction of a matrix using both elementary row and column operations as given in Section 2.9. It was shown there that using both row and column elementary operations, a matrix could be reduced to the simple form

$$\begin{bmatrix} I_r & 0 \\ 0 & 0 \end{bmatrix}$$

Furthermore, the elementary row operations used in the process determine a matrix P whereas the elementary column operations determine a matrix Q such that

$$PAQ = B = \begin{bmatrix} I_r & 0 \\ 0 & 0 \end{bmatrix}$$

If one makes the changes in the variables Y and X using the matrices P and Q that reduce A to canonical form, then the new bilinear form becomes

$$g(V, U) = V'BU = V'\begin{bmatrix} I_r & 0 \\ 0 & 0 \end{bmatrix}U$$

or

$$g(V, U) = v_1u_1 + v_2u_2 + \cdots + v_ru_r$$

This is a much simpler expression for the bilinear form.

Since the P and Q are nonsingular, one can obtain the original form by the second change of variables,

$$V = (P^{-1})'Y \qquad U = Q^{-1}X$$

Substituting these expressions for the variables V and U in $g(V, U)$, it becomes,

$$g(V, U) = V'BU = V'PAQU = (Y'P^{-1})PAQ(Q^{-1}X)$$
$$= Y'AX = f(Y, X)$$

For the example given in this section, it can be shown that under the change of variable

$$Y = \begin{bmatrix} \frac{1}{2} & -\frac{3}{2} \\ 0 & 1 \end{bmatrix} V \qquad X = \begin{bmatrix} 1 & \frac{4}{5} & -\frac{11}{10} \\ 0 & -\frac{1}{5} & \frac{9}{10} \\ 0 & 0 & 1 \end{bmatrix} U$$

the bilinear form will reduce to

$$g(V, U) = v_1 u_1 + v_2 u_2$$

8.3 Quadratic Forms

The most important and useful of the homogeneous forms is the quadratic form. As the name suggests, each term involves exactly two variables x_i and x_j as factors where i and j may or may not be equal. The quadratic form can be thought of as a special kind of bilinear form in which both Y and X are of the same dimension so that the variable Y can be replaced by X. Symbolically, if this were done, then

$$f(X, X) = X'AX$$

where A is now a square matrix. The designation of the form is usually abbreviated to $f(X)$.

For a simple numerical example, consider the form $f(X)$ that is given by

$$3x_1x_1 + 2x_1x_2 + 3x_1x_3 + 4x_2x_1 + 2x_2x_2 + 7x_2x_3 - 5x_3x_1 - 3x_3x_2 - 4x_3x_3$$

For this form the matrix A would be

$$A = \begin{bmatrix} 3 & 2 & 3 \\ 4 & 2 & 7 \\ -5 & -3 & -4 \end{bmatrix}$$

On examining this quadratic form, notice there is a simplification that is possible. Since the sets of variables are the same, terms like $2x_1x_2$ and

$4x_2x_1$ can be combined. These terms that involve two variables with different subscripts are called *mixed variable terms*. This means that for the example, the quadratic form can be written as

$$f(X) = 3x_1^2 + (2 + 4)x_1x_2 + (3 - 5)x_1x_3 + 2x_2^2 + (7 - 3)x_2x_3 - 4x_3^2$$
$$= 3x_1^2 + 6x_1x_2 - 2x_1x_3 + 2x_2^2 + 4x_2x_3 - 4x_3^2$$

Now consider the quadratic form whose matrix is

$$B = \begin{bmatrix} 3 & 8 & 4 \\ -2 & 2 & 1 \\ -6 & 3 & -4 \end{bmatrix}$$

The homogeneous form $g(X)$ associated with this matrix is

$$3x_1x_1 + 8x_1x_2 + 4x_1x_3 - 2x_2x_1 + 2x_2x_2 + x_2x_3 - 6x_3x_1 + 3x_3x_2 - 4x_3x_3$$

This expression can be simplified by combining mixed variable terms to give,

$$g(X) = 3x_1^2 + 6x_1x_2 - 2x_1x_3 + 2x_2^2 + 4x_2x_3 - 4x_3^2$$

Comparing this with $f(X)$ shows they are the same quadratic form! In other words, there is more than one matrix that can be associated with a given simplified quadratic form. In order to avoid this ambiguity, one can specify how to associate a unique matrix with a given quadratic form. A number of possibilities exist, one of these would be to write all mixed variable terms with the smaller subscript variable first. Then the missing mixed variable terms could be added with zero coefficients. This would give a triangular matrix with all zeros below the diagonal as the matrix of the form.

A second possibility is to use half the coefficients of the mixed variable terms for each way of writing the pair of variables. This technique has the advantage that it will give a symmetric matrix for the form. If the coefficients of the mixed variable terms are divided in half,

$$f(X) = 3x_1^2 + (3 + 3)x_1x_2 + (-1 + -1)x_1x_3 + 2x_2^2 + (2 + 2)x_2x_3 - 4x_3^2$$

Written in matrix form,

$$f(X) = \begin{bmatrix} x_1 & x_2 & x_3 \end{bmatrix} \begin{bmatrix} 3 & 3 & -1 \\ 3 & 2 & 2 \\ -1 & 2 & -4 \end{bmatrix} \begin{bmatrix} x_1 \\ x_2 \\ x_3 \end{bmatrix}$$

This latter way of associating a matrix with a given quadratic form is the one that will be used. Hereafter, whenever a quadratic form is written in matrix notation the matrix A will be symmetric.

8.4 Simplification of Quadratic Forms

If the change of variable $X = PY$ is made in a quadratic form, it would become

$$f(X) = (PY)'A(PY) = (Y'P')APY = Y'(P'AP)Y = Y'BY = g(Y)$$

The matrix $B = P'AP$ of the new form $g(Y)$ is related to A in a manner that is different from any relation met so far. If the matrix P is nonsingular, the matrix B is said to be *congruent* to the matrix A. This new matrix B is symmetric since A is symmetric for

$$B' = (P'AP)' = P'A'(P')' = P'AP = B$$

In order to see how this relationship between B and A can be used to simplify a quadratic form, a review of the concepts of elementary matrices is in order. First of all, it was shown that an elementary column operation on a matrix A can be performed by matrix multiplication. The corresponding column operation is performed on the identity matrix to obtain an elementary matrix E. The product $AE = C$ gives the matrix obtained from A by the elementary column operation. By taking transposes this becomes $E'A' = C'$. Since the column vectors of A and C are now the row vectors of A' and C', this says the row vectors of A' are altered by E' in exactly the same manner as the column vectors of A were altered by E. In other words, the transpose of an elementary matrix used on the left will alter the row vectors of a matrix in the same manner as the elementary matrix alters the column vectors when used as a right multiplier.

If a series of column operations are performed on a matrix A, a corresponding set of elementary matrices can be found that will perform these operations when used as right multipliers. If the set of elementary matrices are denoted as $E_1, E_2, \cdots, E_t$, their product can be denoted as P. The product matrix AP would be the matrix obtained by the operations. If the same series of row operations are performed on AP in the same order, the corresponding set of elementary matrices would be $E_t', \cdots, E_2', E_1'$. This product is P' so the matrix obtained by performing both sets of operations on A is $P'AP$. In this simplification it is not necessary to perform all the column operations and then all the corresponding row operations. Instead, one could use a column operation and then its corresponding row operation. The matrix could be altered using pairs of elementary operations consisting of an elementary column operation and its corresponding row operation. Each such pair is called a *congruent elementary operation*. Either the elementary row operation or the elementary column operation can be used first. These congruent elementary operations can be used to obtain a simpler matrix that is congruent to the original matrix. The canonical matrix that can be obtained using the congruent elementary operations is not quite as simple as the canonical matrix for the bilinear form. The simplified matrix is diagonal, but there may be some negative ones on the diagonal.

How one would proceed to obtain the simplified form is best shown by an example. The following series of congruent elementary operations reduces the given matrix to the required canonical form,

$$
\begin{bmatrix} 3 & 3 & -1 \\ 3 & 3 & 2 \\ -1 & 2 & 0 \end{bmatrix}
\xleftrightarrow[\frac{1}{\sqrt{3}}R1]{}
\begin{bmatrix} \sqrt{3} & \sqrt{3} & -\frac{1}{\sqrt{3}} \\ 3 & 3 & 2 \\ -1 & 2 & 0 \end{bmatrix}
\xleftrightarrow[\frac{1}{\sqrt{3}}C1]{}
\begin{bmatrix} 1 & \sqrt{3} & -\frac{1}{\sqrt{3}} \\ \sqrt{3} & 3 & 2 \\ -\frac{1}{\sqrt{3}} & 2 & 0 \end{bmatrix}
$$

$$
\xleftrightarrow[\substack{R2-\sqrt{3}R1 \\ R3+\frac{1}{\sqrt{3}}R1}]{}
\begin{bmatrix} 1 & \sqrt{3} & -\frac{1}{\sqrt{3}} \\ 0 & 0 & 3 \\ 0 & 3 & -\frac{1}{3} \end{bmatrix}
\xleftrightarrow[\substack{C2-\sqrt{3}C1 \\ C3+\frac{1}{\sqrt{3}}C1}]{}
\begin{bmatrix} 1 & 0 & 0 \\ 0 & 0 & 3 \\ 0 & 3 & -\frac{1}{3} \end{bmatrix}
\xleftrightarrow[R(2,3)]{}
\begin{bmatrix} 1 & 0 & 0 \\ 0 & 3 & -\frac{1}{3} \\ 0 & 0 & 3 \end{bmatrix}
$$

$$
\xleftrightarrow[C(2,3)]{}
\begin{bmatrix} 1 & 0 & 0 \\ 0 & -\frac{1}{3} & 3 \\ 0 & 3 & 0 \end{bmatrix}
\xleftrightarrow[\sqrt{3}R2]{}
\begin{bmatrix} 1 & 0 & 0 \\ 0 & -\frac{1}{\sqrt{3}} & 3\sqrt{3} \\ 0 & 3 & 0 \end{bmatrix}
\xleftrightarrow[\sqrt{3}C2]{}
\begin{bmatrix} 1 & 0 & 0 \\ 0 & -1 & 3\sqrt{3} \\ 0 & 3\sqrt{3} & 0 \end{bmatrix}
$$

$$
\xleftrightarrow[R3+3\sqrt{3}R2]{}
\begin{bmatrix} 1 & 0 & 0 \\ 0 & -1 & 3\sqrt{3} \\ 0 & 0 & 27 \end{bmatrix}
\xleftrightarrow[C3+3\sqrt{3}C2]{}
\begin{bmatrix} 1 & 0 & 0 \\ 0 & -1 & 0 \\ 0 & 0 & 27 \end{bmatrix}
$$

$$\xrightarrow[\frac{1}{3\sqrt{3}}R3]{} \begin{bmatrix} 1 & 0 & 0 \\ 0 & -1 & 0 \\ 0 & 0 & 3\sqrt{3} \end{bmatrix} \xrightarrow[\frac{1}{3\sqrt{3}}C3]{} \begin{bmatrix} 1 & 0 & 0 \\ 0 & -1 & 0 \\ 0 & 0 & 1 \end{bmatrix}$$

$$\xrightarrow[R(2,3)]{} \begin{bmatrix} 1 & 0 & 0 \\ 0 & 0 & 1 \\ 0 & -1 & 0 \end{bmatrix} \xrightarrow[C(2,3)]{} \begin{bmatrix} 1 & 0 & 0 \\ 0 & 1 & 0 \\ 0 & 0 & -1 \end{bmatrix}$$

Notice how the matrix is still symmetric after every congruent elementary operation is performed.

There is another way this reduction can be carried out that avoids bringing in the radicals until the final steps. The first steps of this simplification would be,

$$\begin{bmatrix} 3 & 3 & -1 \\ 3 & 3 & 2 \\ -1 & 2 & 0 \end{bmatrix} \xrightarrow[\substack{R2 - 1R1 \\ R3 + \frac{1}{3}R1}]{} \begin{bmatrix} 3 & 3 & -1 \\ 0 & 0 & 3 \\ 0 & 3 & -\frac{1}{3} \end{bmatrix} \xrightarrow[\substack{C2 - 1C1 \\ C3 + \frac{1}{3}C1}]{} \begin{bmatrix} 3 & 0 & 0 \\ 0 & 0 & 3 \\ 0 & 3 & -\frac{1}{3} \end{bmatrix}$$

$$\xrightarrow[R(2,3)]{} \begin{bmatrix} 3 & 0 & 0 \\ 0 & 3 & -\frac{1}{3} \\ 0 & 0 & 3 \end{bmatrix} \xrightarrow[C(2,3)]{} \begin{bmatrix} 3 & 0 & 0 \\ 0 & -\frac{1}{3} & 3 \\ 0 & 3 & 0 \end{bmatrix} \xrightarrow[R3 + 9R2]{} \begin{bmatrix} 3 & 0 & 0 \\ 0 & -\frac{1}{3} & 3 \\ 0 & 0 & 27 \end{bmatrix}$$

$$\xrightarrow[C3 + 9C2]{} \begin{bmatrix} 3 & 0 & 0 \\ 0 & -\frac{1}{3} & 0 \\ 0 & 0 & 27 \end{bmatrix} \xrightarrow[\frac{1}{\sqrt{3}}R1]{} \begin{bmatrix} \sqrt{3} & 0 & 0 \\ 0 & -\frac{1}{3} & 0 \\ 0 & 0 & 27 \end{bmatrix} \xrightarrow[\frac{1}{\sqrt{3}}C1]{} \begin{bmatrix} 1 & 0 & 0 \\ 0 & -\frac{1}{3} & 0 \\ 0 & 0 & 27 \end{bmatrix}$$

$$\xrightarrow[\sqrt{3}R2]{} \begin{bmatrix} 1 & 0 & 0 \\ 0 & -\frac{1}{\sqrt{3}} & 0 \\ 0 & 0 & 27 \end{bmatrix} \xrightarrow[\sqrt{3}C2]{} \begin{bmatrix} 1 & 0 & 0 \\ 0 & -1 & 0 \\ 0 & 0 & 27 \end{bmatrix}$$

The final steps in this reduction are the same as in the previous reduction so are not included.

The process is started in this example by first noting that a_{11} is not 0. A choice is made as to whether to make a_{11} equal to 1 at this point or wait until a diagonal form is obtained. If a_{11} is a perfect square, it can be made 1 without introducing radicals. Whenever it is made 1, the elements of the first row vector are divided by the *square root* of a_{11} and then the elements of the first column vector are also divided by this quantity. Each of these operations will divide a_{11} by the square root of itself. In the resulting matrix, there is a 1 in the first diagonal position.

The next step is to produce zeros below the diagonal in the first column. Since A is symmetric, the corresponding column operations will give zeros in the first row to the right of the diagonal.

At this point in the illustration a new situation arises for the next diagonal element is 0. An interchange of rows and columns moves the nonzero third diagonal element into the desired position. This element is negative so has no real square root and hence this diagonal element cannot be made 1 using congruent elementary operations involving real numbers. However, by using the square root of the absolute value of the element as a divisor, one obtains -1 on the diagonal.

There is another situation that may occur in the reduction process. It might happen that at a certain point all diagonal elements are 0. The procedure to follow in this case is illustrated in the next example. Consider the matrix and its partial reduction,

$$\begin{bmatrix} 0 & 2 & 4 \\ 2 & 0 & -8 \\ 4 & -8 & 0 \end{bmatrix} \overset{\longleftrightarrow}{\underset{R1 + 1R2}{}} \begin{bmatrix} 2 & 2 & -4 \\ 2 & 0 & -8 \\ 4 & -8 & 0 \end{bmatrix} \overset{\longleftrightarrow}{\underset{C1 + 1C2}{}} \begin{bmatrix} 4 & 2 & -4 \\ 2 & 0 & -8 \\ -4 & -8 & 0 \end{bmatrix}$$

The modified form has the required nonzero element in the leading diagonal position so the reduction from here on would proceed as before. This technique could also be used in preference to interchanging the diagonal elements as was done in the example of this section. The choice that is made will depend upon the elements involved. Notice that this procedure involved the congruent operation of adding multiples of vectors with nonzero first component to the first vectors. In this example, the second vectors were added to the first vectors so that the new first diagonal element is a perfect square. One could have added $\frac{1}{2}$ of the third row vectors to the first vectors and also obtained a perfect square in the first diagonal position.

There is one more possible case. All the diagonal elements may be 0 and the first components of all the vectors may be 0. One could follow one of two procedures: either place a nonzero element on the diagonal, or make

a first component of a pair of vectors nonzero. The following examples
show how to do each of these. Consider the simplifications

$$
\begin{bmatrix} 0 & 0 & 0 \\ 0 & 0 & 2 \\ 0 & 2 & 0 \end{bmatrix}
\quad \underset{R2 + 1R3}{\longleftrightarrow} \quad
\begin{bmatrix} 0 & 0 & 0 \\ 0 & 2 & 2 \\ 0 & 2 & 0 \end{bmatrix}
\quad \underset{C2 + 1C3}{\longleftrightarrow} \quad
\begin{bmatrix} 0 & 0 & 0 \\ 0 & 4 & 2 \\ 0 & 2 & 0 \end{bmatrix}
$$

$$
\begin{bmatrix} 0 & 0 & 0 \\ 0 & 0 & 2 \\ 0 & 2 & 0 \end{bmatrix}
\quad \underset{R1 + 1R2}{\longleftrightarrow} \quad
\begin{bmatrix} 0 & 0 & 2 \\ 0 & 0 & 2 \\ 0 & 2 & 0 \end{bmatrix}
\quad \underset{C1 + 1C2}{\longleftrightarrow} \quad
\begin{bmatrix} 0 & 0 & 2 \\ 0 & 0 & 2 \\ 2 & 2 & 0 \end{bmatrix}
$$

The first technique produced a nonzero diagonal element, the second
made the first component of the third vectors nonzero. This reduces the
problem to one of the types just considered. This means that if the first
diagonal element is 0, it is possible to place a nonzero element there when
the matrix is not the zero matrix.

8.5 General Congruent Reduction

The process used in the last section can be extended to the reduction of a
general $n \times n$ symmetric matrix. To begin, the first diagonal element is
checked to determine whether it is nonzero. If it is not, then one of the
techniques of the last section can be used to make the first diagonal element
nonzero. A decision is then made whether to make the diagonal element 1
or -1 at this point or to wait until later. If it is to be simplified now, this
is done. Then multiples of the first row vector are added to the other row
vectors to make all the elements 0 in the first column below the diagonal.
Since the matrix is symmetric, the corresponding column operations make
all the elements 0 in the first row to the right of the diagonal.

One then applies this same process to the submatrix formed by deleting
the first row and column. This cycle is repeated until all diagonal elements
are determined or only a zero submatrix is left. Then the diagonal elements
are changed to 1 or -1 if this was not done before. Finally, the diagonal
elements are reordered to place the positive ones first followed by the negative ones.

There is one situation that might arise where an alteration of the procedure could be used. If a diagonal element under consideration were 0,
it might be that all other elements in its row and column are also 0. One
could just delete this row and column and go on without making the diagonal element nonzero. After the diagonalization is completed, a nonzero

element could be placed in this diagonal position by an interchange of diagonal elements.

The final canonical form will have a series of plus ones, say p of them, followed perhaps by some negative ones on the diagonal. The total number of positive and negative ones will be the rank of the matrix which is denoted as usual by r. This means the number of negative ones is $r - p$. With these designations, one says that the rank of the symmetric matrix is r, and its *index* is p where $p \geq 0$. These are known as the invariants of a symmetric matrix under congruence since they are unchanged under any congruent elementary operations. These designations are also applied to the associated quadratic form.

From the above discussion, it should be apparent that by a change of variable $X = PY$, a quadratic form can be simplified to

$$g(Y) = y_1^2 + \cdots + y_p^2 - y_{p+1}^2 - \cdots - y_r^2$$

To find the matrix that will perform the change of variable, one could perform on the identity matrix, the elementary column operations used in the reduction. For the first reduction given in the previous section this would give

$$
\begin{bmatrix} 1 & 0 & 0 \\ 0 & 1 & 0 \\ 0 & 0 & 1 \end{bmatrix}
\xrightarrow[\frac{1}{\sqrt{3}}C1]{\longleftrightarrow}
\begin{bmatrix} \dfrac{1}{\sqrt{3}} & 0 & 0 \\ 0 & 1 & 0 \\ 0 & 0 & 1 \end{bmatrix}
\begin{matrix} C2 - \sqrt{3}C1 \\[1ex] C3 + \dfrac{1}{\sqrt{3}}C1 \end{matrix}
\begin{bmatrix} \dfrac{1}{\sqrt{3}} & -1 & \dfrac{1}{3} \\ 0 & 1 & 0 \\ 0 & 0 & 1 \end{bmatrix}
$$

$$
\xrightarrow[C(2,3)]{\longleftrightarrow}
\begin{bmatrix} \dfrac{1}{\sqrt{3}} & \dfrac{1}{3} & -1 \\ 0 & 0 & 1 \\ 0 & 1 & 0 \end{bmatrix}
\xrightarrow[\sqrt{3}C2]{\longleftrightarrow}
\begin{bmatrix} \dfrac{1}{\sqrt{3}} & \dfrac{1}{\sqrt{3}} & -1 \\ 0 & 0 & 1 \\ 0 & \sqrt{3} & 0 \end{bmatrix}
\xrightarrow[C3 + 3\sqrt{3}C2]{\longleftrightarrow}
\begin{bmatrix} \dfrac{1}{\sqrt{3}} & \dfrac{1}{\sqrt{3}} & 2 \\ 0 & 0 & 1 \\ 0 & \sqrt{3} & 9 \end{bmatrix}
$$

$$
\xrightarrow[\frac{1}{3\sqrt{3}}C3]{\longleftrightarrow}
\begin{bmatrix} \dfrac{1}{\sqrt{3}} & \dfrac{1}{\sqrt{3}} & \dfrac{2}{3\sqrt{3}} \\ 0 & 0 & \dfrac{1}{3\sqrt{3}} \\ 0 & \sqrt{3} & \sqrt{3} \end{bmatrix}
\xrightarrow[C(2,3)]{\longleftrightarrow}
\begin{bmatrix} \dfrac{1}{\sqrt{3}} & \dfrac{2}{3\sqrt{3}} & \dfrac{1}{\sqrt{3}} \\ 0 & \dfrac{1}{3\sqrt{3}} & 0 \\ 0 & \sqrt{3} & \sqrt{3} \end{bmatrix}
$$

If the following change of variable is made

$$X = \begin{bmatrix} \dfrac{1}{\sqrt3} & \dfrac{2}{3\sqrt3} & \dfrac{1}{\sqrt3} \\[2ex] 0 & \dfrac{1}{3\sqrt3} & 0 \\[2ex] 0 & \sqrt3 & \sqrt3 \end{bmatrix} Y$$

then

$$g(Y) = Y' \begin{bmatrix} \dfrac{1}{\sqrt3} & 0 & 0 \\[2ex] \dfrac{2}{3\sqrt3} & \dfrac{1}{3\sqrt3} & \sqrt3 \\[2ex] \dfrac{1}{\sqrt3} & 0 & \sqrt3 \end{bmatrix} \begin{bmatrix} 3 & 3 & -1 \\ 3 & 3 & 2 \\ -1 & 2 & 0 \end{bmatrix} \begin{bmatrix} \dfrac{1}{\sqrt3} & \dfrac{2}{3\sqrt3} & \dfrac{1}{\sqrt3} \\[2ex] 0 & \dfrac{1}{3\sqrt3} & 0 \\[2ex] 0 & \sqrt3 & \sqrt3 \end{bmatrix} Y$$

$$= Y' \begin{bmatrix} \sqrt3 & \sqrt3 & -\dfrac{1}{\sqrt3} \\[2ex] 0 & 3\sqrt3 & 0 \\[2ex] 0 & 3\sqrt3 & -\dfrac{1}{\sqrt3} \end{bmatrix} \begin{bmatrix} \dfrac{1}{\sqrt3} & \dfrac{2}{3\sqrt3} & \dfrac{1}{\sqrt3} \\[2ex] 0 & \dfrac{1}{3\sqrt3} & 0 \\[2ex] 0 & \sqrt3 & \sqrt3 \end{bmatrix} Y$$

$$= Y' \begin{bmatrix} 1 & 0 & 0 \\ 0 & 1 & 0 \\ 0 & 0 & -1 \end{bmatrix} Y = y_1^2 + y_2^2 - y_3^2$$

For this quadratic form the rank is 3 and the index is 2.

The matrix P can be computed as the matrix A is reduced by augmenting the given matrix on the right with the identity matrix. The elementary row operations will change this identity matrix into P'. Its transpose is the matrix that determines the change of variable needed to simplify the quadratic form.

8.6 Positive Definite Symmetric Matrices

The concept of range of values of a quadratic form is the same as for the bilinear form. In this case, only the one set of variables is needed to give a value to the form. It can be shown that by a change of variable that uses a nonsingular matrix, one obtains a quadratic form with the same range of values as the original one. Thus, since the congruent reduction of symmetric matrices used nonsingular matrices, the corresponding change of variables gives a quadratic form with the same range of values as the original form. It is easy to determine the range of a quadratic form when its matrix is in canonical form. Some quadratic forms can be classified by the nature of their range of values. The classification is determined by the n, r, and p of the canonical matrix. This in turn leads to a classification of symmetric matrices using the same designations as for the corresponding quadratic forms.

Among those quadratic forms of the same size are those whose associated matrix has rank n, that is, the matrix is nonsingular. For these forms the index p can vary from 0 to n. If it is n, then the canonical representation of the quadratic form is

$$g(Y) = y_1^2 + y_2^2 + \cdots + y_n^2$$

As for all quadratic forms, $g(Y)$ is 0 when all the y_i are 0. This is referred to as the trivial case. However, for $g(Y)$ this is the only set of real values for the y_i that will give a zero value. All other values of the form are positive real numbers. A quadratic form whose range of values is positive except for this trivial case is called *positive definite*. The matrix of the form is also denoted as being positive definite. Thus a symmetric matrix is positive definite if its canonical form under congruent operations has $p = r = n$. If the canonical matrix has this property, it is the identity matrix. This means the positive definite symmetric matrix is congruent to the identity matrix.

The next type of special form is one whose matrix is nonsingular, but for which $p = 0$. In other words, in its canonical form all coefficients are -1. That is,

$$g(Y) = -y_1^2 - y_2^2 - \cdots - y_n^2$$

This form now can take on only negative values except for the trivial case. Such a form is called a "negative definite quadratic form." The matrix of the form is also designated as being negative definite. The matrix of the canonical form in this case is the negative of the identity matrix.

For $r = n$ and $0 < p < n$, there is usually no special name attached to the forms. They could take on both positive and negative values.

This leaves the case $r < n$ to be considered, the singular quadratic forms. In case $p = r$ so that the canonical form is

$$g(Y) = y_1^2 + y_2^2 + \cdots + y_r^2$$

the form can only be positive or 0. However, it can be 0 for nonzero values of Y. For instance, letting y_n be arbitrary and the other y_i be 0 will make $g(Y) = 0$. Such a form is called *positive semidefinite* with the same description applied to its matrix. The *negative semidefinite* form is a quadratic form where $r < n$ and $p = 0$. Such a form can never be positive for any vector Y. Sometimes the positive definite form is included in the classification of positive semidefinite forms by requiring only that $p = r$. Similarly, the negative definite form can be considered as a special case of the negative semidefinite forms by specifying only that $p = 0$.

There is an important relationship between the characteristic roots of a symmetric matrix and the r and p of the associated quadratic form. It is true that the number of positive characteristic roots is p, whereas the number of nonzero characteristic roots is r. This is based on a well known result that a symmetric matrix A is also congruent to a diagonal matrix D whose elements are the characteristic roots of A. The nonsingular matrix P that will reduce A under congruence to this diagonal form has the property that $P' = P^{-1}$. In other words,

$$P'AP = P^{-1}AP = D$$

so that A and D are similar as well as congruent. Since A and D are similar, they have the same characteristic roots and these appear as the diagonal elements of D. Because the rank of a diagonal matrix is the number of nonzero elements on the diagonal, the rank of a symmetric matrix is equal to the number of nonzero characteristic roots of the matrix.

For a diagonal matrix to be positive definite, all of its diagonal elements must be positive. This means that if a symmetric matrix has all positive characteristic roots, it will be positive definite since it is congruent to a positive definite matrix. This relationship is valid the other way; for if a symmetric matrix is positive definite its characteristic roots are positive.

For the positive semidefinite matrix, the nonzero characteristic roots must be positive in order for the diagonal matrix of characteristic roots to have this property. Similarly, the negative semidefinite matrix has all nonzero characteristic roots negative whereas the negative definite matrix has all characteristic roots negative.

The diagonal matrix of characteristic roots of a positive definite symmetric matrix has some important properties. Since all of the diagonal elements of the matrix are positive, its determinant is positive. Similarly, all principal minors are positive since all principal submatrices are diagonal with nonzero elements from the main diagonal of D. This says the diagonal form for a positive definite symmetric matrix has all of its principal minors positive. Conversely, if all principal minors of a diagonal matrix are positive, the diagonal elements are positive, so the matrix is positive definite. It can be shown to be true that all principal minors of any positive definite matrix are positive. In contrast, if all the principal minors of a symmetric matrix are positive, the matrix is positive definite. This is a very important test for whether a given symmetric matrix is positive definite or not.

One last observation can be made about a positive definite symmetric matrix A. Because its canonical form is the identity matrix, there exists a nonsingular matrix Q such that

$$Q'AQ = I$$

or, multiplying on the left by $(Q')^{-1}$ and on the right by Q^{-1}, this becomes

$$A = (Q')^{-1}IQ^{-1} = (Q')^{-1}Q^{-1} = (Q^{-1})'Q^{-1}$$

If one lets $Q^{-1} = P$ then

$$A = P'P$$

In other words, a positive definite symmetric matrix can be expressed as a product of a nonsingular matrix and its transpose. In contrast, one can form a positive definite symmetric matrix by taking the product of a nonsingular matrix and its transpose. One might also note that any negative definite matrix A can be expressed as $A = (-1)P'P$ where P is a nonsingular matrix.

8.7 Hermitian Forms

There is an important generalization of the quadratic form that can be made in case the form involves complex numbers. Involved in this generalization are two changes. The first is the replacement of X' by its conjugate $\bar{X}'$, and the second is the use of a Hermitian matrix in place of the symmetric matrix A. Recall that in Section 1.10, a matrix A is said to be Hermitian if $A = \bar{A}'$. This definition implies that a Hermitian matrix has only real numbers on the diagonal as was noted in that section. A Hermitian form can be expressed in matrix notation as

$$f(X) = \bar{X}'AX$$

where A is Hermitian.

There is an important characteristic of the Hermitian form. Although it involves complex numbers, its range of values will consist of only real numbers. To see this, consider the simple case

$$f(X) = a_{11}\bar{x}_1 x_1 + a_{12}\bar{x}_1 x_2 + a_{13}\bar{x}_1 x_3 + a_{21}\bar{x}_2 x_1$$

$$+ a_{22}\bar{x}_2 x_2 + a_{23}\bar{x}_2 x_3 + a_{31}\bar{x}_3 x_1 + a_{32}\bar{x}_3 x_2 + a_{33}\bar{x}_3 x_3$$

Since the product of a complex number and its conjugate is real, the $\bar{x}_i x_i$ are all real numbers. Also, since the a_{ii} are real, the products $a_{ii}\bar{x}_i x_i$ are all real. Consider the sum of the pair of terms

$$a_{12}\bar{x}_1 x_2 + a_{21}\bar{x}_2 x_1$$

The second term is the complex conjugate of the first for

$$\overline{(a_{21}\bar{x}_2 x_1)} = \bar{a}_{21}\bar{\bar{x}}_2 \bar{x}_1 = \bar{a}_{21}x_2 \bar{x}_1 = \bar{a}_{21}\bar{x}_1 x_2$$

Since A was assumed to be Hermitian, $\bar{a}_{21} = a_{12}$, and so

$$\overline{(a_{21}\bar{x}_2 x_1)} = a_{12}\bar{x}_1 x_2$$

Thus the second term is the conjugate of the first. Since the sum of a complex number and its conjugate is a real number, the sum of these two terms is a real number. This same thing is true for all pairs of the form

$$a_{ij}\bar{x}_i x_j + a_{ji}\bar{x}_j x_i$$

where $i \neq j$. Therefore the values of the Hermitian form are always real as can also be shown by noting that

$$\overline{f(X)} = \overline{f(X)'} = \overline{(X'AX)} = (X'\bar{A}\bar{X})'$$

$$= \bar{X}'\bar{A}'X = \bar{X}'AX = f(X)$$

In other words, $f(X)$ is equal to its conjugate for all values of X, hence it must be real.

The next question to consider is the simplification of a Hermitian form by a nonsingular change of variable. If the variable X is replaced by PY, then

$$f(X) = \overline{(PY)'}A(PY) = (\bar{Y}'\bar{P}')APY$$

$$= \bar{Y}'\bar{P}'APY = \bar{Y}'BY = g(Y)$$

where $B = \bar{P}'AP$. The matrix B is said to be *Hermitely congruent* to the matrix A. It is easily shown that B is also Hermitian since A is Hermitian. In terms of performing pairs of elementary operations on A, Hermitian congruence requires a slight change for the congruent elementary operations. One has to use the conjugate of the transpose of the elementary matrix. If the elementary operation interchanged two vectors, its matrix would have only real elements so the conjugate of the transpose would be the same matrix. However, if the matrix performed an operation of type two, there could be a complex constant appearing on the diagonal. In the conjugate of the transpose, the conjugate of this element would have to be used. For type three operations, the multiple appearing in the off diagonal position could be complex so it would have to be replaced by its conjugate in the transpose. This means that if a row vector is multiplied by a constant, its corresponding column vector would be multiplied by the conjugate of that constant. Also, if a multiple of the jth row vector is added to the ith row vector, then the conjugate of the multiple of the corresponding jth column vector is added to the ith column vector. Such a pair of corresponding elementary operations is called a *Hermitely congruent elementary operation*. They will be illustrated in a numerical example. It will be found that the type two operations generally will use real constants, although complex constants could be used.

The problem of simplifying a Hermitian matrix using Hermitely congruent elementary operations is quite similar to that of reducing the symmetric matrix using congruent elementary operations. First of all, one makes the first diagonal element nonzero if it is 0. This can be accomplished in the same manner as for the symmetric matrix. Any nonzero diagonal element can be moved into the first position or one can use any nonzero element in the first row. If all of these elements are 0, one can introduce a nonzero element on the diagonal or in the first row. It might be better to go on to the second diagonal position and obtain the nonzero first diagonal element near the end of the reduction. There is one difference in the reduction of the Hermitian matrix if the nonzero element in the first row is pure imaginary. One then has to add a pure imaginary multiple of the vectors to the first vectors in order to place a real number on the diagonal. This will be illustrated later.

As soon as the first diagonal element is nonzero, then it may be changed to 1 or -1 by type two operations. Again this step can be made after the diagonalization. In either case, multiples of the first row vector can be used to reduce the rest of the elements of the first column vector to 0. The corresponding conjugate column operations will have the same effect on the elements of the first row.

The process is then repeated for the second diagonal element. After this simplification, one works on down the diagonal until all diagonal elements have been simplified or all remaining elements are 0.

One might wonder why there may be negative numbers left on the diagonal since the square root of any negative number exists in the complex field. However, if a row vector is multiplied by i, then the corresponding column vector is multiplied by $-i$. The diagonal element is multiplied by $i \cdot -i = 1$ so it is left unchanged. It is because the operations require the use of the conjugate of the multiple that one cannot change the sign of a diagonal element.

The final canonical form for the Hermitian matrix is the same as the one for the symmetric matrix. On the diagonal there are p positive ones followed by $r - p$ negative ones and all the rest of the elements are 0.

As an example of the reduction, consider the following matrix and its simplification.

$$
\begin{bmatrix} 0 & 2i & 0 \\ -2i & 0 & -3 - 2i \\ 0 & -3 + 2i & 0 \end{bmatrix}
\xrightarrow[R1 + iR2]{\longleftrightarrow}
\begin{bmatrix} 2 & 2i & 2 - 3i \\ -2i & 0 & -3 - 2i \\ 0 & -3 + 2i & 0 \end{bmatrix}
$$

$$
\xrightarrow[C1 - iC2]{\longleftrightarrow}
\begin{bmatrix} 4 & 2i & 2 - 3i \\ -2i & 0 & -3 - 2i \\ 2 + 3i & -3 + 2i & 0 \end{bmatrix}
$$

$$
\xrightarrow[\substack{0.5R1 \\ 0.5C1}]{\longleftrightarrow}
\begin{bmatrix} 1 & i & 1 - 1.5i \\ -i & 0 & -3 - 2i \\ 1 + 1.5i & -3 + 2i & 0 \end{bmatrix}
$$

$$
\xrightarrow[\substack{R2 + iR1 \\ R3 - (1 + 1.5i)R1}]{\longleftrightarrow}
\begin{bmatrix} 1 & i & 1 - 1.5i \\ 0 & -1 & -1.5 - i \\ 0 & -1.5 + i & -3.25 \end{bmatrix}
$$

$$
\xrightarrow[\substack{C2 - iC1 \\ C3 - (1 - 1.5i)C1}]{\longleftrightarrow}
\begin{bmatrix} 1 & 0 & 0 \\ 0 & -1 & -1.5 - i \\ 0 & -1.5 + i & -3.25 \end{bmatrix}
$$

$$
\xrightarrow[R3 + (-1.5 + i)R2]{\longleftrightarrow}
\begin{bmatrix} 1 & 0 & 0 \\ 0 & -1 & -1.5 - i \\ 0 & 0 & 0 \end{bmatrix}
$$

$$
\xrightarrow[C3 + (-1.5 - i)C2]{\longleftrightarrow}
\begin{bmatrix} 1 & 0 & 0 \\ 0 & -1 & 0 \\ 0 & 0 & 0 \end{bmatrix}
$$

If one tried to place the nonzero element $2i$ in the lead diagonal position,

$$\begin{bmatrix} 0 & 2i & 0 \\ -2i & 0 & -3-2i \\ 0 & -3+2i & 0 \end{bmatrix} \xleftrightarrow[R1+1R2]{} \begin{bmatrix} -2i & 2i & -3-2i \\ -2i & 0 & -3-2i \\ 0 & -3+2i & 0 \end{bmatrix}$$

$$\xleftrightarrow[C1+1C2]{} \begin{bmatrix} 0 & 2i & -3-2i \\ -2i & 0 & -3-2i \\ -3+2i & -3+2i & 0 \end{bmatrix}$$

In other words, one cannot place a nonreal number on the diagonal using the Hermitely congruent elementary operations. This is why the multiple i of the second row vector is needed in order to obtain a nonzero element in the first diagonal position.

In the reduction above, the multiple $-i$ of the second row vector could have been used just as well. The verification of this is left as an exercise. In both cases the final form will be the same since the rank and the number of positive ones are invariants. Because these are invariant, the concept of definite, as applied to quadratic forms, can be extended to Hermitian forms.

If a Hermitian matrix is nonsingular, the number of positive ones in the canonical form may vary from 0 to n. If p were equal to n, the corresponding Hermitian form could be reduced to

$$g(Y) = \bar{y}_1 y_1 + \bar{y}_2 y_2 + \cdots + \bar{y}_n y_n$$

Since the product of a complex number and its conjugate is real, the range of values for this form would be the positive real numbers and 0 only for the trivial case. For this reason, this is called a positive definite Hermitian form. The canonical form of the matrix would be the identity matrix. The matrix of a positive definite Hermitian form can be expressed as $A = \bar{P}'P$, where P is nonsingular.

If $p = 0$, the Hermitian form would be negative definite. The range of values of such forms would be the negative real numbers and 0 only in the trivial case. The canonical form for the associated matrix would be the negative of the identity matrix. The matrix of the form could be expressed as $A = -P'P$, where P is a nonsingular matrix.

The concepts of positive semidefinite forms and negative semidefinite forms are the same for Hermitian as for the quadratic forms.

There is also the same relationship between the characteristic roots of a Hermitian matrix and the r and p of the matrix. It is true that a Hermitian matrix is similar to a diagonal matrix which has the characteristic roots on the diagonal. It is also true that the matrix is Hermitely congruent to this same diagonal matrix. This means that the characteristic roots of a Hermitian matrix are real, that there are r of them that are nonzero, and that p of the nonzero characteristic roots are positive and the rest are negative.

PROBLEMS

1. Simplify the following bilinear forms and determine matrices P and Q that can be used to effect the required change in the variables to produce the canonical form.

(a) $f(Y, X) = 2y_1x_1 - 3y_2x_1 + y_3x_1 - y_1x_2 + 5y_3x_2$

$$- 6y_1x_3 + 3y_2x_3 + 19y_3x_3$$

(b)

$$f(Y, X) = Y' \begin{bmatrix} 1 & 1 & 0 & 3 \\ 2 & 0 & 2 & 2 \\ 3 & -2 & 5 & -1 \end{bmatrix} X$$

2. Simplify the following quadratic forms and determine a matrix P that will perform the required change in the variable to produce this canonical form.

(a) $x_1^2 + 2x_1x_2 + 3x_1x_3 + 4x_2^2 + 5x_3^2$

(b) $2x_1^2 + x_1x_2 - 3x_1x_3 + 2x_2x_3 - x_3^2$

3. Simplify the following forms and determine the type of definiteness of each of them.

(a)
$$X' \begin{bmatrix} -4 & 2 & -1 \\ 2 & -4 & 2 \\ -1 & 2 & -4 \end{bmatrix} X$$

(b)
$$X' \begin{bmatrix} 1 & -1 & 0 & 2 \\ -1 & 2 & 1 & -3 \\ 0 & 1 & 1 & -1 \\ 2 & -3 & -1 & 5 \end{bmatrix} X$$

(c)
$$X' \begin{bmatrix} 0 & 1 & 0 & 0 \\ 1 & 0 & 2 & 0 \\ 0 & 2 & 0 & 3 \\ 0 & 0 & 3 & 0 \end{bmatrix} X$$

(d)
$$X' \begin{bmatrix} 4 & 2 & -2 \\ 2 & 4 & 2 \\ -2 & 2 & 4 \end{bmatrix} X$$

(e)
$$\bar{X}' \begin{bmatrix} 4 & i & 0 \\ -i & 2 & -i \\ 0 & i & 4 \end{bmatrix} X$$

(f)
$$\bar{X}' \begin{bmatrix} -4 & 1-i & 2+i \\ 1+i & -1 & 1-2i \\ 2-i & 1+2i & -10 \end{bmatrix}$$

4. Perform the reduction of the illustration of Section 8.6 using the suggested multiple $-i$ of the second vector.

BIBLIOGRAPHY

The following list of references is meant to be selective rather than exhaustive. Not included are any of the many articles on numerical techniques for inverting matrices and solving systems of linear equations. References to these can be found in copies of *Mathematical Reviews*.

Aitken, A. C., *Determinants and Matrices*, 8th ed. New York: Interscience Publishers, Inc., 1954.

Allen, R. G. D., *Mathematical Analysis for Economists*. London: Macmillan & Co. Ltd., 1953.

Beaumont, R. A. and R. W. Ball, *Introduction to Modern Algebra and Matrix Theory*. New York: Rinehart & Co., Inc., 1954.

Beckenbach, E. F. (ed.), *Modern Mathematics for the Engineer*. New York: McGraw-Hill Book Co., Inc., 1956.

Birkhoff, G. and S. MacLane, *A Survey of Modern Algebra*, Rev. ed. New York: Macmillan Co., 1953.

Bodewig, E., *Matrix Calculus*. New York: Interscience Publishers, Inc., 1956.

Bush, R. R. and F. Mosteller, *Stochastic Models for Learning*. New York: John Wiley & Sons, Inc., 1955.

Cramer, H., *Mathematical Methods of Statistics*. Princeton: Princeton University Press, 1946.

Dwyer, P. S., *Linear Computations*. New York: John Wiley & Sons, Inc., 1951.

Faddeeva, V. N., *Computational Methods of Linear Algebra*, translated by C. D. Benster. New York: Dover Publications, Inc., 1959.

Feller, W., *Probability Theory and Its Applications*, 2d ed. New York: John Wiley & Sons, Inc., 1957.

Ferrar, W. L., *Finite Matrices*. London: Clarendon Press, 1951.

Frazer, R. A., W. J. Duncan, and A. R. Collar, *Elementary Matrices*. London: Cambridge University Press, 1950.

Gantmacher, F. R., *Matrix Theory*, translated by K. A. Hirsch, vols. 1 and 2. New York: Chelsea Publishing Co., 1959.

Goldberg, S., *Difference Equations*. New York: John Wiley & Sons, Inc., 1958.

Guillemein, E. H., *Mathematics of Circuit Analysis*. New York: John Wiley & Sons, Inc., 1949.

Halmos, P. R., *Finite-Dimension Vector Spaces*, 2d ed. Princeton: D. Van Nostrand Co., Inc., 1958.

Hildebrand, F. B., *Introduction to Numerical Analysis*. New York: McGraw-Hill Book Co., Inc., 1956.

Hohn, F. E., *Elementary Matrix Algebra*. New York: Macmillan Co., 1958.

Holzinger, K. J. and H. H. Harman, *Factor Analysis*. Chicago: University of Chicago Press, 1941.

Householder, A. S., *Principles of Numerical Analysis*. New York: McGraw-Hill Book Co., Inc., 1953.

Keller, E. G., *Mathematics of Modern Engineering*. New York: John Wiley & Sons, Inc., 1942.

Kemeny, J. G., J. L. Snell, and G. L. Thompson, *Finite Mathematics*. Englewood Cliffs: Prentice-Hall, Inc., 1957.

————, H. Mirkil, J. L. Snell, and G. L. Thompson, *Finite Mathematical Structures*. Englewood Cliffs: Prentice-Hall, Inc., 1959.

Kempthorne, O., *Genetic Statistics*. New York: John Wiley & Sons, Inc., 1957.

Koopmans, T., *Statistical Inference in Dynamic Economic Models*. New York: John Wiley & Sons, Inc., 1950.

Lanczos, C., *Applied Analysis*. Englewood Cliffs: Prentice-Hall, Inc., 1956.

Luce, R. D. and H. Raiffa, *Games and Decisions*. New York: John Wiley & Sons, Inc., 1957.

MacDuffee, C. C., *Theory of Matrices*, 2d ed. New York: Chelsea Publishing Co. 1946.

————, *Vectors and Matrices*. Ithaca: Mathematical Association of America, 1943.

Margenau, H. and G. M. Murphy, *The Mathematics of Physics and Chemistry*, 2d ed. Princeton: D. Van Nostrand Co., Inc., 1956.

Murdoch, D. C., *Linear Algebra for the Undergraduate*. New York: John Wiley & Sons, Inc., 1957.

Perlis, S., *Theory of Matrices*. Reading: Addison-Wesley Publishing Co., Inc., 1952.

Reed, M. B. and G. B. Reed, *Mathematical Methods in Electrical Engineering*. New York: Harper & Bros., 1951.

Salvadori, M. G. and K. S. Miller, *Mathematical Solution of Engineering Problems*. New York: McGraw-Hill Book Co., Inc., 1948.

Samuelson, P. A., *Foundations of Economic Analysis*. Cambridge: Harvard University Press, 1948.

Schreier, O. and E. Sperner, *An Introduction to Modern Algebra and Matrix Theory*. New York: Chelsea Publishing Co., 1952.

Thrall, R. M. and L. Tornheim, *Vector Spaces and Matrices*. New York: John Wiley & Sons, Inc., 1957.

Tintner, G., *Econometrics*. New York: John Wiley & Sons, Inc., 1952.

————, *Mathematics and Statistics for Economists*. New York: Rinehart & Co., Inc., 1953.

Wade, T. L., *The Algebra of Vectors and Matrices*. Cambridge: Addison-Wesley Publishing Co., Inc., 1951.

Chapter 1

1. (a) $\begin{bmatrix} a_{11} & a_{12} & a_{13} & a_{14} & a_{15} \\ a_{21} & a_{22} & a_{23} & a_{24} & a_{25} \\ a_{31} & a_{32} & a_{33} & a_{34} & a_{35} \end{bmatrix}$ (b) $\begin{bmatrix} b_{11} & b_{12} & b_{13} \\ b_{21} & b_{22} & b_{23} \\ b_{31} & b_{32} & b_{33} \end{bmatrix}$ (c) $\begin{bmatrix} c_{11} & c_{12} \\ c_{21} & c_{22} \\ c_{31} & c_{32} \\ c_{41} & c_{42} \\ c_{51} & c_{52} \end{bmatrix}$

(d) $\begin{bmatrix} d_{11} \\ d_{21} \\ d_{31} \\ d_{41} \\ d_{51} \end{bmatrix}$ (e) $\begin{bmatrix} e_{11} & e_{12} & e_{13} & e_{14} & e_{15} \end{bmatrix}$

2. $1 \times 4, 4 \times 1, 3 \times 4, 4 \times 3, 4 \times 4$.

4.
$$A' = \begin{bmatrix} a_{11} & a_{21} & a_{31} \\ a_{12} & a_{22} & a_{32} \\ a_{13} & a_{23} & a_{33} \\ a_{14} & a_{24} & a_{34} \\ a_{15} & a_{25} & a_{35} \end{bmatrix}$$

$$C' = \begin{bmatrix} c_{11} & c_{21} & c_{31} & c_{41} & c_{51} \\ c_{12} & c_{22} & c_{32} & c_{42} & c_{52} \end{bmatrix}$$

$$E' = \begin{bmatrix} e_{11} \\ e_{12} \\ e_{13} \\ e_{14} \\ e_{15} \end{bmatrix}$$

$$G' = \begin{bmatrix} -3 & 2 & 0 & 1 \end{bmatrix}$$

$$J' = \begin{bmatrix} 2 & 2 & 4 & 1 \\ 1 & -1 & 4 & 0 \\ -4 & 3 & -1 & -1 \end{bmatrix}$$

10. $FG = -3 - 6 + 0 + 4 = -5$ $FJ = \begin{bmatrix} 8 & 12 & -19 \end{bmatrix}$

$$KG = \begin{bmatrix} -14 \\ 0 \\ -13 \\ -4 \end{bmatrix}$$

$$EC = \begin{bmatrix} \sum_{k=1}^{5} e_{1k}c_{k1} & \sum_{k=1}^{5} e_{1k}c_{k2} \end{bmatrix}$$

$$HK = \begin{bmatrix} 37 & -21 & -4 & 28 \\ 2 & -20 & -10 & -21 \\ 10 & -1 & 7 & 18 \end{bmatrix}$$

$$DE = \begin{bmatrix} d_{11}e_{11} & d_{11}e_{12} & d_{11}e_{13} & d_{11}e_{14} & d_{11}e_{15} \\ d_{21}e_{11} & d_{21}e_{12} & d_{21}e_{13} & d_{21}e_{14} & d_{21}e_{15} \\ d_{31}e_{11} & d_{31}e_{12} & d_{31}e_{13} & d_{31}e_{14} & d_{31}e_{15} \\ d_{41}e_{11} & d_{41}e_{12} & d_{41}e_{13} & d_{41}e_{14} & d_{41}e_{15} \\ d_{51}e_{11} & d_{51}e_{12} & d_{51}e_{13} & d_{51}e_{14} & d_{51}e_{15} \end{bmatrix}$$

$$AC = \begin{bmatrix} \sum_{k=1}^{5} a_{1k}c_{k1} & \sum_{k=1}^{5} a_{1k}c_{k2} \\ \sum_{k=1}^{5} a_{2k}c_{k1} & \sum_{k=1}^{5} a_{2k}c_{k2} \\ \sum_{k=1}^{5} a_{3k}c_{k1} & \sum_{k=1}^{5} a_{3k}c_{k2} \end{bmatrix}$$

16.

$$K = \begin{bmatrix} 5 & 0 & \frac{1}{2} & 3 \\ 0 & 1 & -\frac{1}{2} & \frac{3}{2} \\ \frac{1}{2} & -\frac{1}{2} & 2 & \frac{3}{2} \\ 3 & \frac{3}{2} & \frac{3}{2} & 1 \end{bmatrix} + \begin{bmatrix} 0 & -2 & -\frac{7}{2} & 2 \\ 2 & 0 & \frac{3}{2} & \frac{5}{2} \\ \frac{7}{2} & -\frac{3}{2} & 0 & \frac{3}{2} \\ -2 & -\frac{5}{2} & -\frac{3}{2} & 0 \end{bmatrix}$$

17. (a)
$$\begin{bmatrix} 12 & -6 & 15 & 3 \\ -2 & 10 & -3 & 0 \\ -2 & 8 & 0 & 14 \end{bmatrix}$$
(b)
$$\begin{bmatrix} 6 & -1 & -8 \\ 6 & 1 & 6 \\ 12 & -4 & -2 \\ 3 & 0 & -2 \end{bmatrix}$$

(c)
$$\begin{bmatrix} 3b_{11} & 3b_{12} & 3b_{13} \\ -b_{21} & -b_{22} & -b_{23} \\ 2b_{31} & 2b_{32} & 2b_{33} \end{bmatrix}$$

18. (a) and (b)
$$\begin{bmatrix} 15 & -6 & -9 & 15 \\ 6 & 3 & 3 & 12 \\ 12 & -6 & 6 & 9 \\ 3 & -3 & 0 & 3 \end{bmatrix}$$
(c)
$$\begin{bmatrix} 6 & 3 & -12 \\ 6 & -3 & 9 \\ 12 & 12 & -3 \\ 3 & 0 & -3 \end{bmatrix}$$

(d)
$$\begin{bmatrix} 12 & -6 & 15 & 3 \\ 6 & -30 & 9 & 0 \\ -3 & 12 & 0 & 21 \end{bmatrix}$$

19.

$$Q^{-1} = \begin{bmatrix} \frac{1}{3} & 0 & 0 \\ 0 & -1 & 0 \\ 0 & 0 & \frac{1}{2} \end{bmatrix} \qquad R^{-1} = \begin{bmatrix} \frac{1}{3} & 0 & 0 & 0 \\ 0 & \frac{1}{3} & 0 & 0 \\ 0 & 0 & \frac{1}{3} & 0 \\ 0 & 0 & 0 & \frac{1}{3} \end{bmatrix}$$

20. The matrix S is skew Hermitian and the matrix T is Hermitian.

Chapter 2

1. (a) $\begin{bmatrix} 3 & -1 & 6 \\ 1 & 2 & -3 \\ 2 & -3 & -1 \end{bmatrix} \begin{bmatrix} x_1 \\ x_2 \\ x_3 \end{bmatrix} = \begin{bmatrix} 1 \\ 0 \\ -9 \end{bmatrix}$ (b) $\begin{bmatrix} 2 & -1 & -2 \\ 4 & 1 & 2 \\ 8 & -1 & 1 \end{bmatrix} \begin{bmatrix} x_1 \\ x_2 \\ x_3 \end{bmatrix} = \begin{bmatrix} 5 \\ 1 \\ 5 \end{bmatrix}$

(c) $\begin{bmatrix} 1 & -1 & 4 & -2 \\ -1 & -1 & -2 & 4 \\ 0 & 2 & -4 & 3 \\ -1 & 0 & 3 & 1 \end{bmatrix} \begin{bmatrix} x_1 \\ x_2 \\ x_3 \\ x_4 \end{bmatrix} = \begin{bmatrix} 3 \\ 1 \\ -5 \\ 2 \end{bmatrix}$

2. (a) $x_1 = -1, x_2 = 2, x_3 = 1$ (b) $x_1 = 1, x_2 = 1, x_3 = -2$

(c) $x_1 = -(1/2), x_2 = -(3/2), x_3 = 1/2, x_4 = 0.$

4. (a) $\begin{bmatrix} \frac{1}{2} \\ -\frac{1}{3} \\ -\frac{1}{2} \end{bmatrix}$ (b) $\begin{bmatrix} 2 \\ -1 \\ -2 \\ 3 \end{bmatrix}$ (c) $\begin{bmatrix} -2 \\ 1 \\ 2 \\ -1 \\ -1 \end{bmatrix}$ (d) $\begin{bmatrix} 1+\lambda \\ -1 \\ \lambda \end{bmatrix}$

(e) $\begin{bmatrix} -10 \\ -6 \\ 0 \end{bmatrix}$ (f) $\begin{bmatrix} 9 \\ -38 \\ -6 \end{bmatrix}$ (g) $\begin{bmatrix} \frac{12}{5} - \lambda_1 - \frac{2}{5}\lambda_2 \\ \frac{19}{5} - \lambda_1 - \frac{9}{5}\lambda_2 \\ \lambda_1 \\ \lambda_2 \end{bmatrix}$

(h) $\begin{bmatrix} -1 + 11\lambda \\ -2 + 14\lambda \\ \lambda \end{bmatrix}$ (i) and (j) inconsistent,   (k) $\begin{bmatrix} -7\lambda \\ -5\lambda \\ \lambda \end{bmatrix}$

(m) only the trivial solution.

5. (a) $\begin{bmatrix} \frac{3}{2} & -\frac{1}{4} & -\frac{1}{4} \\ \frac{3}{2} & -\frac{3}{4} & \frac{1}{4} \\ 1 & -\frac{1}{2} & \frac{1}{2} \end{bmatrix} \begin{bmatrix} 1 & -1 & 1 \\ 2 & -4 & 3 \\ 0 & -2 & 3 \end{bmatrix} = \begin{bmatrix} 1 & 0 & 0 \\ 0 & 1 & 0 \\ 0 & 0 & 1 \end{bmatrix}$ rank is **3**

(b) $\begin{bmatrix} \frac{1}{6} & \frac{5}{12} & -\frac{11}{24} \\ \frac{1}{6} & -\frac{1}{12} & \frac{7}{24} \\ -\frac{1}{3} & \frac{1}{6} & -\frac{1}{12} \end{bmatrix} \begin{bmatrix} 1 & 1 & 1 & -2 \\ 2 & 4 & 3 & 3 \\ 0 & 4 & 2 & 2 \end{bmatrix} = \begin{bmatrix} 1 & 0 & \frac{1}{2} & 0 \\ 0 & 1 & \frac{1}{2} & 0 \\ 0 & 0 & 0 & 1 \end{bmatrix}$ rank is **3**

(c) $\begin{bmatrix} \frac{1}{6} & \frac{1}{6} & 0 & 0 \\ \frac{2}{3} & -\frac{1}{3} & 0 & 0 \\ \frac{7}{3} & -\frac{2}{3} & 1 & 0 \\ -\frac{13}{3} & \frac{2}{3} & 0 & 1 \end{bmatrix} \begin{bmatrix} 2 & -1 & 1 & 2 \\ 4 & -2 & -1 & 16 \\ -2 & 1 & -3 & 6 \\ 6 & -3 & 5 & -2 \end{bmatrix} = \begin{bmatrix} 1 & -\frac{1}{2} & 0 & 3 \\ 0 & 0 & 1 & -4 \\ 0 & 0 & 0 & 0 \\ 0 & 0 & 0 & 0 \end{bmatrix}$

rank is 2.

6. (a) Itself   (b) $\begin{bmatrix} 1 & 0 & 0 & 0 \\ 0 & 1 & 0 & 0 \\ 0 & 0 & 1 & 0 \\ 0 & 0 & 0 & \frac{1}{3} \end{bmatrix}$ (c) $\begin{bmatrix} 1 & 0 & 0 & 0 \\ 5 & 1 & 0 & 0 \\ 0 & 0 & 1 & 0 \\ 0 & 0 & 0 & 1 \end{bmatrix}$

(d) $\begin{bmatrix} 1 & 0 & 0 & 0 \\ 0 & 0 & 1 & 0 \\ 0 & 1 & 0 & 0 \\ 0 & 0 & 0 & \frac{1}{3} \end{bmatrix}$

7.
$$\begin{bmatrix} 1 & 0 & 0 & 0 \\ 0 & 0 & 1 & 0 \\ 0 & 1 & 0 & 0 \\ 0 & 0 & 0 & \frac{1}{3} \end{bmatrix} \quad \begin{bmatrix} 1 & 0 & 0 & 0 \\ 5 & 1 & 0 & 0 \\ 0 & 0 & 1 & 0 \\ 0 & 0 & 0 & \frac{1}{3} \end{bmatrix} \text{ and } \begin{bmatrix} 1 & 0 & 0 & 0 \\ 5 & 0 & 1 & 0 \\ 0 & 1 & 0 & 0 \\ 0 & 0 & 0 & \frac{1}{3} \end{bmatrix}$$

8. (a) I_3, rank 3,
$$Q = \begin{bmatrix} \frac{3}{2} & -\frac{1}{4} & -\frac{1}{4} \\ \frac{3}{2} & -\frac{3}{4} & \frac{1}{4} \\ 1 & -\frac{1}{2} & \frac{1}{2} \end{bmatrix}$$

(b) $[I_3 \ \ 0]$ rank 3,
$$Q = \begin{bmatrix} \frac{1}{6} & \frac{5}{12} & -\frac{11}{24} & -\frac{1}{2} \\ \frac{1}{6} & -\frac{1}{12} & \frac{7}{24} & -\frac{1}{2} \\ 0 & 0 & 0 & 1 \\ -\frac{1}{3} & \frac{1}{6} & -\frac{1}{12} & 0 \end{bmatrix}$$

(c)
$$\begin{bmatrix} 1 & 0 & 0 & 0 \\ 0 & 1 & 0 & 0 \\ -\frac{7}{3} & \frac{2}{3} & 0 & 0 \\ \frac{13}{3} & -\frac{2}{3} & 0 & 0 \end{bmatrix} \text{ rank 2,} \quad Q = \begin{bmatrix} \frac{1}{6} & \frac{1}{6} & \frac{1}{2} & -3 \\ 0 & 0 & 1 & 0 \\ \frac{2}{3} & -\frac{1}{3} & 0 & 4 \\ 0 & 0 & 0 & 1 \end{bmatrix}$$

10. $x_1 = 7/4$, $x_2 = -5/4$, $x_3 = -3/4$.

12. $\begin{bmatrix} I_2 & 0 \\ 0 & 0 \end{bmatrix}$

Chapter 3

1. (a) $[1 \ 0 \ 0 \ 0] \quad [0 \ 1 \ 0 \ 0] \quad [0 \ 0 \ 1 \ 1]$ dimension is 3

(b) $[1 \ 0 \ 0] \quad [0 \ 1 \ 0] \quad [0 \ 0 \ 1]$ dimension is 3

(c) The unit column vectors, dimension is 3

(d) $\begin{bmatrix} 1 \\ 1 \\ 0 \end{bmatrix} \quad \begin{bmatrix} 0 \\ 0 \\ 1 \end{bmatrix}$ dimension is 2

2. (a) $\sqrt{2}, \sqrt{3}, 2, \sqrt{2}$ (b) $\sqrt{2}, \sqrt{13}, 1, \sqrt{38}$ (c) $\sqrt{14}, \sqrt{5}, \sqrt{14}$

(d) $\sqrt{19}, \sqrt{2}, 1.$

7. $\begin{bmatrix} 3 \\ -5 \\ -4 \end{bmatrix}$ $\begin{bmatrix} 3 \\ -1 \\ 0 \end{bmatrix}$ $\begin{bmatrix} 3 \\ 1 \\ 6 \end{bmatrix}$

8. (a) $\begin{bmatrix} -8 \\ -15 \\ -1 \end{bmatrix}$ $\begin{bmatrix} -5 \\ -10 \\ 0 \end{bmatrix}$ $\begin{bmatrix} 2 \\ -11 \\ 15 \end{bmatrix}$ (b) $\begin{bmatrix} -5 \\ -21 \\ -28 \end{bmatrix}$ $\begin{bmatrix} -2 \\ -11 \\ -12 \end{bmatrix}$ $\begin{bmatrix} 5 \\ -10 \\ 12 \end{bmatrix}$

(c) $\begin{bmatrix} 5 \\ 28 \\ 82 \end{bmatrix}$ $\begin{bmatrix} 5 \\ 20 \\ 55 \end{bmatrix}$ $\begin{bmatrix} 43 \\ 52 \\ 68 \end{bmatrix}$ (d) $\begin{bmatrix} 10 \\ 23 \\ -3 \end{bmatrix}$ $\begin{bmatrix} 2 \\ -1 \\ 5 \end{bmatrix}$ $\begin{bmatrix} -14 \\ -29 \\ 1 \end{bmatrix}$

Chapter 4

1. (a) -24 (b) -1540 (c) $-12 + 24i$ (d) 24   (e) 0   (f) 21
(g) 1   (h) -410 (i) 243.

4. 1(d)

$$\text{adj } A = \begin{bmatrix} -8 & -24 & 16 & 0 \\ 3 & -30 & 15 & -6 \\ 10 & -12 & 10 & -12 \\ 5 & 6 & -7 & 6 \end{bmatrix}$$

1(g)

$$\text{adj } A = \begin{bmatrix} -2 & 0 & 0 & 1 \\ 5 & 3 & 2 & -4 \\ 4 & 2 & 1 & -3 \\ -12 & -3 & -2 & 8 \end{bmatrix} = A^{-1}$$

Inverse in 1(d) is $\frac{1}{24}$ adj A.

5. (a) $x_1 = -1$, $x_2 = 2$, $x_3 = 1$ (b) $x_1 = 3/2$, $x_2 = 4$, $x_3 = -3.$

Chapter 5

5.
$$P = \begin{bmatrix} -7 & -1 & 0 \\ 9 & -1 & -1 \\ 31 & 1 & 2 \end{bmatrix}$$

6. $r_1 = 23.11323$, $r_2 = -3.1271$, $r_3 = 0.014$.

$$P_1 = \begin{bmatrix} 1.00000 \\ 0.68253 \\ 2.80384 \end{bmatrix} \quad P_2 = \begin{bmatrix} -0.4630 \\ 1.0000 \\ 0.0560 \end{bmatrix}$$

7. (a)
$$A^8 = \begin{bmatrix} 650691 & 315621 & 168732 \\ 315621 & 188181 & 146889 \\ 168732 & 146889 & 166338 \end{bmatrix} \quad \begin{array}{l} r_1 = 5.5321 \\ r_2 = 4.347 \\ r_3 = 2.12 \end{array}$$

$$P_1 = \begin{bmatrix} 1.0000 \\ 0.5321 \\ 0.3473 \end{bmatrix} \quad P_2 = \begin{bmatrix} -1.532 \\ 1.000 \\ 2.879 \end{bmatrix}$$

8. $r_1 = 10$, $r_2 = -5$, $r_3 = 2$.

Chapter 6

1. (a)
$$\begin{bmatrix} 0.16 & 0.07 & -0.04 & -0.04 \\ 0.07 & -0.03 & 0.06 & 0.07 \\ -0.04 & 0.06 & -0.02 & 0.10 \\ -0.04 & 0.07 & 0.10 & 0.01 \end{bmatrix}$$

(b)
$$\begin{bmatrix} 0.20 & 0.13 & -0.16 & -0.06 \\ 0.24 & 0.10 & -0.27 & 0.05 \\ -0.06 & -0.02 & 0.20 & 0.07 \\ 0.21 & -0.10 & -0.07 & -0.07 \end{bmatrix}$$

(c) $\begin{bmatrix} -0.5 & -0.5 & 0.5 & 0.5 \\ -1 & 0 & 0 & 1 \\ 4.5 & 1.5 & -2.5 & -2.5 \\ -1.5 & -0.5 & 1.5 & 0.5 \end{bmatrix}$

2. (b) $\begin{bmatrix} 0.04 & 0.17 & -0.04 & 0.02 \\ 0.17 & -0.21 & -0.03 & -0.30 \\ -0.04 & 0.03 & 0.04 & 0.18 \\ 0.02 & -0.30 & 0.18 & -0.39 \end{bmatrix}$

4. (b) $\begin{bmatrix} 0.14 & -0.14 & 0.16 & 0.39 \\ 0.10 & -0.03 & 0.02 & -0.18 \\ -0.06 & 0.05 & 0.10 & -0.09 \\ 0.10 & 0.08 & -0.01 & -0.01 \end{bmatrix}$ (c) $\begin{bmatrix} -0.15 & 0.05 & 0.16 \\ 0.09 & -0.05 & 0.05 \\ 0.21 & 0.08 & -0.17 \end{bmatrix}$

Chapter 7

1. $\begin{bmatrix} -0.1524 & 0.0502 & 0.1624 \\ 0.0886 & -0.0527 & 0.0537 \\ 0.2086 & 0.0822 & -0.1729 \end{bmatrix}$

2. $\begin{bmatrix} 0.00810 & -0.00810 & 0.09901 & -0.00990 \\ -0.10121 & -0.00990 & 0.00990 & -0.01210 \\ 0.00990 & -0.00990 & 0.00990 & 0.09901 \\ 0.01030 & 0.10081 & -0.00990 & 0.01210 \end{bmatrix}$

3. (a) $x_1 = 2$, $x_2 = 1$, $x_3 = 1$ (b) $x_1 = 2$, $x_2 = -1$, $x_3 = -1$.

Chapter 8

1. (a) $g(V, U) = v_1 u_1 + v_2 u_2$

$$P = \begin{bmatrix} 1 & 0 & 0 \\ 0 & -\frac{1}{3} & 0 \\ 5 & \frac{11}{3} & 1 \end{bmatrix} \quad Q = \begin{bmatrix} 0 & 1 & 1 \\ -1 & 2 & -4 \\ 0 & 0 & 1 \end{bmatrix}$$

(b) $g(V, U) = v_1 u_1 + v_2 u_2$

$$P = \begin{bmatrix} 1 & 0 & 0 \\ 1 & -\frac{1}{2} & 0 \\ \frac{2}{5} & -\frac{1}{2} & \frac{1}{5} \end{bmatrix} \quad Q = \begin{bmatrix} 1 & -1 & -1 & -1 \\ 0 & 1 & 1 & -2 \\ 0 & 0 & 1 & 0 \\ 0 & 0 & 0 & 1 \end{bmatrix}$$

2. (a) $y_1^2 + y_2^2 + y_3^2$

$$P = \begin{bmatrix} 1 & -\dfrac{1}{\sqrt{3}} & -\sqrt{2} \\ 0 & \dfrac{1}{\sqrt{3}} & \dfrac{1}{2\sqrt{2}} \\ 0 & 0 & \dfrac{1}{\sqrt{2}} \end{bmatrix}$$

(b) $y_1^2 + y_2^2 - y_3^2$

$$P = \begin{bmatrix} \dfrac{1}{\sqrt{2}} & -\dfrac{2}{\sqrt{13}} & -\dfrac{\sqrt{2}}{2} \\ 0 & \dfrac{11}{\sqrt{13}} & 2\sqrt{2} \\ 0 & \dfrac{1}{\sqrt{13}} & 0 \end{bmatrix}$$

3. (a) Negative definite   (b) $p = r = 2$, positive semidefinite

    (c) $p = 2$, $r = 4$ (d) $p = r = 2$, positive semidefinite

    (e) $p = r = n = 3$, positive definite   (f) $p = 0$, $r = n = 3$, negative definite.

Index

Index

A

Addition
elementwise, 10–12
of linear transformations, 85
of matrices, 7, 10–12, 70
of real numbers, 8–9
vector, 80
Additive inverse, 9, 85, 86
Address, of element of a matrix, 3
Adjoint matrix, 103–108
Algebraic systems, 2–3, 7–10, 18
Arbitrary element, 50
Arbitrary parameters
in homogeneous systems, 111, 118–121, 123
linear equations, solution of, 49–52, 54
vector space, determination of, 74–75
Associative law of matrices, 85
Associative law of matrix multiplication, 36–38
Associativity, in matrix multiplication, 15, 18, 57

B

Bilinear forms, 204–207
Binary operations, 8–9

C

Calculators, desk, determining inverse of a matrix, 152, 162
Canonical form, of a matrix, 54–66, 115
Cayley-Hamilton theorem, 125
Characteristic equation, of a matrix, 122, 123–126, 128
Characteristic vectors, of a matrix, 118–150
Coefficient matrix, 40
Cofactor matrix, 104–106
Cofactors, expansion by, 98–102
Column, of a matrix, defined, 2
Column operations, elementary. *See* Elementary column operations
Column vector, defined, 3–4
Commutative group, 9, 18
Commutativity, 18
Computers
digital, finding dominant root of matrix, 143
high-speed, in inversion of matrices, 201
Congruent elementary operations, Hermitian form, 220–222
Congruent reduction, general, 213–216
Conjugate, of a complex number, 22
Conjugate roots, of polynominal equation, 149